H.T.

The Revolt of Asia

THE REVOLT
OF ASIA

ROBERT PAYNE

an ASIA book

THE JOHN DAY COMPANY · NEW YORK

For
JAWAHARLAL NEHRU
and
CLEMENT ATTLEE

Contents

The Revolt of Asia

The Rebirth of Asia

THIS book is about the greatest single event in human history—the revolt of Asia. Long before the two gray ships steamed into mid-Atlantic and the Four Freedoms were announced, the revolt had become inevitable, as much a part of the historic atmosphere of our times as the invention of radio and the atomic bomb. The main father of the revolt was a French musician and educationalist who died 150 years ago; his Asiatic successors were two lawyers, one born in India and the other in Sumatra, and a self-educated Chinese scholar who had been for a short while librarian in Peking University. Under their impulse a billion peasants from the Asiatic heartlands are determined that they will never again suffer the humiliation of colonization, and they are hammering out for themselves a way of life that is neither capitalist nor communist, but adopts the benefits of both. The Asiatic revolt is in full tide, and its potential power and resources are incalculable.

Asia is one, and from now on must be regarded as one; there are connecting links between the new revolutionary states that give a grave unity to the whole. But the Asiatic revolution has many facets —though almost wholly a sociological revolution, it is also a revolt against the Asiatic past and against the cultural and political domination of the West. In this revolution economics are subordinated to social reorganization, nationalisms are less important than the survival of the whole, the individual is submerged within the community, and the pressures of three centuries of foreign domination are finally released. Huge powers, which once belonged to the West, have now been acquired by the Asiatics, and though we can calculate with fair precision many of the consequences of the revolt in the future, all the directions it will take are not yet known.

The war is not the direct cause of the revolution, but it has made the initial stages easier and less calamitous than they might have been if Western pressure had still been applied. In the short breathing space between the defeat of Japan and the new orientations of Western politics, the revolt swung into furious energy, became canalized, and in many cases owed its successes to the fact that the new governments were armed with captured Japanese guns. In those countries where village life has most closely approximated to democratic and communalistic government, the revolt has been most successful; in the countries where feudal organizations persisted, the revolt has been temporarily held; but so widespread is the social revolution in its effects on the peasants that it cannot be held much longer. Here and there—in the cities of south China and Formosa, in Korea and British Malaya—forces are at work to stem the relentless tide; they will fail, if only because the social revolution spills over frontiers and grows most quickly among those who are least conscious of the existence of frontiers, among peasants and farmers whose loyalties are to their own valleys, their hearths, the streams where they bathe, the forests where they have gone courting, and the fields they have tilled. National boundaries can mean little in the East where one village may speak a dialect unintelligible to the village over the river; differing national characteristics can mean little when nearly all are farmers living on the same hideous level of primitive subsistence. Beyond the next hill may lie the end of the world. They are not conscious of rigid national barriers, but they are conscious that they are Asiatics who refuse any longer to be exploited.

To these villagers a capital may be as remote and meaningless as the desert places marked on medieval maps with the inscription: "Here are tigers." Unaccustomed to self-government, they will have to be taught to rule themselves. Illiterate, without sanitation or health services, they will have to learn to read, to dig latrines, and to train nurses. These things will come, are already coming as the result of the determined efforts of those who are politically conscious. There is no lack of trained Asiatic minds. Illiteracy in the Dutch East Indies has never been less than 90 per cent, but the most successful revolt in Asia has been that of the Nationalist party in Java, led by Javanese who had often pursued rigorous studies in Dutch universities. The traditions of the West have found their seed ground in the Far East; and if the whole of the West perishes, its best ideas will survive among the Asiatics. The Chinese revolution of 1911 owed its impetus to the overseas Chinese; nearly all the leaders of the present revolution have been educated abroad.

Six hundred years ago Europe went through a similar cataclysmic revolt against the tyrannies of the Holy Roman Empire, but the nations that then came to birth hardened their national frontiers while they crystallized their national languages; by attaching the utmost significance to their boundaries and cultures, they set the stage for centuries of civil war. In Asia no such process seems likely to come into being. Their sovereignties have been more easily acquired and they will tend inevitably to group themselves against the West, in the same way that the Holy Roman Empire found stability only when it could encompass the whole of Europe against the Saracens. The world is now divided cleanly into two—Asia and the West; it is significant that Russian influence has played almost no part in the revolts of recent years.

For centuries these farmers have lived by the sweat of their brows, worshiping the village gods, without contact with the outside world except when the tax collectors came or when they watched their sons conscripted into rabble armies. There were no hospitals, or so few that disease spread unchecked. Their education was haphazard, and they were powerless against drought or famine, powerless against the inefficiency of their governments, which allowed them to starve in Bengal and central China not because there was insufficient food in the world, but because distribution was faulty and the governments were not prepared to assume their most immediate responsibility to the people. In a million villages of Asia there are no houses—only thatch sheds barely strong enough to shelter the villagers from the spring rains, inadequate against monsoons. The farmer went to his field at dawn and returned at sunset, content until recently with a fate that would strike Westerners dumb with horror. Gradually he has come to realize that an average life expectancy of twenty-seven years, as in India, and thirty, as in China, and thirty-two as in Java, is a reflection on his own moral courage —he has it in his power to raise the level of his own health and subsistence; and if the existing colonial or feudal governments fail to raise him from his misery, he can raise himself from his misery. Fed only on the terrible certainties of hunger, the seasons, and remorse, he knows that he can tame them all, even the seasons, if he sets his mind to it, and if the technological advances of the West are put to his service. He has learned from Rousseau or from some wandering students that his own dignity must be reinforced by government; and though he may hate the West passionately for the indignities of cheap labor and servitude that have been sometimes forced on him, he is prepared to recognize that salvation comes from applied science. More than anything else, during the critical years that lie ahead, does he need our technological assistance.

The revolt is triple-pronged. The revolt against the past is also a revolt against religion, for the new values of Western science are incompatible with the worship of the gods of fertility. If fertilizers improve his crops, there will be less need to pray for rain; fertilizers, rather than communism, are the main enemies of Oriental religion. His moral codes may remain relatively unchanged, his religious fervors may be exchanged for a fervent worship of science, libraries may take the place of temples, but the religions of India and Java are so powerfully interwoven with the nature of the people that they will not entirely disappear. Trimmed of their excesses and deprived of their superabundant authority, they may work for good and may do no harm. The most successful leader of any Asiatic revolt, Soetan Shjarir, is a Christian who passionately distrusts the more Calvinist Christian Chiang Kai-shek. Christianity in the East may well cancel itself out, but it should not be forgotten that the missionaries are also partly responsible for the revolt, if only because they spoke of the brotherhood of man at a time when merchants spoke only of profits.

In the East traditions are dying hard, but they have a habit of reviving during times of revolution. In a single generation the old Chinese traditions of scholarship almost perished with the disappearance of the imperial examinations, but already great scholars like Wen Yi-tuo have shown that scholarship deserves a place in the government. In the West the scholars have betrayed the cause of government, and they are no longer appointed to embassies as they were in the time of Boccaccio and Dante. It is significant that Soetan Shjarir, Jawaharlal Nehru, and Mao Tse-tung are scholars in their own right, with the historian's understanding of the political forces at work and the poet's sensitivity. Democracy, decaying in the West, is being revived in the East. If democracy can be maintained on its new soil, the war will not have been fought in vain.

Since the day when the first Portuguese settlers landed on Ternate, the strategy of conquest has continued to pay its illusory dividends. Only once, during the end of the first Dutch occupation of the Indies, was any revolutionary measure taken to free the original inhabitants from the domination of the Western powers. This occurred significantly at the time of the French Revolution, when the Committee of East Asian Affairs at The Hague wrote to Batavia ordering that the system of liberty and rights of the people be introduced into the Indies. The measure failed, as a result of the opposition of the Batavian authorities. For the rest the story is one of unparalleled exploitation. In India, in the Dutch East Indies, and to a lesser extent in China native princes and native groups have been set against each other on the principle of divide and rule. The wheel has turned full circle. The Indians, watching the Japanese and British Empires quarreling over India, could reflect at the end of the war that the same process was at work in the opposite direction—the Western-trained civilizations had fought themselves to a standstill, and become so weakened that Indian independence could be achieved.

Yet the contribution of the West to the East should not be minimized. Good men went to the East in increasing numbers, when the first tide of colonization was over. The missionaries, when they were scholars or doctors, the students and the professors of Asiatic customs, the technologists and the lawyers have left their imprint. Congress was founded by an Englishman. In Hawaii Sun Yat-sen was taught by Englishmen, and his release from captivity in London was effected by a host of English sympathizers. The Chinese Communists owe their strength largely to a leadership trained in France. American colleges in China have produced some of the best democratic leaders. A strained and unconvincing marriage between East and West has already been brought about, but the marriage ceremonies have still to be performed.

There has been an Atlantic Charter; there has been no Pacific Charter. Now, when the world center of gravity is shifting from the Atlantic to the Pacific, where the greatest areas of manpower confront the greatest areas of industrialization, nothing could be more necessary, yet already there is so much agreement upon the principles to be introduced in the Far East that an unspoken charter can be said to exist. The bonds connecting the democratic forces of China, India, and Indonesia are close; the Chinese democrats speak in the same voice, and employ the same terminology, as the Indonesians and the Indians. In the history of modern revolutionary movements—the movements that change the course of events—no date could be more important than that of the Pan-Asiatic conference held in the Spring of 1947, at the invitation of Jawaharlal Nehru.

The march of freedom during the last 150 years has reached the gates of Asia. The American Revolution of 1775, the French revolutions of 1792 and 1832, the German revolution of 1848, and the Russian Revolution of 1917 failed to penetrate the East. For the first time we are witnessing a revolt that includes within its scope half the population of the world—a revolt so widespread, so fraught with dangers, and at the same time so hopeful for the future that the West must take account of it, because we are *directly* concerned. The implications of the revolt do not affect Asia alone. They affect power politics already; they will affect our standards of living and our whole economy later. It would be the greatest misunderstanding to imagine the Asiatic revolt as dependent upon the uneven balance between Russia and America. The pattern of the revolt includes elements of socialism and capitalism. Not socialist Great Britain only, but the whole of Asia will provide the bridge between the Russian and American way of life.

It is necessary to see clearly what forces are at work. The temptation to regard all revolutionaries as agents of Moscow must be overcome. In these vast agricultural areas foreign capital becomes a necessity in order that the productivity of the land and the mineral resources should be properly exploited. Nehru, Shjarir, and Mao Tse-tung have all called for foreign capital, but they are tempted to demand, as one of the conditions of foreign investment, that native youth shall receive technological training abroad. The greater the amount of capital available for the nascent industries of the East, the greater the stability of those countries in the future and the greater the prospects of harmony between the East and the West. Asia is becoming industrialized. The temple is no longer the focus of city life. Flying from Kalgan to Peiping, I came down at Chining on the Inner Mongolian plain. The crenelated walls of the city, which was to be fought over by the Communist and Kuomintang armies a month later, were dwarfed by the huge powerhouse, the water tower, and the fantastically large railway station. Chi-ning is hardly a city; it is a small town with a population of about twenty thousand on the Japanese-built railway to Pailingmiao, but it is the pattern of all the Asiatic towns of the future. The heartlands are being conquered for industry, and over the whole of Asia the powerhouse is introducing the new civilization. We may regret its coming, but we cannot afford to regret that the Inner Mongolian plains have been opened up and that wealth is passing from the hands of fuedal princes into the hands of skilled laborers. "Religion," said Lenin, "is the opium of the people." It was an unwise remark, for in the East the essential simplicities of worship remain, but a new element has entered the consciousness of the people—a deep respect for the resources of power. A new vision and a new doctrine are being enunciated; in their simplest form they say that from one end of Asia to another there will be electric light.

We can neither frustrate nor delay the rebirth of Asia. Sun Yat-sen, in a moment of despair, spoke of the Chinese people as "shifting sand without power of cohesion," people so anarchic that no form of government was tolerable by them, and therefore they were incapable of governing themselves. There was some truth in the remark—the implicit anarchism that derives from Taoism remains, and with it there goes inevitably the tight complex of the family system derived from Confucian tradition with its appalling tolerance of nepotism; but the East cannot be measured by China, and it would be a mistake to believe that Chinese tolerance is always a virtue. Neither India nor China, the two most potentially powerful nations of the East, has succeeded in their revolution so quietly as Buddhist Burma and Mohammedan Indonesia. Religion has cut across the Indian revolt; the extremes of feudalism and a form of communism have cut across the Chinese revolt. In the Philippines, in Japan, in British Malaya, and in Korea foreign influence still dams the normal flow of revolutionary fervor. But the main patterns are already clear, and the example of Indonesia, already closely linked to India and Burma, will be followed by the other nations of the Far East. I asked a Chinese scholar what he meant when he spoke of democracy in the East. "It is electric light for the villagers, and milk for children, and better diet, and free ballot, and no more secret prisons and torture chambers." There is a sense in which the whole of the revolt in the Far East is simply for these things.

With the war there came the last great scattering of Asiatic forces; with the peace comes a consolidation. The islands of the Indies were artificially scattered as the result of centuries of conflicting rule by Spaniards, Dutch, Portuguese, and British—the tendency will now be in the reverse direction, not only in Indonesia, where a national consciousness has been aroused extending to the farthest islands of the Great East, but in Indo-China, where the French maintained one colony, an empire, two kingdoms, and a protectorate, and even in India, where despite the artificial friction of religions, there is growing among the educated a sense of the necessity of compromise at the same time that there is growing a determination that India shall remain one. A few years ago only one Asiatic nation possessed effective armed power; now every nation of the East has the arms it wants, not to fight civil wars, but to prevent the colonial powers from ever again assuming mastery. None of the colonial powers has the men, the arms, or the finance to keep Asia any longer in subjection. Except in China the Asiatics have a common enemy, and they are united against him.

The desire to be free of alien control does not mean that they are preparing war against us; it means only that like children who have grown to adolescence, they are determined to set up house for themselves. They will make their own laws and fashion their own civilizations, with weapons poised against interference; and here and there men will suffer from a smoldering indignation against the Westerners, who have too often subjugated them or behaved toward them with ill-concealed hostility. When in 1908 the Balinese saw themselves outnumbered in soldiers and fire power by the Dutch, they robed themselves in gold and silks, carried their most splendid creeses, painted their faces, and marched to the sound of the music of gamelans straight at the Dutch troops, asking to be killed. Less than forty years later the republics of Java and Viet-nam announced that if the colonial powers landed it would be war to the death; once again they were heavily outnumbered in men and fire power. But it was the last time. There can never again be opportunities of subjection. Too many young students have read the copybook phrase "Give me liberty or give me death," and too many older students have read the Atlantic Charter, the Communist Manifesto, and President Wilson's Fourteen Points. Colonial governments, by doing nothing or nearly nothing to raise the standard of literacy, may have considered that the Asiatic countries could be kept in perpetual bondage to themselves, but the Japanese brought radios to the village kampongs of Java and the walled villages of China; the problem of literacy disintegrated, and for the first time the Asiatics spoke to Asiatics across the ether. By opposing the colonial powers, Japan welded the colonial people together; by giving them arms and radios and a slogan of incalculable reverberation, she gave them the courage to revolt. Originally the slogan had been: "The four corners of the universe at peace under the Emperor," a phrase derived from the Confucian classics; then it became "Asia for the Asiatics"; then there occurred the fatal change: "The East Asia Coprosperity Sphere." The Asiatics caught the ball halfway and used it for their own device, and though they continue to speak of "Burma for the Burmese" and "India for the Indians," the vision of a united Asia remains, more glamorous than the vision of the individual nations.

For centuries the Asiatics feared the West. When the Japanese exploded the myth of military and social invulnerability, sank the *Prince of Wales* and the *Renown,* and treated white prisoners with calculated indignity and barbarity, the day of Western domination was already over. What is surprising is that the West seemed totally unconscious of its inevitable retreat. Queen Wilhelmina of the Netherlands, Churchill, General de Gaulle after the Brazzaville Conference, all continued to speak of their future Asiatic empires as though the relations betweeen the subject races and the conquering powers had suffered only a slight strain; the Asiatics would be offered increased representation in government counsels, and perhaps the rate of literacy would be improved. Nor did America behave in any better light toward the Philippines, for the Filipinos were left to their dubious freedom without complete powers of representation within their own government, the shadow of America looming heavily over them. The West had been an expanding and aggressive civilization at all times; even to pause in its expansion it was compelled to suffer psychological changes for which it possessed no aptitude. That other nations should expand or even demand their freedom had never occurred to us.

The Japanese wrought a greater revolution than they ever dreamed of, and one that destroys the basis of their economy, for the cheap labor markets of Asia will not fall again into Japanese hands; and with luck there will be no cheap labor markets at all. The future economy of Asia will be based on the rural co-operatives, to be numbered in millions, on heavy industries owned by government, and the minor industries left in capitalist hands. The arts will be reborn. If there is peace in China, within ten years more books will be printed in Asia than in the whole of America and Europe put together. With the success of the great revolt, there follows inevitably a cultural renaissance of Asia, whose cultures are so much older than our own. Macaulay's awakened Englishman in New Zealand will see between his islands and the towers of Westminster vast new empires of fantastic populations—at the end of the century the population of Asia cannot be less than the present total population of the world—where all that survives of three centuries of domination may be a few English and American professors and engineers, and something of our social system. The Chinese bought time with space; now that in the greater part of Asia the space is their own, time is less expensive; it is not only that innumerable peasants have sprung from the paleolithic into the atomic age, but that they have sprung fully armed like Athena from the head of Zeus, and their psychological adaptation to the new forms of power may be easier than our own. Yet predominantly they remain peaceful in their intentions upon the world; internal problems will remain for some time to come; the stresses are not yet released; they are nations in a stage of adolescence while we are nations in a state of old age, hoping to be reborn.

The major tasks that confront our generation are two: the understanding of Asia and the resolve to make all frontiers void. If the world is to avoid another war, the frontiers must be dissolved and become once again geographical rather than national expressions. Only a few countries possess natural frontiers. In Asia the frontiers are least natural; between all Asiatic nations there are broad belts of no man's land where sovereignity is hardly upheld. "Europe for the Europeans" is at least as natural a demand as "Asia for the Asiatics" or "America for the Americans." But in the end these slogans are meaningless in comparison with "Brothers for brothers." There are capitalists, agricultural workers, proletariat; the vertical

divisions have historic roots, but the greatest divisions are those between men and women and between parents and children. In the
East these divisions are more subtly harmonized, and even now,
at a time of revolutionary and national wars, the Oriental has not
attached, as we have, importance to natural boundaries. Sovereignty
is a myth invented in the thirteenth century; it is unlikely that the
Orientals, who have better myths, will consistently pursue it.

In the span of the next ten years the Asiatic countries must attempt to evolve through political and sociological patterns that have
taken the West seven hundred years of constant striving. There
seems little doubt that they will succeed; the advantages are on their
side. If the moderates in Delhi, Jacarta, Hanoi, Rangoon, and Nanking have their way, the future is more hopeful for Asia than for
the West. The first of the Asiatic countries to receive its independence was Indonesia, and the rest will follow. There is happening
now an event of such importance that it eclipses all our delibera-
tions in the United Nations, though almost none of the revolutionary states of Asia are represented there. What is happening is the
rebirth of Asia and of a kind of consciousness that has never existed
before. As always, the burden of understanding lies with us. We
must understand, or perish.

In this new world the stakes could not be higher. The marriage
of East and West was the dream of Alexander the Great; it has
taken more than two thousand years to come near to fulfillment.
When we have realized that the Asiatics are our kin, and that we
complement each other, when our attitude toward the Asiatics has
changed from indifference to sympathy and understanding, we
shall be nearer to peace. The prize is conquest—that each man may
own the whole world.

Chapter 2

<hr>

The Coming of the
Indonesian Republic

O
UT of the turbulence of two thousand years of invasions the
Indonesians have made their republic. The original inhabitants of the thousands of islands scattered from the
coasts of Malaya to northern Australia came probably from the red
basin of Yünnan in southwest China, drawn there by the promise
of the sun and the great rivers that once flowed down the Malay
Peninsula; the dark-skinned, beautifully made people who inhabit
Indonesia have distant roots in the Chinese heartland. The great
box-shaped empire that the Dutch carved out of the equatorial
islands was not the first empire to come to fulfillment there, or to
decay. Great waves of Indians, Arabs, Spanish, Portuguese, and
Englishmen have attempted to rule the islands, but it was only on
August 17, 1945, that the Indonesians themselves were able to proclaim an empire over their own territory. This empire contains over
seventy million people, and if it retained full sovereignty over its
outermost possessions, it would extend over a land and sea area
larger than the United States of America.

For long centuries, till about five hundred years ago, Hindu
civilization flourished in the Indies; great temples arose; Palembang
is known to have had at one time two million inhabitants; there
was trade with China, Arabia, the coast of Africa, and Madagascar
on a scale unrivaled until modern times. The wealth of the Indies
came from the stability of the Hindu governments that ruled first
from Sumatra, then from Java, and finally from Malaya. For centuries religious tolerance gave graciousness to the wealth of the
empire; Buddhism and Hinduism were practiced together, but

both fell before the iconoclastic fervor of the Mohammedan-Indian invasions of the Middle Ages, yet increasing Moslem influence has done little to change the nature of the people who retain, as in Bali, a cultivated animism together with a worship of the one God. In such an atmosphere it is not surprising that the two leading artificers of the revolution should be Christians at the same time that the most powerful political party should be exclusively Mohammedan.

A traveler in a ship voyaging eastward in the Indies loses count of the number of islands he passes, some no larger than molehills with a single date palm growing from blue water, others hugely continental in size. A traveler on the mainland of Java or Sumatra, seeing the fields ripening with their two yearly crops, the complicated irrigation through mazes of split-bamboo pipes, every inch of the earth fertile, would be wrong in thinking that this was the richest earth in the world—the basin of Szechuan is far richer. Except for geographically recent volcanic areas, where tobacco, coffee, tea, and cinchona can be grown, and the silt-covered lowlands, where rice and sugar flourish, there are vast stretches of barren land destroyed by violent rains, unexplored and nearly inpenetrable forests, and sandy deserts. In Timor, Bali, and some parts of Sumatra natural meadows allow dairy farming, but there are few cattle except buffaloes in Indonesia. The tremendous rate of increase of the population under Dutch rule has led to a dangerous balance between agricultural and forest land; the limit of deforestation has been reached. In spite of the natural wealth of the Indies, the Indonesians still live on the border line of poverty, though not of famine. An hour of labor will bring in only one and a half kilograms of thrashed rice, at a prewar value of five cents a kilogram. Little of the natural wealth of the country went into profits for the natives. Vast export surpluses accumulated, ranging between 1920 and 1939 from $400,000,000 to $100,000,000, whereas India, two and a half times as large as the Indies, could produce only an export surplus of $50,000,000 in 1938. In spite of the large export surplus, little effort was made by the Dutch to educate the Indonesians; on the whole the Indonesians were left to their own resources, allowed to obey their own customary law, the *adat,* and to provide their own village education, their own sanitation, and even their own hospitals. The Dutch gave them a quasi-benevolent rule by residencies (*resi-*

dentschappen) and did not impose too strongly upon the habits and customs of the native inhabitants. Three watertight divisions cut the country asunder, which for administrative purposes was divided into European, native, and foreign Asiatic. The Japanese were included among the Europeans. This arrangement protected the Indonesians from the laws that would otherwise affect their customary rights, but the implications of the division were endless and confusing. The Indonesans resented their deprivation from the elementary rights offered to the Europeans; their duties were laid clearly before them, they possessed none of the advantages defined by Roman-Dutch law. Feudalism remained, harsher than in any other country in the Far East.

Up to 1941 great feudal estates existed in Java where the landowners demanded from the peasants the full fifty-two days' labor to which they were entitled by law; in Java alone nearly a quarter of a million people lived out their precarious peon lives in virtual slavery. Public pressure on the government at Buitenzorg compelled the authorities to attempt to buy lands for redistribution among the peasants, but it is significant that at the time nationalism was strongest, during the mid-thirties, no appropriations were made for this purpose. Feudalism in Sumatra survived till the spring of 1946, when the sultans were deprived of their power by an armed rising of the peasants led by students. Forced labor persisted to the very end of Dutch rule: all able-bodied men up to the age of fifty were compelled to work a certain number of days a year on roads or public works, or pay a head tax. More than 600,000 men in Java paid their taxes in this way. Nothing quite comparable to this can be found in the histories of modern India, Burma, the Philippines, or Malaya.

There were difficulties and dangers in the "paternalistic" rule of the Dutch. The policy of gradualism slowed down; four large-scale efforts during a hundred years failed to improve either the education or the progress of the peasants. The hierarchies of sultanates remained, deliberately fostered even when it seemed inevitable that one day the land should be returned to its owners. The basic mistake of Dutch policy was to imagine that the owners were the sultans, who possessed the land by hereditary right, rather than the people, who had tilled the land through all historic time.

The peasant lived sparsely on two bowls of rice a day. He was short and thin, stunted in growth, his body lacking in carbohydrates and vitamins, his intellectual resources limited to the delicate art of shadow play, batik, and obedience to the adat. At the lowest income levels he paid taxes. An annual income of 120 florins (roughly $50) placed him within the tax bracket; less than one twentieth of 1 per cent of the Indonesians received $450 a year. The Dutch could say that on the whole the Indonesian was content with his lot; his wants were few and the more necessary desires could easily be fulfilled. Under a benevolent autocracy completely separated from the outside world, with a stable population, the contentment might have remained; but more quickly than the Dutch had realized there was seeping into Indonesia a knowledge of the more complicated wants of the West. A bicycle would save many back-breaking tasks, but the great majority of the peasants earned less than $50 a year, and could not pay for one. Few villages had radios. There were almost no mechanical tractors. The Dutch could point to the fantastic increase of population under their rule (it was estimated that between 1845 and 1930 the population of the islands of Java and Madura had increased from four and a half million to nearly forty-one million), and ask what would happen if labor-saving devices and more sanitation penetrated the Indies.

The rule of the Dutch in the Indies, like the rule of the British in India was harsh and just; neither its harshness nor its justice commended it to the native inhabitants. The Indonesian was not different in his conception of honor from all the other Asiatics; he claimed full recognition of his status, and this claim was personal and intimate, coming from a fierce pride in his intangible culture and his physical person. A Chinese dies quietly because he is too proud to demand assistance; Conrad has shown the effervescent depths of pride in the Malay princes. But the pride of the poor farmer might be fiercer even than his sultan's, and foreign rule touched the quick of his most personal feelings. The Dutch did not flaunt their rule as openly as other conquerors, but their quiet determination was as dangerous as the regal parades in India; they came at their best as scholars, but they rarely came as friends.

The lives of the Indonesian peasants were simple and revolved around the seasons. They were deft in their agriculture, and this deftness entered into all aspects of their lives. Their homes were small shelters of bamboo, sometimes surrounded by low walls, but they had long ago lost the use of brick. Today, small huts of palm huddle under the vast stone temples of the Madjapahit Empire. The eastern rainless monsoon blows on the volcanic soil, but rain falls heavily among these equatorial islands, with the result that the richness of the earth is slowly petering away; there are almost no water conservation schemes.

An Indonesian kampong has none of the ordered beauty of a Chinese village; there are no sculptured marble memorials to dead virgins, no camel-back bridges, no decorated temples with gold leaf on the flared roofs. The Mohammedan temple is bare of ornament; the Mohammedan gravestones are simple plinths standing forlornly in the earth. As dusk falls, the village becomes almost indistinguishable from the surrounding fields, the palm-leaf huts merging into the somber colors of the countryside. But it would be a mistake to paint the communities of Indonesia in somber colors. Under the stern volcanic mountains, nothing could be lovelier than the terraced fields, the slow-walking buffaloes, the hollow stems of bamboo through which spring water bubbles over fields. Wearing patterned sarongs, barefoot, with a wisp of dark-colored turban round their heads, the industrious peasants live in the fields, gently propitiating the animistic gods who have been retained even under iconoclastic Mohammedanism. There are special prayers to be spoken to trees, to the rice, to passing wayfarers, to the carabao, to the priests; there are gentle curses for foreigners. The Indonesians sometimes run amuck, but they are more gentle in their daily lives, and more tolerant even than the Chinese. At night there are shadow plays, storytellers who recount the endless epic of the courts, dances; their lives are full to overflowing in spite of the poverty that pursues them, so that few villagers are out of debt, and in spite of the Dutch imposition of the *herrendienst* (service to the masters), which survived till the end of Dutch rule. They eat cakes made of the fried hide of water buffaloes, they embroider their sarongs with a perfection unimaginable elsewhere, for they have a peculiar feeling for the quality of native cloth and the patterns that can be woven or melted into it; they are still warlike if necessary, and the tempered blades of their creeses owe something to the Arabs and the crusaders who first evoked a method of producing an infinitely keen sharpness. "Sharpness" is one of their favorite words.

Though Mohammedanism is present everywhere, the Indonesians

have retained elements of Hinduism, and animism comes naturally to these people who have been peasants all their lives. The Javanese is not a perfect Mohammedan; he will not always think it necessary to pray in the direction of Mecca, unlike the sternly religious Minankabaus of western Sumatra and the Atchenese of north Sumatra. He remains even now half in love with magic, believing it is possible with sufficient will power to fly into the clouds, become invisible, be raised from the dead. He believes in ghosts because he has seen them, or at least heard them. Women who have died in childbirth, from whom the placentae stream in the winds, can be heard in the evening, and some have seen them, perhaps confusing them with green will-o'-the-wisps of the hills. Shamanism is still common, and at the approach of the shaman the whole village may be induced to take part in ceremonial drum-beating and incantations. At the beginning of the revolution the present president, Achmed Soekarno, was credited with possessing shamanistic powers. Like the Boxers before them, the fiercely independent revolutionary soldiers of East Java inscribed passages from the Koran on their shirts and thought they would be protected from bullets. The famous gun barrel in Batavia was strewn with flowers, and never more than when the Japanese were present. For years men had unconsciously believed that the rule of the foreigners was nearly over; it was said that when the gun barrels of Batavia and Semarang were brought together, the last foreigner would go. And every villager reading the Koran could find some prophecy of final freedom.

Of all the races in the East, the Indonesians are most similar to the Indo-Chinese, who are partly of the same stock. Though Indo-China was opened to the West by a great Christian missionary, Monseigneur Pigneau de Béhaine, the French like the Dutch have failed to convert more than a small percentage of the natives, content with their syncretic worship that includes the cult of the ancestors, mysterious communion between the living and the dead, and a belief in the existence of benevolent and improvident spirits who must be appeased. The great Khmer temples of Ankhor Vat and Bayon, like the Borobudur in Java, were built at a time when Brahmanism and Buddhism existed contentedly side by side. Religious tolerance becomes a positive thing in the East—a man's honor is at stake, you cannot mercilessly deprive him of the religion he cherishes.

The majority of the Indonesians speak a language so simple that it can be learned in three months, unlike the Chinese, who must spend all their youth grappling with Chinese ideograms. The problem of illiteracy in the future will therefore be easier to solve in Indonesia than in India or China. The deft mind of the Indonesian, trained to agriculture, possessing a hard practical temper as well as the intellectual subtlety of the Indian, adept at intrigue like all those who live so much of their lives within the family, dutifully believing in the simple precepts of the Koran and still half fearful of the animistic gods in the volcanic hills and forest surrounding him, may be more capable of dealing with the problems of the new revolutionary age than the Chinese or the Indian. His hatred for his Occidental taskmaster has been a simple hatred, not confused by other loyalties, though sometimes the loyalty to the sultan and the princely house may remain.

The Indonesian is conscious of the past glory of the Indies; the stories that are told in the evening around the kampong fires may relate to events in a remote India, but the situations have been transposed. They say that Alexander was once king of the Indies; their legends are full of memories of epics that took place beyond the seas. A sense of exile hangs over the Indies; their spiritual home is India or the wastelands of Mecca, and they have long ago forgotten the tangible glories of the past, for the intangible glories go deeper and last longer. When Sir Stamford Raffles was lieutenant governor in 1819, he set out to explore the buried temples near Djodjacarta. It was only with the greatest difficulty that he could find headmen who knew of their existence. He was puzzled to find that they were as unapproachable as Mayan temples; they were lost almost completely, and no worship was offered at the stupa of the Buddha at Chandi Mendut, perhaps the greatest Buddhist sculpture in the world.

A profound sense of exile may lead to an extraordinary sense of balance; the communal life of the Indies, raised to perfection in Bali, has firmer roots than our mechanical Western civilization. Seventy per cent of the people work for themselves; over wide areas no idea of exclusive private property prevails. The territory of the community is owned collectively; property cannot be bequeathed, but belongs to the village as a whole. Land may be reapportioned annually, or every five years, but the hoes, the carabao, the whole resources of the village are held in common; and the village is ruled by the elected headman. The adat or customary law does not allow absentee ownership; the farmer must be close to the soil, which he owns only temporarily, according to the needs of the village as a whole, not according to his own needs. When Serakat Islam, the cautiously revolutionary party that represented Mohammedan interests, began to become prominent in the twenties, its greatest claim to affection was that it insisted on the laws of the adat against the rising strength of the socialists. An almost perfect form of communism already existed in Indonesia. Presiding over the Congress of Serakat Islam, the venerable Hadji Agoes Salim could say with some show of truth, against the objectors of the extreme left, that Mohammed had taught the doctrine of historical materialism twelve centuries before Marx was born. Today, with the Republic dedicated to a form of socialism, Shjarir has been at pains to suggest that no great changes are contemplated in the form of village government, except to make the franchise wider. What is strange is that no one before 1945 realized that the theoretical possibilities of a successful socialist revolution existed in Indonesia to an extent unparalleled anywhere else in the East. Feudalism existed, but the native forms of government existed as well. The human pattern was the village, not the family, though the rights of the family are included in the adat. The pressures and tensions of a rigid religion did not exist, the products of a shared economy were shared nearly equally over vast areas; and though their lives were frugal, and frugality governed all their actions, a sense of community gave them a sense of contact with the blossoming land as a whole. In Indonesia there were no outcasts; all were part of the pattern of the whole.

A closed economy inevitably produces dangers. Faced with modern industrialization, it may break completely. The youths will go to the towns, the contact with the soil may be completely obliterated. In the Yangtze valley whole villages have fallen into decay because the young have made their way to Shanghai or the industrially richer coastal areas; no new economy, except the wildest speculation in human productivity, takes the place of the narrow encircled ritual of village economy. The problem, for Indonesia, as for the rest of the East, is to find the balance between industrialization and agriculture. The time of the tractors will come. No one has yet discovered, outside Russia, how men will employ their lives when the task of agriculture is given over to machines.

Industrialization in Indonesia came largely from America, less from the Dutch. Characteristically, the Japanese invaders made the slogan of the Java Defense Corps: "Down with Anglo-American Imperialism! Live or die together with Japan!" The immensity of British and American investments frightened even the Dutch. The still unexplored industrial wealth of Indonesia may be greater than India's. Below the green and silver rice lakes lie rich deposits of tin, oil, bauxite, manganese, sulphur, nickel, gold, silver, diamonds, copper, and zinc. The great bauxite belt that stretches through Yünnan and upper Burma appears to continue down through Sumatra. Diamonds are mined in Borneo; sulphur in Java, Sumatra, and Celebes; coal in Borneo and Sumatra; manganese and phosphates are found in Java. Tin, oil, and coal exist in vast untapped quantites. Before the war Malaya and Indonesia supplied 65 per cent of the world's tin. The early conquerors went east in search of gold and spices, but gold takes eighteenth place in the list of Indonesian capital products today. Though the main wealth lies in unfabricated products, assembly plants were already being introduced, largely with American capital, before the war. In 1941, the last year for which reliable statistics are available, 61,000,000 barrels of oil were taken from the earth, and only 10 per cent was exported as crude oil, the rest being refined in the Indies. As a result of the growth of the Technical College in Batavia, trained mechanics have been increasingly available. The colleges were founded by the Dutch. The irony remains that it was the Dutch-educated revolutionaries from the three major colleges of Batavia who led the revolution.

No one has even begun to calculate the industrial possibilities of the Indies. Cinchona bark, of which Indonesia produced almost the entire world supply, may no longer have medical uses, since synthetic products are at hand to take its place; but Indonesia with its rich grasslands, volcanic earth, and huge timber forests may provide one of the great world centers for plastics, and it will remain with Cuba the greatest producer of sugar. There are islands off Borneo that are known to be "resting on oil." The undeveloped capital of the Indonesian earth could support a population at least five times as great. No republic ever came to birth with so prodigious a heritage. Like the Chinese and the Indian peasants, but with greater luck, the Indonesian enters the modern industrial world with his weapons concealed, so multitudinous that they may well disturb the Western world. At various times the Chinese and the Indians have laid claim to the leadership of Asia forfeited by industrialized Japan; within the next twenty years we shall probably discover that the leadership has fallen to the people who made the first successful revolution in the Far East. Vast factories will take the place of the nipa palms on the Javanese shores. The Dutch, who called their little outposts "factories" in the past, though nothing was fabricated there, will see immense industrial cities in a hundred places in the islands.

The Indonesians have gone through revolutionary phases in the past, not always against foreign aggressors. When they built six universities to commemorate the success of the Republic, they named them after Gadja Mada, the revolutionary prime minister of the declining Madjapahit Empire who lifted the Indonesian islands into the greatest empire it had ever known, invaded Bali, received forced tributes from north and central Sumatra, and even took over the kingdom of Palembang, which had succeeded the Sri-vijaya Empire. He commanded a large fleet which ruled over all neighboring waters, sent expeditions to Borneo, Macassar, and Flores; the princes of the Moluccas paid obeisance to him, and before he died all of New Guinea and the far southeastern islands were under the sway of the Madjapahit emperor. Gadja Mada, who had started his career as an officer in the imperial household, has become the epitome of the soldier-scholar. He wrote vast epics, or at least ordered them to be written; and around his name, and the name of Prince Diponegro, who attempted a revolution against the Dutch shortly after the British interregnum, the revolutionaries of 1945 wove the fabric of their revolution. Neither the Indians nor the Chinese have invoked the names of their past emperors, and something of the feudal atmosphere that still remains in Indonesia helped the revolutionaries for a while; the princes, descendants of Madjapahit, helped the revolutionary movement to birth in spite of the constant presence of Dutch Residents.

Prince Diponegro might have had an even greater claim to their affections. Like King Airlangga before him, he had lived for long years in hermit-like solitude. The Javanese, who delight in the good things of life, have always half worshiped hermits; but the hermit

Chapter 3

The Rise to Power

THE history of the rise of Indonesian nationalism in its modern form begins with a young Javanese princess who died in childbirth at the age of twenty-five in 1911. Raden Adjeng Kartini made no claims to fame. The letters she wrote to her friends were not published till six years after her death. She wrote with a clear cold brilliance, with something of Katherine Mansfield's power of evoking landscapes in terms of persons. She wrote about life at court, her occasional visits beyond the palace gates, the terrible "lean years" between the ages of twelve and sixteen when she was compelled to remain within high walls, the books she read, her love for her father, and her worship of the land, complaining sometimes, but nearly always caught up in an almost ecstatic delight in the things around her. Conscious of the exquisite delicacy of Javanese civilization, she could not understand why the Dutch always referred to the Javanese as "the little people."

We do not expect the European world to make us happier [she wrote]. The time has long passed when we seriously believed that the European is the only civilization, supreme and unsurpassed. . . . The clever, educated Dutchmen say the Javanese are born liars—utterly untrustworthy. We do not reply to the accusation. We only ask that when a child sins through ignorance, and when a grown-up person commits the same sin with deliberate calculation, which of the two is the most guilty? Sometimes we ask ourselves quite reasonably—what is civilization? Does it consist only of a commanding tone, or hypocrisy?

Her letters are rarely attacks against the Dutch; the young princess speaks of the Dutch with pity, amusement, and sometimes with an overwhelming sense of love, wondering why "the Javanese, in whom politeness is a natural heritage," should be beaten by Dutch officers. She had seen young girls and women beaten; she was torn between the desire to love and the necessity not to hate. She cried: "Do not Europeans live with us in our inmost hearts? And do we not share the same life as the Europeans?" Conscious of the role she could play in educating Javanese women, she asked her father to send her to Holland; her father refused, afraid she would marry a Dutchman, afraid the traditions she had acquired slowly at court would be lost. She cried out against the injustice of his fears, but in the end accepted them, knowing they were valid. Her whole happiness lay in the thought of a school where she could teach young Indonesians with the help of Western and Javanese textbooks. Sanctity touched her, and one has the desperate feeling, when she says: "I want to make myself worthy of the highest title, and that is a Child of God," that we are in the presence of a saint. Gay, faintly malicious, always noble in manner, living, like Nehru, "between two worlds, one dead, the other powerless to be born," beautiful and accomplished, she seems to have possessed all the gifts that the fertile soil of Java could provide. Couperous has spoken of the quiet, mysterious, and unyielding strength of the Javanese people, who seemed to be half slumbering in the shades of the volcanoes, but Raden Adjeng Kartini gave proof that there were Javanese who were wide-awake. In comparison with the fire of her brief letters, the rise of the Javanese nationalist parties to slow maturity, and then to fruition in the revolution, seems almost a reaction. When she died, her child also died; the movement for nationalism and social democracy was stillborn.

In nearly all her letters she complains gently of the lack of education in Java. At the time of her death there were only eight Javanese students in Leyden, and a few years before only five in all Holland. Higher education had been introduced into the Philippines by the Spanish three centuries before; Lord Macaulay had introduced higher education into India during the previous century, but nothing comparable had been brought about in Indonesia. The adat remained to temper Dutch rule, but at no time before the turn of the century had there been any emergence of intellectuals from Indonesia.

Partly, it was the deliberate policy of the Dutch government, which feared the power of the sultanates would increase if the princes were sent to Holland. At all stages in the rise of nationalism in Indonesia the nationalists have been assisted by the sultans. To this extent the fears of the Dutch were justified, but already the native societies were being laid open to Western influence; Western technology was entering the field of commerce and administration, and telegraph poles were being raised across the landscape of Java, where all communications previously had been made at the speed of the bullock cart. Primitive societies, which had lived hardly above the technological development of the Stone Age, were suddenly being brought into the current of Western thought.

The first native society to be formed was the Boedi Oetomo, which characteristically meant "beautiful striving." No one knew exactly what it was striving for. It represented the large, scattered, and unspoken demand for national fulfillment. Led by a pensioned government doctor, Mas Wahadin Sudiro Husodo, the movement seemed at first to be dedicated only to establishing scholarships for Javanese boys. By 1908 there were already 10,000 members in Java and Madura, mostly from among the Javanese aristocracy, government officials, and intellectuals. The movement possessed no political credo. Essentially scholastic, it looked toward India, deriving strength not from the nascent Moslem nationalism but from Rabindranath Tagore's vision of a self-governing Asia at peace. The "striving" was purely intellectual striving. It was typical of the times that the foreigners most revered by Boedi Oetomo were Tagore, Gandhi, and Mme Montessori. The masses could be influenced more easily by the vigorous possibilities of an Islamic revival; the intellectuals turned toward the Hindus, who were even then mapping out their plans for a concert of Far Eastern congresses.

Boedi Oetomo lived up to its name; the natural idealism of the Javanese, which sprang from the adat and the simplicities of an agricultural civilization, provided a springboard for further conquests, but it was still hoped that the famous declaration from the throne of September 1, 1901, would be implemented. Queen Wilhelmina had said: "The Netherlands have a moral duty to perform toward the people of the Indies." When she made a similar statement forty years later, it was too late—the men who founded Boedi

Oetomo had disappeared from the scene, and in their place there were young intellectuals determined upon political action.

The splendid logical minds of the Netherlands governors had produced an "ethical policy" for the government of the Indies that subscribed to a gradual widening of the franchise and of native rule; but it worked too slowly, and in the place of the former idealistic movement there appeared another, more vigorously Islamic, dedicated now not to educational ends, but to the social reorganization of the Indonesian people. The aims of the new movement were originally reactionary, violently in favor of Islam and violently against the growing economic wealth of foreigners, among whom they included the Chinese. But in 1912 the earlier iconoclasm had vanished in the mists of controversy, and in its place Serakat Islam announced a co-ordinated policy of assistance to commercial enterprise among the Indonesians (based on a rising co-operative movement), education, and the promotion of Mohammedanism. The three aims were not irreconcilable. The original leaders proclaimed their dubious loyalty to the government. Within five years the movement grew to include more than 800,000 members. While the more rigidly Mohammedan inhabitants of the outer territories believed that the movement aimed at a holy war against the West, the leaders of the movement were more modest in their demands. They wanted peace, time to develop, time to search out the possibilities of a movement that already encompassed all the sultans and nearly all the potential intellectual leaders. Its Mohammedanism was tempered with a traditional regard for co-operatives. The *pesantrans* of religious schools had insisted that the pupils should be given religious instruction as well as work in the fields under technical overseers. This tradition survived until the war years, and gave to the Indonesians a greater technical strength than they would have otherwise possessed.

The Dutch watched the growth of the movement with apprehension. Their apprehension was justified when, at the second congress of Serakat Islam, demands began to be made for self-government. The demands were refused, as Serakat Islam expected they would be, but the iron had entered their souls, and a political character began gradually to color the movement. For the first time "sinful foreign capitalism" began to be mentioned. The second congress, held in 1917, demanded outright independence. The Indonesians were closing their ranks. Once again they were turning their eyes to India.

The Dutch were not refusing to compromise, but they were wary of every effort toward a political understanding with Serakat Islam; compromise would lead inevitably to political defeats. New measures were introduced. In 1920 the number of Indonesians on the People's Council (Volksraad) was increased, the revival of democratic principles was accepted by law, and for the first time the Dutch acknowledged that they would be compelled to open the People's Council till it included eventually an overwhelming proportion of Indonesians.

Among the members of Serakat Islam, Hadji Agoes Salim was outstanding. A tall man with a pointed beard, wearing yellow horn-rimmed spectacles, white blouse, and green cap, he would have been outstanding at any time. He spoke seven languages—Javanese, Malay, Dutch, English, French, German, and Arabic—with ease; he knew perhaps twenty dialects, and was said to have a nodding acquaintance with Hindi. His wife was a Menankabau, and therefore an extreme Moslem, but Hadji Agoes Salim was known for his moderation. Born in 1884, the son of a magistrate in Kota Gadeng, then the intellectual center of Sumatra, he studied in Batavia and passed some years as interpreter in the Dutch Consulate at Jidda, a position of considerable importance because Indonesian pilgrims to Mecca had to pass through the Consulate. Returning to Menankabau, he established elementary schools, and in 1918 he founded a Dutch newspaper for young Javanese intellectuals called the *Bataviaasch Nieuwsblad*. He formed the Young Islamic League (Yong-Islamieten Bond) almost singlehanded. In 1924 he became the representative of the Serakat Islam on the People's Council. Seven years later he organized the nation-wide demonstrations against the *herrendienst,* which in his youth he had sworn to abolish. Meanwhile he helped to organize the trade unions, and attended the International Labor Conference in Geneva as an official delegate in 1929 and 1930.

The significance of his rise to maturity was not lost on the Dutch, who were finally able to employ him as their chief Indonesian spokesman, and to convince him that the Indonesians should help Holland to regain her lost territory after the surrender to Germany. His usefulness toward the Indonesian independence movement had passed; from being one of the principal architects he became one of its principal enemies. It was not perhaps his fault. As he grew older, his sympathies for the Dutch increased, and like the still more famous Dr. Raden Soetomo he thought a common victory might lead to a common alliance. Intellectually he based his claim for Dutch rule on the advisability of continuing the long tradition; without Dutch assistance the far vaster impact of Western thought after the war might rock the foundations of Indonesian society, and he preferred the more cautious impact of Dutch thought than the brutalities of the Japanese. He was loyalist to the last, retaining in isolation the qualities that had made the beginning of Serakat Islam so exciting, forgetting that a new generation would arise more critical of Dutch hegemony, and more bitter in its political convictions.

It is fair to the Dutch to insist that until the defeat of the Dutch armies in Java, the two most famous intellectual leaders were in favor of retaining Indonesia within the framework of the Dutch empire. The dying words of Raden Soetomo in 1941 were: "Beware of the Japanese! Fight for a better existence, for your rights and a higher standard of living. But do this within the framework of the Dutch empire." When the framework collapsed, it was already too late.

Dr. Raden Soetomo had been one of the founders of Boedi Oetomo. He had made a prolonged study of educational methods, become a professor of medicine and founded in 1924 the powerful Indonesian Study Club, which established schools, co-operative societies, and banks. Like Hadji Agoes Salim, he assisted the birth of the trade union and struggled unsuccessfully against *herrendienst,* usurers, and government expropriations. With more European learning than Hadji Agoes Salim and a greater gift for diplomacy, he was able by 1935 to form the Partai Indonesia Raja (Parindra), which absorbed a number of independent nationalist movements. By November 1939, when Holland was not yet attacked by the Germans, but the danger seemed imminent, the time had come for a more comprehensive scheme of federation. At the end of the year there was held in Batavia the first All-Indonesia Congress.

The consequences of the federation were far-reaching, for the mere fact of federation at such a moment was an implicit demand for independence. The resolutions followed in the main the pattern set by the All-India Congress. The red-white flag was adopted as a symbol of national unity, the people were urged to use their own language, their own newspapers and news agencies, to adopt the national song, and to subscribe to the insistent demands of the leaders for independence. The national movement could now be canalized. Future leaders appeared from comparative obscurity— Amir Sjarifoedin, who was to assume great powers later, became chairman of the committee of action. A deeply religious Islamic atmosphere—the federal assembly ordered all its members to fast on December 20, 1939, and to offer prayers to Allah at midnight *— remained, but the focus of attention had already swung from the older Islamic societies with their demand for small groups of active scholarly partisans to a demand for concrete independence. By a resolution of December 24, the All-Indonesia Congress was to be maintained as a permanent body whose purpose was "to give happiness and prosperity to the Indonesian peoples." Among their aims was the institution of parliament.

The federation had come about with almost reckless speed, largely as a result of the fears expressed by Javanese students in Holland that Holland would be overrun. The new federation demanded the arming of a native militia. After Germany struck, the Dutch government in Batavia possessed more power than the Dutch government in exile in London. The fear of a Japanese invasion increased; defenses were hastily put up; missions were exchanged with Singapore; the inevitable arrests of Indonesian leaders followed, but Dutch plans seem to have been tempered by a last-minute recognition that the Dutch armies in Indonesia would be helpless in the event of invasion without the active support of the people. The war had created a boom in the materials in which Indonesia was most abundant—rubber, tin, and oil. Though the boom continued to the end, no one doubted that the wealth of the Indies seemed to the Japanese a justifiable reason for desiring that Indonesia should enter the "East Asia Coprosperity Sphere." The Indonesians themselves had no such desire; there was nothing to be gained by accepting one form of imperialism in exchange for another. On July 30, 1941, Queen Wilhelmina announced the new orientation of Dutch policy:

* Ten years previously the All-India National Congress had also declared independence at midnight. The symbolism was clear.

As soon as the Netherlands are liberated from the oppressor, a new Cabinet will be formed. . . . This new Cabinet must immediately prepare a revision of the constitution, a revision by which the relations between the mother country and the other parts of the Kingdom shall be appointed. . . . In this manner we can lay the foundation for a happier and more prosperous future for the entire Kingdom.

The speech tacitly assumed that the government had been unduly unrepresentative in the past, but there was no indication of the methods by which a more representative government would be brought about. How would the representatives be chosen? What powers would they possess? Would the demands of the federation be recognized, or would there be only a slight shift in the powers of the governor general, whose powers were endless? Mr. Wirja-pratno, leader of the nationalist Parindra, accepted the statement with gratitude; others were more reserved. But the menace of Japan was closer than the menace of Germany; two weeks before Queen Wilhelmina's speech a bill had at last been passed to allow the formation of a native militia in Indonesia, but it was already too late, though the Dutch had greater sense than the British in Malaya, who refused the offers of the Chinese to form an army until the last moment.

The speech of July 30 had been written with the help of Dr. Hubertus van Mook, who had been born in Java and educated at Leyden University. Unlike Charles van der Plaas, whom he was later to succeed as governor general of the Indies, he possessed a deep sympathy and understanding of the Indonesians, and had helped to found a study circle called the Society for the Promotion of the Social and Political Development of the Netherlands East Indies, which as early as 1930 was promoting the idea of the Indonesian Commonwealth. Though he was appointed Director of Economic Affairs in 1937, he was unpopular with the Dutch in The Hague to the same extent that he was popular with the Dutch in Java. He was fat and chubby, smoked cigars continually, liked reading detective novels, and spoke Javanese perfectly; even in Holland he was continually employing Javanese words, and would answer inquiries for elucidation: "But my dear fellow, haven't you heard of Javanese-Dutch? This is our national language." He was a scholar of old Javanese texts, and this particularly endeared him to the Javanese. He suffered from an almost pathological admiration of ancient Javanese civilization. Yet the declaration of Queen Wilhelmina was of no very great assistance. It opened the gate a little, but did not differ from the recommendations of the Brazzaville Conference where General de Gaulle outlined the new French empire.

When war seemed inevitable, frantic efforts were made to protect Indonesia, but since no one had foreseen a simultaneous attack on the American, Dutch, and British outposts in the Pacific, it was decided that the main center of resistance should be Singapore. No modern fighters were available for Indonesia; the first Catalina flying boats did not arrive till late September 1941. The native militia in Java, Amboina, and Minahassa was placed on a war footing. A call for 18,000 volunteers was made; 100,000 volunteers offered themselves, but of these only 6,000 could be armed, with Italian rifles captured by Lord Wavell in the Libyan desert. With six thousand Indonesian militia, three cruisers, five destroyers, fifteen submarines, less than a hundred airplanes, and considerably less than a hundred thousand troops under arms, the Dutch East Indies faced Japan. In the dockyard at Soerabaya, where there were inadequate and ancient aircraft guns, the chief protection came from poisoned stakes dug into the ground and pointed upward—against a parachute landing. The possibility of invasion by parachute jumpers, on the model of the German invasion of Poland, seemed to be so great that similar primitive methods were employed throughout southeast Asia.

The effect of the Japanese attack was to unite the Indonesians. They could complain with justice that the Dutch had failed to protect them as they should have been protected. They were bitter against the Dutch, but infinitely more bitter against the Japanese, whose economic penetration in every sphere of Indonesian life had reduced the native middlemen to little more than servitors of the Japanese—by 1934 the imports of the Indies from Japan exceeded the exports to Japan by 74,000,000 guilders. After and during the world depression they flooded the Indonesian market with light bulbs, sheet iron, bicycles, fish preserves, beer, earthenware, cloth of all kinds; they were haughty, they counted as Europeans in the courts, and they spoke a little too often of their undeclared war with China. The Indonesian revolutionary societies saw themselves in a dilemma. If they supported the Dutch, they would find themselves in another kind of bondage; if the Japanese won, they would find themselves in the worst bondage of all. Characteristically Dr. Mohammed Hatta, a nationalist leader and a graduate of Rotterdam University, declared: "The Indonesian people, except for a small minority now in the armed forces, have not been taught to use arms, and therefore are not responsible for their present fate. Yet they should not think that the war does not affect them. If we are convinced that the Japanese aggression endangers our ideals, then we must resist Japanese imperialism; and even if we were to believe that the Japanese might win, it would still be our duty to come to the defense of our endangered ideals. It is better to die standing than to kneel living." Though Dr. Mohammed Hatta was later to become vice-president of the Indonesian Republic and took service under the Japanese, he represented at this time the general opinion of the Indonesian peoples, who saw little hope that Indonesian nationalism could survive without deliberate resistance.

For a month the war hardly touched Indonesia. Pontianak was bombed, scouting planes appeared on mysterious missions, but it became clear that the main brunt of the attack was to be on Malaya. On January 1 the Netherlands government received through the Swedish government an official proposal by the Japanese government that "in the name of humanity our two nations should avoid bloodshed and every kind of inhumanity." The peace offer was refused. By January 20, when the Japanese and the British were engaged along the Endau-Muar line north of Johore, the Japanese began an encircling movement to cut the communications between Singapore and Batavia. It was the beginning of the end. The oil wells of Balik Papan were destroyed by the Dutch, who still thought it might be possible to put a scorched-earth policy into effect. The Japanese landed at Amboina and penetrated the Banda Sea; by February 7 the airfield of Kupang on Timor was being bombed; by February 20 they had landed on Timor, occupied Bali, and cut the communications line to Australia. A last battle, directed by General ter Porten at Bandoeng, led to the surrender of the Dutch forces under his command on March 8. The governor general was captured, and the lieutenant governor, Dr. Hubertus van Mook, escaped a few hours before the fall of Bandoeng and fled to Australia. By July the Japanese could claim that all the outermost islands of the empire were flying the flag of the rising sun.

The condition of the Indonesians was appalling in the places where the battle had passed. For weeks there was anarchy. Japanese garrison troops were celebrating as they celebrated in Nanking; and over large areas the peasants took to the hills. In places where there was almost no Japanese influence, there was little change; the Javanese kampongs had been self-supporting for so long that administration or the lack of administration hardly affected them. As in Malaya, the Japanese attempted to offer their friendly services to the sultans, who kept themselves remote wherever possible, their lives endangered by the new associations. Dr. Soekarno was flown back from exile in Sumatra and persuaded to accept the presidency of the "Java Central Council," though Shjarir has declared that he accepted with secret reservations and attempted wherever possible to maintain underground connections with the resistance movement. Shjarir was also flown back, and disappeared immediately into hiding. The Japanese began to organize a pro-Japanese militia, sent radio receiving sets into the villages, and promised independence at the conclusion of the war. The militia was taught the goose step and ordered to shout Japanese slogans; they obeyed, but occasionally Japanese disappeared into wells, or their bodies were found in rivers. Occasionally there was more active resistance. At Indramajoe, Blitar and Tasikmalaja in Sumatra, and in Pontianak in West Borneo there were large-scale acts of sabotage against Japanese arsenals. There were some Javanese nationalists who hoped to advance their cause by playing the Japanese against the Dutch, but the members of the Java Central Council all possessed records of nationalist activity dating back to 1926. Soekarno, influenced by the early India Congress leaders Tilak, Gokhale, Aurobindo Gosh, and Gandhi, justified himself in his own eyes and in the eyes of many of his compatriots by attempting a policy of nonresistance. There was in fact almost nothing he could do except keep a watchful eye on Japanese attempts to disrupt the nationalist movement at its source by killing the young intellectuals. Amir Sjarifoedin was arrested and sentenced to death. This sentence was changed to life imprisonment at the request of Soekarno.

Meanwhile the Japanese continued to export food, cattle, and raw materials without bringing imports in exchange; for the first two years of the occupation they enjoyed an Oriental holiday of pillage, which began to decrease only when the Americans had so far advanced their bomber bases that they could cut off ships sailing from Java to Japan. Even then, by hugging the coast and building wooden ships in Javanese shipyards, the Japanese were able to deprive the country of much of its wealth.

In November 1943, after the visit of Dr. Soekarno and Dr. Hatta to Tokyo, the Japanese promised to give Indonesia an advisory council; a year later, in September 1944, the Japanese made their first definite offer of independence, but it was not until July 1945 that they convened a conference to discuss problems connected with the independence. The date was significant. The Japanese were fearing Russia's entry into the war, and Count Terauchi in his headquarters at Saigon had previously been informed that the moment Russia entered the war he would be empowered to sign a declaration of Indonesia's independence in the name of the Emperor. On August 5 a telegram announcing that Japan would be fighting Russia within a few hours was received. Four days later three Indonesian leaders, Soekarno, Mohammed Hatta, and Rajiman left for Dalat in Indo-China, where they remained until the end of the war. On August 16, when the war was over and Japan had announced her surrender, they were flown back. Japan had played consciously the same role that the Germans had played; the airplane that brought the three Indonesian leaders to Djodjakarta fulfilled the same function that the sealed train containing Lenin fulfilled in 1917. The Japanese acted in cold blood. Months later Nathan Broch, interviewing Colonel Yano, a leading Japanese commander in southeast Asia, learned that Soekarno was flown back in a deliberate effort to prolong the war. Having told the story of the flight of the Indonesian leaders to Dalat, Colonel Yano concluded: "Anyhow, in the fall of 1943 our army chiefs in Java had established the 'Java Volunteer Defense Corps,' which was immediately expanded all over the islands. This should allow the Indonesians to fight for their independence as our allies or alone—if necessary."

But if the Japanese had not sent the airplane from Dalat, the Indonesians would still have declared their independence, for there were others besides Soekarno who thought in the same terms. The suspicion that Japan had contrived the whole revolt remained for some months, but a year later Hubertus van Mook recognized that "looking back on the history of the past years, forces were at work in Indonesia more significant than Japanese machinations; they had deeper roots than any mere surge of terrorism, and on the whole we must accept that these forces resisted the Japanese." The statement of Soekarno was briefer. Stepping from the airplane he declared: "Indonesian independence has now come into force. Orders to this effect will be issued in due course." Within the next three days activity was feverish. An Indonesian army was not formed officially until October, but all over Java soldiers were marching and the red-white flags were streaming. On the walls of houses there appeared for the first time the first words of the provisional constitution, written while the Japanese were still in power, though it contains no trace of Japanese sentiment and springs directly from the French Revolution and the American War of Independence:

We, the Indonesian people, hereby declare our independence. Independence is the right of every nation. Any form of subjugation, being contrary to humanity, must be abolished. Our struggle has reached a state of glory, in which the Indonesian people are led to the gate of the Free Indonesian State which is independent, just and prosperous. With the blessing of Allah and led by the highest ideals of a free national life, the Indonesian people do hereby forever declare their lasting freedom. In the Republic of Indonesia the people are sovereign. The Republic is for righteous and moral humanity, for the unity of Indonesia and for democracy.

Chapter 4

The Red Bull, Unchained

WHEN the Indonesian Republic was declared on August 17, 1945, exactly a week before a similar declaration by the Viet-nam in Indo-China, hardly anyone in the outside world knew of the existence of the signers of the declaration of independence, Achmed Soekarno and Mohammed Hatta. They were known to the Dutch, who had imprisoned both of them as leaders of the underground independence movement—a movement that had been gaining strength since the defective revolution of 1927, when cruisers in the hands of young Indonesians were compelled to surrender. The Dutch knew that neither was communist or even socialist, but so little was known about them abroad that news editors ransacked their files in vain for information about the leaders of a new nation of 70,000,000.

Handsome and clean-jawed, wearing always a plain black Moslem cap and a white drill coat, Achmed Soekarno with all his faults is the father of the revolution. Born on June 6, 1900, the son of a Javanese schoolmaster and a Balinese mother, he made himself at the age of twenty-six the founder and first chairman of the Indonesian Nationalist party, only a few months after his graduation from the Technical University at Bandoeng with a degree in civil engineering. Tall for a Javanese, graceful and lithe, with a deep speaking voice and extraordinary powers of oratory, he was the first to insist vehemently and convincingly on the necessity of national unity. There was something of the actor in him, something of the mob politician, and something of the traditional gaiety of the Javanese revolutionary. He moved among princes and peasants, collected European paintings, campaigned steadily, organized "fighting squads" against the government, delighted in living illegally. He was glib, but possessed incredible energy. He traveled widely and developed a vast knowledge of the problems facing the Indonesian farmers. He could make decisions and invent slogans. He was responsible for the introduction of the national red-white flag with its rampant and unchained bull in the center, and for the national anthem. He likes to quote Shakespeare. His scholarship is not deep or firmly grounded like Soetan Shjarir's, but the energy behind it makes up for its inconsistencies. He is not in any sense a great man, but it is inconceivable that anyone without his qualifications could have taken his place. In the early days of the revolution he represented the Indonesian desire for independence on a scale unreached by anyone else; he *was* Indonesian independence; and when the presidential train made its historic journey through the Javanese hinterland after the declaration of independence, the previous opponents of his extremism crowded round him, garlanded him, touched the hem of his sarong, and laughed intoxicatedly at the jokes of the young architect and engineering student who had suddenly grown to the stature reached before only by Gadja Mada and Prince Diponegro. Almost singlehanded, by his assumption of the presidency, he had united the Javanese and the Sumatrans, who had been united only three times before, once under the Majapahit Empire, once under the Srivijaya Empire, and once for a short period in 1628 under Sultan Agung, who raised the same red-white flag and organized a new system of government by the complete extermination of the nobility.

Achmed Soekarno had no immediate desire to suppress the nobility; they had helped him in the past by financing his movement and protecting him. After the short-lived uprising in 1926, when nearly five thousand Indonesians were arrested and deported without trial to prison camps in New Guinea, his nationalism became uncompromising, while the death of some of his friends under revolting conditions in the camps at Tanah Merah made him for the first time a bitter opponent of the Dutch. In 1928 he was arrested in Djodjakarta after giving a speech in the palace of one of the minor princes. He was never put on trial, though a year later, in December 1929, he was placed before an examining committee that ordered his deportation to the Soeka Miskin jail in Bandoeng. He was released in the following year, formed a new party under the name Partindo (Partai Indonesia), and was again arrested in 1933.

This time he was exiled to the island of Flores. He remained there until 1937, when he was transferred to Benkoelen in south Sumatra, where he stayed until the Japanese released him.

Soekarno is a deliberate opportunist. He said: "I call my social political philosophy *marhaenism* [common-man-ism], or the guide to action for the seventy million impoverished Indonesians." He wrote in *The Torch of Young Indonesia*: "The party in its struggle for the attainment of its objective will not follow fixed lines of action, but will use policies depending upon ever changing circumstances." He believed in Allied victory and sent from his imprisonment in Benkoelen a telegram to the Netherlands government after the Japanese invasion, requesting his release and transfer to Australia, where he would be able to rally the Indonesian forces abroad. For some reason the request was denied. He accepted a position of considerable power under the Japanese, but seems to have acted with distrust of their pretensions to grant Indonesia independence. During the occupation he helped to organize the Java Volunteer Labor Corps, which assisted the Japanese in the defense of the island; he has excused himself by saying that this was forced on him and that if he had not done this, others would.

A capable architect who has designed houses and mosques, a connoisseur of paintings, he has read widely and fallen under the influence of Gandhi, from whom in the early days of the Indonesian revolt he borrowed the idea of "non-co-operation." He likes to quote Santayana and Dewey, but his ideas on the complexities of government are not so well informed as those of the much younger Soetan Shjarir. His main resource lies in his capacity to canalize the emotions of the Indonesians with simple slogans delivered with tremendous repetitive force. John Thompson, who accompanied the presidential train through Java, has explained how he could rouse the masses to the wildest enthusiasm:

Soekarno put on an act. If more constructive speakers had not proceeded him there would have been confusion in the public mind. As it was, however, he left the crowd in a thoroughly good temper. He made fun of the great long titles with which, he said, some people endeavored to honor him; for he regarded himself just as a simple man, a plain man of the people, and the only title he desired was the title of "brother Karno."

He kept the crowd in an ecstasy of laughter and fervor. "Will you accept the dominion status?" The crowd replied "Tieda," that is to say, "No." "Will you accept eighty per cent independence?" "Tieda." "Ninety-nine per cent independence?" "Tieda, tieda, tieda!"

Soekarno was delighted. He enjoyed nothing so much as this kind of audience participation, and his next flight of fun was to teach the whole assembly to say after him in English (for the benefit of the foreign correspondents), "Everything is running well." He asked the Indonesians, "What about the sugar factories?" A section of the crowd replied, "Everything is running well." He called for a louder response: "What about the railways?" The response in English was louder. "What about the electric light? What about the food supply? What about the water supply? What about the oil refineries?" And before he completed his questions, thousands of people were roaring with one voice, "Everything is running well."

Soekarno's greatest contribution to the Republic was that he succeeded, during the interval of six weeks between the Japanese capitulation and the first British landing under Lieutenant General Sir Philip Christison, in developing and inflaming the popular will for the independence to a point where there could be no surrender. Christison is reported to have said: "I have not come to give Java over to the Dutch," with the result that the Indonesians began to take it for granted that their demand had been heard; the tragedies of war-torn Java and Bali followed, but the initial impulse had been strong enough to leave no doubt that independence was assured, whether the Dutch liked it or not.

Revolutions are brought about by a happy combination of popular representative figures and shock troops. When the revolution is consolidated, it often happens that both must be removed; the technicians come into power. Both Achmed Soekarno and Mohammed Hatta, though they had been recognized by the Indonesians, were regarded by the Dutch as collaborators. Dr. Hubertus van Mook, who had returned to Java as acting governor general, was prepared to make concessions, but he stated publicly that he would refuse to carry on conversations with anyone who had collaborated with the Japanese. Soekarno retained his title as president and disappeared to Djodjakarta, leaving plenipotentiary powers in the hands of Soetan Shjarir, who held in the new government the portfolios of Prime Minister and Minister of Foreign Affairs. The first technician had arrived.

Shjarir, an infinitely more complex figure than Soekarno, possesses qualities entirely lacking in the President. He likes to reason, and distrusts Javanese mysticism and magic. (Soekarno was credited with having made a study of magic under his intimate friend Raden Sosrokartno, who possessed healing powers and was able to converse with the dead.) Shjarir has a nimble, swift mind that remains prodigiously logical. A small man, even for an Indonesian, five feet tall, clear-skinned, with sharp bright eyes, he speaks with professorial calm, and has never been known to lose his temper. He speaks English, Dutch, and Javanese with almost equal fluency. With none of Soekarno's personal power, he can make his points only by reasoning. He admires André Malraux, Joseph Conrad, and Ernest Hemingway. He is married to a Dutch wife, whom he has not seen since his arrest in 1936 for underground political activities. He has never seen his twelve-year-old son. In spite of the fact that he was treated more harshly than Soekarno in prison—he was sent to the Digul River internment camps and then later to the island of Banda—he has almost no bitterness. In January 1942 he was flown from Banda to Java by the Dutch, who locked him up in a police station for fear that he might contact the Japanese; but of all the political leaders thrown up by the Indonesian revolt, he was the least suspected of collaborating with the Japanese. During the war he fled to the hills, organized resistance, published illegal pamphlets, and opened a hospital. A deliberate humanist, he is closer in spirit to Nehru than to the Chinese leader Mao Tse-tung.

Shjarir the technician is probably the most brilliant figure in the whole Far Eastern revolt. Where Soekarno attempts to lift the peasants into frenzied ecstasy, Shjarir's efforts are always toward calm and firmness. He is tragically aware of the destructive forces awakened by revolution. In a broadcast to the Indonesian people from Batavia in December 1945 he said:

"We have summoned up unknown and unsuspected reserves of spiritual strength, and sometimes find ourselves borne rudderless over a wave of emotion. At such times a film descends over our eyes, and we are blinded by the aims of our national struggle. But we must beware always lest passion overcome our reason."

The theme is repeated continually; he demands urgently that people think before they act. In the early days of the revolt he employed a figure of speech that became popular throughout student circles in Indonesia: "Let us canalize and store these explosive forces, so that as occasion demands they can be solidified, cooled, and tempered." He likes scientific analogies and uses them often, and in the introduction to *Indonesia's Fight* he says characteristically that he wrote it in order to perfect the *technique* of the fight for independence.

The pamphlet is of incalculable importance to the future of Asia. Analyzing the cause of the revolt, the disorders and mistakes that marked the beginning, the various stages that the revolt must pursue till the country reaches a stable democracy, he spoke with a voice of authority. The pamphlet was well timed. Written in October 1945, when the uncompromising tempers of the President and Vice-President were leading to war with the Dutch, it showed that compromise was possible as long as wider objectives were held in view. It was a call for sobriety and vigor; nothing quite like it had appeared since Thomas Paine summoned the American revolutionaries to the fight. It is necessary to quote it at some length, because it provides the intellectual basis for the whole of the Asiatic revolt:

In this pamphlet I intend to present certain matters that are thought to be of essential importance to our present struggle. I intend to place them before you calmly and objectively; and because our struggle affects the livelihood and fate of all the millions of our people, it must be considered as a whole. The problem of guiding a people politically is clearly a matter for Reason, and not for one's own private wishes. . . .

We know now that it is the general desire of all classes of our community to keep and protect our independence. Never before has the desire for independence reached such a peak as today. Especially among the young it is clear that their whole lives revolve around the idea of independence; and sooner or later, even the masses, in the towns and in the villages, will be compelled to join in the struggle. The common people will inevitably be drawn into the conflict, and for them it is clear that the slogan *"Merdeka"* * does not mean only a sovereign Indonesia, nor does the red and white flag mean to them only a symbol of the unity and ideals of our race and country; to them it means especially freedom itself—freedom from tyranny, hunger, and oppression, and the red and white flag means for them the struggle for democracy. . . .

During those three and a half years of domination by Japan, the fundamentals of our life in the villages were turned upside down by forced labor, by bribing the villagers to become slave workers, by putting them

* Freedom.

in uniform to fight with the Japanese, by seizures of harvest, forced labor in fields, and indescribable tyrannies. There came to this country a reign of uncertainty and tyranny, causing wide unrest. Thousands lost their jobs. Tens of thousands of peasants ran to the towns to avoid starvation and forced exactions. Tens of thousands became slaves in *Heiho* gangs. Disturbances increased, and inevitably continued over into the time when the Japanese were compelled to surrender. . . .

The Japanese influenced our youth to take part in racial agitation; and indeed nationalist agitation did satisfy the hearts of some of our youth and intellectuals who were living in the midst of this unrest and uncertainty. Secret Japanese societies, known by the names of Black Dragon and Black Fan, their secret police, the *Kempeitai* and *Kaigun,* aimed their propaganda particularly toward the young, and did indeed influence their thoughts, although the majority of our young men instinctively hated the Japanese. The Japanese attempted to make us the enemies of the Dutch, of all the Allied Nations, of the Eurasians, who are of our own race, the Ambonese and Menadonese, both of whom belong to our own people, the Chinese and the government officials; and their intention was that all the races of the world should be hated by us, except the Japanese!

This was the position before the Declaration of Independence; out of this material we had to build up a free Indonesia. When the Republic began, the average government official was someone who had taken office under the Japanese. There had been little political education under the Dutch colonization; during the Japanese interregnum there was none at all. Our youth had been accustomed only to receiving orders; never had it been accustomed to responsibility. We had bowed to the Japanese as though they were gods, as the Japanese bowed to their Emperor—and that was all.

Militant awareness, essential to democratic action, did not exist. So we were unable to make use of the possibilities that existed in our society, and all the unrest was concentrated by our young men against the foreigners who lived in our country; they paraded as robbers, crept hither and thither with knives and guns after all kinds of futile ends. As we saw them, it seemed that their struggle was meaningless, even reactionary, almost a fascist reaction. Then gradually the Allied armies took over from the Japanese, who could rule no longer, and it is true that they gave the government of the Indonesian Republic the chance to consolidate its power. But the opportunity was never taken.

The primary reason for this defeat was that those who had taken over power were not men of strong spirit. Most of them were accustomed to bowing and scraping before the Dutch or the Japanese command; their souls were fearful; clearly they were unwilling to accept their responsibilities.

Secondly, many of them felt their indebtedness to the Japanese, who had unintentionally presented them with the possibility of attaining a free Indonesia. Ultimately, they thought they would be the government because they had worked with the Japanese. It followed that when the Japanese power weakened, they did nothing to introduce a strong government of their own; the country appeared to have no rulers; the untutored peasants had no idea how they would rule themselves, because they had never received any political education. The confusion increased. The killing of foreigners, murder, and arson can be understood in the light of political condition of the people, but they inevitably proved the weakness of the Indonesian Republic, which could not yet acquire the respect of the people. The medicine to remedy all problems was thought to be action, till action itself became a drug on the market. . . .

All these signs of confusion disappointed the Western world; they disappointed capital, but they also disappointed the working people. Capital was disappointed because it hoped for possibilities of investment when the country was at peace. The working people were disappointed because they saw signs of fascist violence, and they could not understand the murder of foreigners and Eurasians in our country. World capital is based on profit and loss. Providing they lose nothing, they are neutral. If we profit them, they are in our favor, and if they think they are likely to lose money invested here, they will be against us. If they think they will certainly lose money, they will concentrate their forces against us, and they will not hesitate to use military force to save their investments. Indonesian governments must make it a firm duty to stop this confusion. . . .

For ourselves, our revolution is both a national awakening and a democratic revolution, made inevitable by the feudal nature of our country and society. We cannot compare our revolution with the French revolution. We live in a world that knows the power of the atomic bomb, and possesses technical knowledge, resources, and industrial methods on a scale that cannot be compared with anything that has gone before. Our age is familiar with trust and cartel, telegraph, radio, factories, heavy industries. Although ours is a democratic revolution, we face different forces; there was neither capitalism nor real imperialism at the time of the French revolution. Also, the structure of French society was altogether different from the structure of Indonesian society.

The French during the French revolution were the unwitting pioneers of the road that led to capitalism and imperialism; our own revolution may justly be regarded as assisting the end of that same period. . . .

The Indonesian Republic is therefore an instrument of the democratic revolution. All laws that are not yet perfectly democratic must be made so; and we must prove that the essence of our country's belief is that our people should have freedom of thought, speech, religion, writing, choice of livelihood, and education, and that all governing bodies should be elected by popular vote. . . .

As quickly as possible the whole government must be democratized, so that the whole people feel the new influence. This can be done by creating or putting real life into the people's representative councils from the villages right up to the heads of the government. High government departments must also be democratized again in order to help make smaller the gulfs between the communities of people. Temporarily the old civil servants must be given positions as advisers, but inevitably power must come into the hands of the representative councils themselves. All laws and rights of citizens must be drawn up democratically, with humanity and socialism.

Because ultimately all nations must form one humanity embracing the whole world, becoming one race—the whole human race living in one society based on justice and truth—we must no longer be ruled by the narrow prejudice that divides human beings into different strata according to the color of their skins, or their differing traditions and inheritances. In the end these narrow feelings must cease to influence our lives. Once free of these bonds forged in a raw period of our evolution, we shall know that there is a vast difference between loving the land of our birth and hating foreigners. . . .

Government in the villages would be made healthier by the introduction of a true democracy that will use the old means of government of the "elected assembly," and receive full power. Its efficiency will be increased with the general rise of learning and education in the villages; rationalization and efficiency will break down some village traditions. Peasant trade unions, which must be created, will become the pioneers in equating the old traditions with the necessities of modern times.

People are altogether wrong if they imagine that the young men in the army, or our military leaders, will lead our political revolution. This misunderstanding can be understood—in recent years we have had altogether too much experience of military power. Our military education has suggested to too many people that our fight for independence relies on military power, but our youth must never be influenced by feudal or fascist militarism. Knowledge, still lacking in all spheres, must be increased. Let men learn to become revolutionary, not military leaders, idealistic, possessing the consciousness and the knowledge necessary for them to be clear that they are fighting also for the rest of humanity.

Indonesia's Fight, in spite of its undisguised attack against the Indonesian Army and President Soekarno, altered the course of the revolution. This young Dutch-educated lawyer from Sumatra, who was not even included in the cabinet of the provisional government announced on October 11, 1945, immediately attracted the attention of the more responsible and moderate revolutionaries. Dr. Hubertus van Mook had repeatedly refused to discuss policy with Soekarno or Hatta. The provisional cabinet included men like Dr. Soebardjo, a doctor of law who graduated in Holland, whom no amount of cajolery could acquit of the charge that he had been an active co-operator with the Japanese; it also included, as Minister of Information, Amir Sjarifoedin, another doctor of law, who had escaped execution by the Japanese only by a hair's breadth. The cabinet was re-formed. Soekarno and Hatta retained their titles and some of their power, but under the new government Shjarir, who had been chairman of the working committee of the National Council, joined forces with Sjarifoedin, the former president of the Gerindo party and the acknowledged leader of Indonesian resistance during the occupation. Shjarir held the portfolios of Premier and Minister for Foreign Affairs; Sjarifoedin became Minister of National Defense and Internal Security. Both were outstanding socialists, at the head of the socialist bloc, which included the trade-union group and the Socialist Youth Movement.

Their problems were not easy. Soekarno and Hatta remained in central Java, with undefined powers; Shjarir was given full plenipotentiary powers to deal with the British and the Dutch. But an intercepted British telegram from Lord Killearn during the protracted negotiations suggests that his power was largely based on the force of his personality and not on arms. "It is easy to give orders," he said ruefully, "but how shall I know that they are being carried out?" There was still occasional mob violence; early in 1946 there were risings led by youthful nationalists against the Sumatran princes, with heavy loss of life. Shjarir admitted that the killings were not all on the side of the Dutch. Tan Malakka, the hero of the 1920 Communist risings, and Soebardjo, for a brief while Minister of

Foreign Affairs, attempted a *putsch,* in which Shjarir himself was arrested; the *putsch* failed only with the direct intervention of Sjarifoedin. He was a socialist premier holding a precarious balance between three widely differing major parties: the Partai Nasional Indonesia, which had been led by Soekarno until it was repressed in 1929; the Masjoemi, a federation of purely Moslem parties; and the Socialist party. The Pemoeda youth corps, sponsored by the Japanese, was still in existence. The Tentara Republiek Indonesia, the Army of Republican Indonesia, was still insufficiently trained and equipped, and in spite of Sjarifoedin's technical competence, its organization was still at the mercy of the general confusion. Islamic extremists were determined to fight a holy war against infidels—the Khalifat had received its deathblow under Kemal Ataturk, but Indonesia was still sufficiently Moslem to relish the sensation of a holy war. In Sumatra the governor appointed by Soekarno, Dr. Hassan, had produced order out of chaos, but there were still signs that the confusion in Java might be lasting.

The combination of Shjarir and Sjarifoedin proved to be far-reaching. They are nearly the same age, they have both studied law in Holland, both are Sumatrans and have edited newspapers and taken part in the underground resistance. Sjarifoedin is short, darker than Shjarir, wearing yellow-rimmed spectacles, always carrying a brief case (Shjarir never seems to carry anything more permanent than a pocket handkerchief); he is a family man and a Christian, and plays the violin. The two Christians, representing 70,000,000 Mohammedans, are not puppets. Sjarifoedin has been arrested three times, twice by the Dutch in Batavia and Bandoeng, and once by the Japanese in January 1943, when he was forced to submit to the water torture. He retained even during the presidential tour through Java the air of an earnest student. He has no great oratorical gifts, but he possesses a persuasive simplicity of character and a capacity to understand the root of a problem quickly.

The first fourteen years of his life were spent in Holland, and though he speaks the dialects of Haarlem and Leyden, he says he distrusted most Dutchmen from the beginning, found them over-bearing and inefficient, without the depth of sympathy that might have given vigor to their scholarly understanding; the best came as scholars, the worst were the merchants and the police, who arrested him in 1940 on the charge that he was in illegal contact with the

Partai Komoenis Indonesia (Indonesian Communist Party). It was perfectly true; he had been in contact with the Communists, but only in an effort to make a common front against the imminent possibility of Japanese invasion. Immediately after his release he was appointed a research student in the Department of Economic Affairs by one Dutchman whom he admired, Dr. Hubertus van Mook.

More versatile than Shjarir, a good swimmer, an excellent tennis player, delighting in the theater, he has none of Shjarir's inflexibility. There are moments when even Shjarir appears inhuman beside the more laughter-loving Sjarifoedin, who describes himself as a man who came to Christianity "because it was the religion of love and pity." Shjarir, whose humanism comes from the intellect as much as from the heart, lives by the values that moved André Malraux to write *L'Espoir* and *La Condition Humaine,* two books that he unreservedly admires. It is characteristic of Sjarifoedin that he deliberately took the portfolio of internal defense because he knew there would be violence and he was determined that it should be tempered with charity.

Under the original draft constitution the Komite Nasional would have become an appendage of the presidential powers. Sjarifoedin was a member of the Executive Committee, which insisted on the broadening of the basis of government, so whittling down the powers of the president that the real power reverted to the premier and the cabinet. When Shjarir accepted the premiership, he did so only on the clear understanding that a high portfolio should be given to Sjarifoedin.

Order began to appear. Fewer bodies floated in the canals of Batavia. The British troops were showing signs of weariness, and the Dutch troops were no longer a great force to be reckoned with, though fighting was to continue sporadically for months.

The revolution had followed the lines of European revolutions in the past. No regime is ever in danger unless weakened from within; the long process of weakening, unnoticed by the Dutch, had begun thirty years before; the boast of the Dutch empire—*Je maintiendrai* —had long ceased to possess the significance it possessed in the early days of the empire. Revolutions do not occur during eras of desperation, but at moments when hope becomes manifest and when the young intellectuals are prepared to act as leaders. The students of the law, medical, and engineering colleges of Batavia were the intellectual elite that drove the revolution beyond the limits of a minor revolt.

For a revolution to remain stable it is necessary that the extremists should be expelled at the earliest possible moment; this, too, had occurred within a year of the Declaration of Independence. Organized violence there had been—Shjarir was at pains as early as October to express his fears that the revolution might lose its impetus from the employment of too great strength. But the days of violence were short-lived, the Dutch on the whole received commendable treatment, the violence was not always from the side of the Dutch, and Shjarir himself was often caught between the two fires of Indonesian extremism and Dutch misunderstanding—at least once he was fired on by Dutch soldiers. What is remarkable is that the revolt should have passed with so little loss of life, and that it should have followed in so many respects the typical pattern of European revolution. A process of consolidation followed. Hardly a year after the Declaration of Independence, the Dutch educator P. J. Koets could point to a society solidifying around the new government. "What struck me," he said, "was the quiet and peacefulness. The farmer is busy on the farm, the women planting or harvesting, the people gathered in the market place, peddlers with heavy loads along the roads, the dogtrot of the carrier with his load on his back, a merchant on his way to the next village. . . . I had a long talk with a republican leader whom I had known in Holland. He used the comparison with water in the course of freezing. Consolidation, he said, is like water that freezes at the top; there are large stretches where one can walk over in safety because the ice is thick and strong. There are parts where one can walk, but hear the threatening sound of cracking, and there are sections where only a thin skin of ice is forming, and over the deepest spots there are still open cracks. But the process of freezing continues, consolidation is progressing." * Shjarir had used the same analogy in *Indonesia Fight*. More than the French and Russian revolutions, the Indonesian revolt had been planned; it was a *technical* revolt, perhaps the last that will ever occur now that we have entered the historical stage when overwhelming power must lie on one or other of the two contending sides.

It was necessary from the beginning that the revolt should be

* Quoted from *Time*, December 23, 1946.

harnessed to something more powerful, more explosive than simple independence. It is to Shjarir's credit that he saw this from the first. So much of the Indian Congress's weakness lay in the fact that it could obtain unity only on the subject of independence; when power came finally, all other problems were still unresolved. On the anniversary of the revolt, broadcasting over Radio Indonesia, Shjarir could look back on the successful accomplishment of nearly all his aims and show that still wider issues were involved:

"We must pause now and think over the problems of our life as a nation. For one year we have struggled, not only to secure the status of nationhood among other nations, but also, and to a still larger degree, we have struggled to find a new basis for our nationhood, a basis more closely approaching the perfect life according to the principles of humanity. We have struggled to free ourselves by action from the influences that have harmed our souls.

"Though our present struggle must sometimes appear to have been roughly hewn, it was nothing but a struggle to obtain individual freedom of the spirit, through the growth of national freedom. Our national maturity was a means to obtain personal maturity.

"Because we are a nation in process of renewing our life and spirit, we have full confidence in humanity and the future. *We have learned to handle instruments of power, but we neither worship nor swear allegiance to power. We have faith in a future of humanity in which life on humane principles will no longer be suppressed by power, in which there will be no wars and no reasons for hostility among human beings.*

"As a renewed nation we seek our strength as a people in high and pure ideals. We do not believe in the possibility or the advantages of a life dominated by a thirst for power. And in our endeavors to secure a place among other nations, we remain true to the principles of life, which we desire for our people. We are prepared to exert to the utmost our energies, and we are prepared to sacrifice all we have, even our lives, to obtain the high and pure ideals of our people, but we must not use deceit and intrigues in our struggle. We fight by the code of the Kshatriyas.*

"Our nationalism serves only as a bridge to reach a human level that nears perfection, not to gratify ourselves, far less to do damage to human intercourse. We keep firmly to our faith in humanity in general. We are

* The Kshatriyas were the members of the Hindu caste dedicated to fighting. The most famous Kshatriya was Gautama Buddha.

no enemies of humanity. Our nationality is only one facet of our respect for humanity.

"Consequently our relations with other nations will be good if others can appreciate or at least understand our national ideals, but will be difficult to develop favorably if they still continue to worship an outdated nationalism, adhering to a narrow-minded national egoism and imperialism that has proved to be harmful to the world and humanity."

The simplicity of such statements may be bewildering, but nothing could be further from the truth that they were made in a spirit of intrigue. The curious evolutions in the thought of Sun Yat-sen are absent; firmness here is not dogmatism; he can foresee a world without national boundaries, and regards all boundaries as hinderances to human intercourse. The merit of Shjarir's approach lay in the philosophical background perfectly co-ordinated with the practical; he was making history, but at the same time he was seeing history being made with philosophical detachment. Neither Nehru nor Mao Tse-tung had spoken so affirmatively of the necessary path that the whole of the East would be compelled to follow. On the same day that he spoke over Radio Indonesia he made a statement to the press on the negotiations: "The republic will not collapse of itself, and will not be crushed by military action. Anyone who is sincere in his desire for a peaceful outcome should beware of relying upon our collapse either from internal causes or as a result of military or other pressure. This is bad thinking." It was a characteristic conclusion to the first year of revolution; consolidation had come to stay.

The Constitution of the Indonesian Republic was already in existence before the Republic was proclaimed. It was a tentative constitution, written during the occupation by the Japanese-sponsored Indonesian Independence Preparatory Commission, largely under the influence of Dr. Hatta. The constitution was based on the American pattern. It was a formidable document, showing no signs of Japanese influence. The president and vice-president were to be elected for five years; the president was *ipso facto* commander in chief of the Army, Navy, and Air Forces, with power to declare war, make peace, and sign treaties with other countries, to appoint and receive ambassadors. The Council of Representatives was to meet every year. Freedom of assembly, speech, and press were guaranteed; the people had the right to form unions and to strike. Every citizen had the right to receive education. Moslem insistence led to the concept of the state's being in the service of the Almighty, but "the state guarantees freedom for every citizen to embrace the religion he prefers and to carry out its rituals and prescriptions. Those religions that proclaim high morality and human principles become important factors in uniting the various groups of our society on the basis of mutual respect and understanding." The inevitable high-flying character of all constitutional documents is preserved, but certain passages stand in relief as embodying principles that are not included in the 1936 constitution of China, or in any similar Oriental charter. The right of free education, the right to strike, the right and duty to worship, the insistence on the state as the servant of divinity were new; nothing comparable to these are visible in the statutes and ordinances issued by the Dutch government. For the first time the constitution itself had become a weapon in the struggle for independence in the Far East; there was no likelihood that it would serve as a point of discord, as so often in China, where seventeen constitutions have been attempted since 1911.

A socialist aim was proclaimed in the first draft of the constitution and retained in the second. Article 33 reads:

1. The economy shall be organized co-operatively.
2. Branches of production that are important to the State and that affect the life of most of the people shall be controlled by the State.
3. Land and water, and the natural riches therein, shall be controlled by the State, and shall be exploited for the greatest welfare of the people.

Complete freedom of worship, speech, assembly, and movement are given in the constitution, as a constitutional right; it has not been found necessary to insert, as in the Chinese constitution, a clause restricting these freedoms when it is necessary to restrict rights to prevent infringement of the freedom of other persons, or to avert an imminent crisis, or to maintain social order, or promote the public interest." The Chinese constitution designated to come into affect on Christmas Day 1947 has neither the simplicity nor the relevance to the present times that characterizes the Indonesian constitution. Restrictions appear everywhere, subtly disguised by a government made cautious through its own use of unrestricted rights. That no such disguise has been found necessary in Indonesia speaks well for the intentions of the government, for the simplicity of a constitution is a measure of the willingness of a government to conform to rights as well as to duties.

The constitution was a weapon; it was also, in the early stages of the revolution, an appeal to justice. Broadcasting from Djakarta (Batavia) on October 11, 1945, Hatta and Soekarno appealed to the United States, Great Britain, the Philippines, New Zealand, Australia, the Netherlands, China, Canada, France, India, and Soviet Russia, demanding that Indonesian independence should be recognized. The appeal was based upon the Atlantic Charter and the constitutional rights of a democratic government, and like the original declaration, it was modeled on the American Declaration of Independence:

We are determined to break off all ties forever with Dutch colonial rule. The National Government of the Republic of Indonesia is an effective and stable government based on democratic principles. The Indonesians are opposed to any form whatsoever of autocratic or fascist rule as evidenced by the Constitution, which places the emphasis on the sovereignty of the people, nor do they recognize any other civil government in this country other than their own Republic.

The declaration pointed out that four contending governments were employing power in Indonesia—the government of the Republic, the Allied Military Administration, the Netherlands Indies Civil Administration, and the Japanese Military Administration. The Republic had been established on August 17, 1945. A month later the British, accompanied by a small group of Netherlands Indies Civil Affairs officers, landed in Batavia. The British announced that their sole aim was "to disarm the Japanese and evacuate the prisoners and internees." For two weeks there were probably less than fifty Allied soldiers in Java; the Indonesians had already a force of 9,000 soldiers of the Peace Preservation Corps and 1,800 armed police in Batavia alone. Dr. Charles van der Plas was refusing to negotiate with the Indonesian Republican government on the grounds that Soekarno and Hatta had been puppet officials under the Japanese. "I will not discuss government affairs," he said, "with a handful of brigands and traitors." In the state of confusion that existed at the time, the remark was not calculated to make the picture of Dutch rule more inspiring. He was placed in protective custody by the British; until the arrival of Dr. Hubertus van Mook, negotiations continued with the British alone.

The presence of the Japanese in large numbers was encouraged by the British as long as fighting continued. They were used as guards, police, and soldiers. In at least one case they were employed to attack Indonesian outposts. While the fighting continued the President and Vice-president continually insisted upon the prerogatives of the Republic. Dr. Hatta stated over the radio on October 4: "It is true that we formed the Constitution while the Japanese were in power. We held discussions continually on the future form and shape of the Indonesian state, but you will notice that we did not copy Japanese principles or ideas." A strange interlude occurred on October 7 when he announced dramatically that the five policies of the new state would be belief in God, nationalism, universalism, democracy, and social security. What was strange was that he had followed precisely the three principles of Dr. Sun Yat-sen, adding belief in God and universalism as make-weights. As a Moslem, he could believe strictly in the necessity of founding the state upon divinity—the impetus of the revolution came from the Islamic societies—but the order in which he placed the new five principles suggested that the President and Vice-President still represented the middle and upper classes of Indonesia. With the arrival of Soetan Shjarir to full power, the emphasis was reversed; social security and democracy became the new watchwords.

For Soetan Shjarir and the Socialist party they were far more than watchwords; the success of the revolution depended upon the application of a demonstrable form of social order under socialist principles. Shjarir had studied John Stuart Mill's *Principals of Political Economy* during his long imprisonment. He had a clean, sharp, humanistic brain; he admired the West "for its indestructible vitality, its love of and desire for life," and he was apt to regard the worst evils of capitalism as better than the mysterious myopia of Oriental mysticism, or even of Islamism. From the West he derived a singular capacity to put his ideas in order, and a practical determination to see that there did not exist a large gap between ideals and their realization. In a speech at a conference in Solo to government officials delivered on February 7, 1946, after the reconstruction of his second cabinet, he spoke of "the gulf that is being formed" between vision and fact. He said:

"A common mistake in all great revolutions occurs when the leading men in the revolution measure social possibilities by their vision, seeing all things in terms of aims and ideals; so that they tend to base their calculations on what they imagine to be possible, not on things as they are. To every student of history and sociology, the most important thing of all is the gulf that is formed between the people's struggle, and all its potentialities, and the ideals of the revolutionary actors. The modern revolutionary should be continually conscious of the existence of this gulf between subject and object. It follows that his actions should be based upon objective possibilities and not on subjective ideals."

The speech at Solo contained another scarcely veiled attack on Hatta and Soekarno, who were prepared to think of the revolution in terms of personalities and ideals. The elaboration of a socialist, democratic community would not come about as the result of chanting *"Merdeka,"* or invoking universalism. It would come about only as the result of a careful analysis of people's needs.

A direct determination to deal with things as they are characterized Shjarir's thinking. He had read Mao Tse-tung's *New Democracy,* and attached quite extraordinary importance to Mao's determination to pursue the revolution along its historical stages rather than to attempt the visionary feat of altering the whole pattern of an Oriental nation in a single overthrow of established customs. "Some malicious propagandists," Mao Tse-tung had written, "intentionally mix the two different stages, and in order to deceive the people speak of 'revolution in one stage.' It is an illusion to believe that the democratic stage does not also have its own historical tasks. It is absurd to believe that we can accomplish at a lower stage tasks that rightly belong to a higher one, and it would be foolhardy to try to accomplish the tasks of the socialist stage at the level of the democratic stage." Shjarir held such a high opinion of Mao's acceptance of the two necessary stages that he inserted them in the official platform of the Socialist party, of which he remains the chairman. Democracy must come first; then, perhaps—socialism.

The same battle had been fought before, for nearly all revolutions suffer from the presence of the visionaries who are helpless once the kingdom is placed in their hands. Soekarno alone had made the Republic possible; Shjarir was responsible for its continuance, its amplitude, and its form. The great cry of Serakat Islam in the past had been "To worship the country is to worship God"; by identifying nationalism and religion, the hard core of revolutionary fervor had been formed. The welfare and happiness of a country does not depend upon an alliance of nationalism and religion; it depends upon ballot boxes, organization of factories, trade unions, a clear-cut agrarian policy. There were still no signs that the government had elaborated an agrarian policy. The socialists insisted upon introducing fixed paddy prices and an Indonesian currency; it was too early in the process of revolution to decide matters affecting property rights of land, though in theory the state was the sole depository of all rights over the land, and in the early stages of the revolt the workers of east Java had taken over all enterprises and factories, declaring them the property of the Republic.

Vast problems remained; they could not be solved in the atmosphere of civil war that was encouraged by the presence of four theoretical governments on Indonesian soil. The main problems facing the young republic concerned the wealth that could be obtained from the available land rather than efforts to partition the land among the peasants, or the institution of large-scale co-operative enterprises on the Russian model. During the parliamentary debate on the budget of the East Indies in 1898, the liberal van Gennep had said: "The main point is and shall remain the increase in the people's welfare. . . . The two principal measures that may be employed for it are, as I see them, railways and irrigation works."

By 1940 great changes had appeared; neither railways nor irrigation works retained importance; emphasis was placed on emigration to the outlying islands of the Great East, and on education. Van Deventer could say in 1940: "Our main task now is to spread a knowledge of education, emigration, and irrigation. We must remember there are great virgin forests in the Outer Provinces waiting for men to cultivate." Already it was too late. The experiment had been tried, notably during the "ethical system" that was being practiced by Idenburg during his period as Minister of the Colonies (1902-05), when the Dutch government subscribed 40,000,000 guilders for the settlement of Javanese farmers in the Outer Provinces. The experiment failed because the increase of population was

such that the settlements could not keep pace with the new births.
The Dutch contented themselves with resettling 25,000 farmers between 1905 and 1940; meanwhile the population of Java had increased by five million. Emigration remained the only possibility,
and it could be organized on a vast scale only when the Indonesians
possessed their own government and were not restricted by budget.
Politically, the task of the new government was to form a democratic
society. Practically, it was faced with the task of large-scale plans of
irrigations, so that two crops could be grown, and of extensive plans
for emigration. But for the moment all these would have to wait.

But much had been accomplished. On February 22, 1946, an Indonesian People's Bank was formed, new industries were beginning,
the universities were open for the students; an inflation, due largely
to the Dutch capture of two billion guilders' worth of Japanese
scrip, was beginning to be controlled; though Soerabaya remained
even till Feburary 1947 a storm center of Dutch and Indonesian
guerrilla warfare, large areas were now at peace, and the agreements
reached at the Malino Conference, where 39 delegates representing
some 12,000,000 peoples of the "Outer Islands" (that is, the whole
of the Dutch Indies except Java, Sumatra, and Madura) declared
unanimously for the formation of a new self-governing dominion
within the Dutch empire to be called the United States of Indonesia,
showed that temporizing with the Dutch could prove no more in-
convenient than temporizing with the British. The talks between
Lord Inverchapel and Lord Killearn and the Indonesian leaders
were fruitful; there had been more agreement than disagreement,
and the British could leave the island with the conviction that
though much harm had been done by some of their troops, they
were the first to have understood the valid revolutionary causes of
the struggle. Food was cheap and plentiful in the villages, though in
the towns it could be bought only at inflation prices; clothes were
ragged, but in a climate as warm as Indonesia's this was not a matter of great importance. The political leaders sometimes wore ragged
shirts and shorts simply because they had no other clothes.

Other things contributed to the peaceful solution. The heated political atmosphere of Holland, which had reached at times heights
of venom unknown to England since the days of Gilray and Row-
landson, had abated. Dr Hubertus van Mook, in spite of occasional
outbursts, had shown a spirit of conciliation. Shjarir, reinstated four

times in the premiership, had shown diplomacy, some guile, and so much readiness to understand the Dutch point of view that Lord Killearn once telegraphed: "He is beginning to do everything we ask him, when it is reasonable." The internees were being withdrawn by rail, the roads to Bandeong, Malang, and Linggardjati were no longer infested with guerrillas, and the government was being increasingly widened to include all parties. By February 1947 plans were already being made for the long overdue emigration of from fifteen to twenty million Javanese to underpopulated Sumatra; if this succeeded it would be the greatest mass movement known to history, for nearly a third of the population of Java would be transported bodily to the neighboring island, and if the Dutch (who retain Borneo) approved, another ten million would be transported to Borneo, and another five million might be removed to some of the outermost islands. The possibilities were dazzling; where now there are forests and head-hunters, the industrious Javanese would make plains and towns.

From the beginning of the revolution the government had declared that the native co-operative societies remained "the cornerstone of Indonesian economic life." They were preparing to demobilize half a million men and settle them on the land. They hoped that foreign technicians and advisers would come to serve the Javanese people. The whole of southeast Asia had fallen in ninety days; it would take longer than ninety days for these countries to arise.

There were encouraging signs abroad, and not the least encouraging was that the Dutch at last were viewing eventual Indonesian independence without too great a horror. By the agreement with the Indonesians, the right to secede from the kingdom was hedged around with innumerable provisos; but independence does not depend upon words, and the Indonesians themselves seemed perfectly content to experiment with the fiction of Dutch rule. More important than the political advances were the theoretical advances. Soetan Shjarir had discovered the path that Asia would have to follow, but his most important pronouncements did not appear in the official speeches he delivered from the Djakarta radio. They appeared anonymously in three issues of *The Voice of Free Indonesia* published in April and May 1946, under the title: "Our Nationalism and Its Substance: Freedom, Social Justice, and Human Dignity."

Beginning with a review of the causes that brought about the accusation that the revolutionary movement was inspired by the Japanese, Shjarir says, borrowing a phrase of the Dutch philosopher Ter Braak, that the movement has nothing in common with the "rancor doctrines" that brought about Nazi fascism: "We absolutely deny that our movement springs from rancor. Without hatred, without resentment, but as keen as ever, and with no less passion, do we stand in this struggle for principles and values that in the long run determine the sense of human life." Thereupon he traces abstractly, in philosophical terms, how Asiatics, in striving to decide their own destiny and protect themselves, attempted to master the technical and organizational methods that were the outward manifestations of Western culture; and in so far as they allowed themselves to be influenced by Western culture, they were attracted to one special phase—positivism. He concludes that this regard for positivism is wholly to be understood when we consider the circumstances under which the meeting of the two cultures (which has the character of a culture collision with all the inevitable consequences of assimilation and elimination) took place. The Asiatics, faced with a relentless struggle for survival, saw in positivism "an insight into that tendency which makes it possible to determine the future beforehand, and eventually to interfere in coming events and compel the future to obey our will." But though the Asiatics could see the manifestations of Western power, and attempted to copy it, they did not know how Western power had developed, and suffered from irresolution and indecision. Desperately attempting to copy the West, they still could not understand the springs of its action. Thereupon resentment grew, and those who possessed no particular resentment were confirmed in their abhorrence of the West, and simply lived in the seclusion of religious beliefs or visions of empires of the past. Japan, concludes Shjarir, was never able to reach beyond that phase.

It is at this point that Shjarir's analysis becomes most interesting, and his criticism most illuminating. Unable to cope with the problems produced by the West, the Asiatics failed for a long time to employ their full strength. The contradictions were only resolved by *"a widening of the mental horizon, by which the struggle could be fought against the background of the universality of the values."*

It is at this point that Shjarir's major contribution to the understanding between East and West arises, for he continues:

In penetrating deeper and being made more receptive to the overwhelming riches of the Western mind, they regained their inner certainty. They allowed themselves to be influenced by those elements of culture which could be fertilizing and developing, to form free and harmonious personalities. And at the same time they realized that it also belonged to the Western tasks to conform to standards of truth, beauty, and goodness. These were the same ideas that had already been proclaimed for ages by the prophetic figures of the East, though differently formulated and applied.

The West itself has also been in a process of revision and purification for a long time. Among themselves they knew that the application of knowledge and technique could have fatal results, if at the same time moral standards were allowed to be overthrown. The chaotic condition existing among the world powers with all that it implies (annihilation by the atomic bomb) arises from man's self-doubt and from the lack of inner moral resistance.

The essential task of the modern man today, whether he comes from the East or the West, is to rescue himself from this abyss by endeavoring to fix again his known position, and re-establish his absolute presence, his destination in the cosmos. In all this he must be led by standards of truth, beauty, and kindness, which form together the components of human dignity.

These universal values are today no monopoly of the East, nor of the West; these are the tasks of fundamental man, and are valid whether he considers he is obeying the orders of the Almighty, or whether he considers man as a being finding his center in himself.

In all this we keenly experience and are fully aware that the realization and maintenance of human dignity are not possible within the space of servility and submission of one people to another; for there is no human dignity without freedom to determine one's fate.

Hence our fierce resistance against all that hampers and hinders our freedom, and our strong will, and hence our determination to form the new society we have in view.

So we resisted, not primarily because we were driven by hatred, resentment, or aversion to foreigners, but because we consider freedom as a *conditio sine qua non,* without which it is impossible for us to be ourselves, to form ourselves and our community.

Freedom is the condition for human dignity. But freedom and human dignity are ideas that remain sterile if they do not find concretion and application in the society in which we live.

At this point, armed with Spinoza, Shjarir pauses to describe briefly, but with amazing skill, the progress of the historical evolution of the West. He demands to know why the West has failed to maintain its historic mission, and comes to the conclusion that "freedom without social content is freedom in a vacuum, and meaningless." Obsessed with ideas of sovereignty, the nations after the French Revolution neglected the political freedom of the individual and turned it into the reverse. Individual freedom was replaced by freedom for unlimited exploitation. Free markets were in effect the negation of freedom whenever they assaulted the political freedom of the individual, and deprived him of necessary dignity. By colonizing the Indies, the Dutch increased production, built a banking system, installed hotels, and made good roads, but while production and exports amounted to an annual value of millions of guilders, the peasant still led a bare existence on a halfpenny a day. The problem was one of distribution contending against the element of power, of the marginal upper limit acceptable to the entrepreneurs, and the lower limit that was all the peasant was allowed to receive. Between these two limits the struggle was waged. There were two economies, the economy of the margin, adopted by the exploiting forces, and the economy of the lower limit, adopted by the peasants whose renumeration obeyed the laws of classical economy, but failed to obey the laws of human dignity. What is necessary, according to Shjarir, is "the just distribution," and he concludes: "A planned economy, led by the socialistic idea, is therefore necessary, because it is only in the atmosphere of socialism that a just distribution of the social product is conceivable, so fulfilling the demands of human dignity."

In the final paragraphs he looks toward a world where the greatest of all values will be human dignity, the disease of nationalism forgotten, and all major issues of planning decided by international co-operation. Only by equalizing the standards of living of the people in the world can we have real guarantees of peace, and only by surrendering sovereignty can we abandon wars. He quotes Jawaharlal Nehru approvingly: "We suffer from the disease of nationalism and that absorbs our attention and it will continue to do so until we get political freedom." To him it seems inevitable that this is the direction that the world will have to pursue, and he points to Bretton Woods, the International Monetary Fund, and the International Bank for Reconstruction and Development as of major importance to this end.

It is significant that Shjarir should have used Spinoza with such disarming force against the Dutch, who could claim Spinoza as their own. The relentless logic is sharper than Nehru's, more penetrating in discussing the causes and the changing psychologies that have brought the revolution about; unlike Mao Tse-tung, he is not obsessed with Marxist doctrine, though he is by no means its enemy. But neither Marx nor the classical sociologists of the West have studied the field of the Far East so brilliantly as the young Sumatran, who signed the three articles mysteriously with a single letter —S. (He published his prison diaries in 1946 in Holland under still another name—Sharazad.) Of all the phenomena that the war has brought from obscurity, Shjarir may well be the most important. His intellectual leadership of Indonesia is undisputed; and Indonesia itself has accomplished more than the other countries in the Far East. These small dark people have become the leaders in the struggle for the emancipation of subject peoples all over the earth, and the fate of the human world may well be determined, not by the prime ministers of the powers or the delegations at Lake Success, but by the decisions of the anonymous millions who read history through the eyes of Shjarir and take part in the village councils of Java and Sumatra.

Chapter 5

The Indian Scene

ALL three of the great nations that are leading the revolt of Asia have great histories; all have seen empires flourishing on their soil. Though the Chinese might demur, and the Indonesians have nearly forgotten the naked impact of Indian thought upon themselves, it is India that has held the Asiatic leading strings through history. The Madjapahit and Srivijaya empires in Indonesia were both Indian in origin; China owes more to the two peaceful scholarly invasions of Buddhism during the Han and T'ang dynasties than to any other outside source. India is the seedbed of the East, luxuriantly fertile, seething with intellectual curiosity and unrest, a country so astonishingly various that it is almost inconceivable that any one man should know more than a fraction of its vast culture, or even of its prodigious history. In India the shapes are so vast that Westerners are confused by its mere immensity.

But some things can be said which are roughly true about India: in almost every way Indian civilization is complementary to Chinese civilization. The Chinese were practical people who could invent paper and gunpowder; their ideographs are foursquare; they accepted the earth as it was, and never attempted to fight against nature, believing that a man could harness nature best by finding his own place on the ancestral soil, and staying there. They did not, like the Indians, carve gigantic caves out of their hills; they had no desire to leave permanent relics of themselves. They liked to be dignified, and their courts were so arranged that orders of nobility died out in four or five generations. The Indians invented a deliberate caste system and gloried in nobility—their heroes are nearly always princes. The heroes of the early Chinese stories are cunning peasants. The earliest Chinese poems are love poems or simple feudal odes to a king, while the earliest Indian poems invoke the gods of thunder and rain, the sun and the moon, the vast visionary creatures of their continually effervescing imaginations. The Indians invented the numerals we call Arabic, but the Arabs call them *hinduq,* testifying to their Indian origin; it is characteristic of the Indians that they should have pushed thought to its furthest extreme and have developed extraordinarily complicated logical systems. The Chinese did not begin to develop a logic until recent times, and their philosophies are expressed almost wholly in anecdotes; they lack the capacity for thinking in abstract terms, which seems to have been present among the Indians from the beginning. The longer one stays in China and India, the more inevitable it seems that the Indians and the Chinese share nothing in common, and it is precisely because of the dissimilarity between them that they are complementary. They represent extreme aspects of the Far Eastern scene. Yet both have one thing of enormous consequence in common—a landless peasantry.

We may never know the origins of India, but the earliest settlements suggest an ordered refinement of civilization absent from the earliest known Chinese settlements. The inhabitants of Mohenjo-Daro worshiped the cow, as their descendants do today; but the buried city of Mohenjo-Daro suggests a far higher standard of cultivation and civilization than one can find in present-day Indian villages. The sanitation was carefully planned; the huge bathhouses, ancestors of the tanks, the carefully wrought seals, and the tremendous depths of the fortification, belong to a race of warrior-craftsmen. Not far from Mohenjo-Daro there grew up in early historical times the great university city of Taxila. Religions, which begin in the West between the desert and the sown, seem to have begun in India between the mountains and the cultivated land. The traditions of religion flourished; the bull and Vishnu's ancestral chariot can be seen in the earliest seal engravings. They had houses of burned brick, with flat roofs; they turned out finely burnished pottery on fast lathes; they were skilled metalworkers employing gold, silver, lead, copper, and bronze. They appear to have been pacific people, and the discovery of skeletons of women and children in rooms or staircases suggest that like the Minoan Cretans they were suddenly overwhelmed, perhaps by the Aryans coming down from the north. There is evidence that the workmen organized themselves in guilds, and that men worshiped the Mother Goddess as they worship Kali today. They lived four thousand five hundred years ago, but if we compare the lives of the villagers of Mohenjo-Daro with the lives of the Indian villagers today, there seems to have been a long, slow decline. Nine out of every ten of the houses in which the Indian villagers live are hovels with thatched roofs and mud floors. The simple architecture of the forerunners has gone; instead, there is overwhelming evidence that the Indian peasant is deprived of the skills possessed by his ancestors, and of their comforts and settled mode of living.

The Chinese peasant preserves in his remote villages a sense of quiet decorum. His house is built according to the principles of geomancy; and since geomancy demands a necessary beauty of site in relation to wind and water, hills and forests, he tends to build better than the Indian villager, who must build according to a complex law of caste which insists that the main houses should be occupied by men of higher caste and that there shall be a simple gradation from palace to hut according to the caste system. The ordered hierarchic life that has been the basis of Indian civilization for centuries puts the agricultural worker at a disadvantage; he is the least in the ascending scale that rises through the artisans and the traders to the rulers and the priests. The hierarchic control makes for social peace. It is not always rigid, and in the deltas of the Ganges members of lower castes can enter higher ones by changing their names or by bribery; but the strength of the caste remains, with its social obligations sharpened against the poorest and the least educated. The Indian peasant lives slowly to the rhythm of the ripening of crops and the slow movement of the bullock cart. He dare not often go to the town, for he lives in an almost moneyless economy, but already there are rumors of radios and phonographs and films and books that can be bought there. The isolation is breaking down, but the caste system remains. Gandhi, in spite of his professional support of the *harijans,* has done little to remove caste barriers, partly in his fear that the removal of caste would only introduce violent class warfare.

The Indian peasant lives to an ordered routine, following the movement of sun, rain, and growth, and the seasons of the gods. He rarely moves more than eight miles from his home; his horizon is the market, which is closely associated with the gods. By Western standards his life may be miserable, but his misery cannot be compared with the misery of the small industrial worker who receives money wages but is excluded from any proprietary right in the seasons, and whose gods are reconciled uneasily with modern machines. The dictated peace of the village community ruled by Brahmans may be unpleasant to the foreigners, but the peasant has advantages that are denied to the city dweller. There are long periods of laziness; and the sensuous beauty of Indian village life, the girls on swings, the blue ponds reflecting the fabulous green parrots in the sky, the lakes with their red rocks, the white goats, the vermilion monkeys, and the spectacle of passing trains and caravans, belong to almost legendary existence. Animism prevails; the gods are everywhere.

"In the East," wrote Professor Radhakamal Mukerjee, "group action is social, social progress is evolved through the co-operation of the social group. In the West one group tends to coerce another, and all coerce society." This generalization is at least partly true; but the very rigidity of the village social group suggests profound instability in the face of technical progress. The tractors will come— what then? What will happen when all codes and hereditary customs are assailed by industrialism? The prevalent Indian Congress answer is that the transference from rule by the local landlord to rule by self-government will take place without dislocating village life, because the Indian village possesses advantages denied to the West—there is a close-knit group already in existence, with its power defined, its functions enumerated, and its history known. The English medieval parish with its feudal rule of landlord and priest, revolving around the alehouse, the vicarage, and the manor, provides a comparison. In modern England only the alehouse remains as a pivot, but two others have taken the place of the manor and the vicarage—the nearest movie and the nearest Woolworth.

Some kind of similar transformation is due in the Indian village. The nearest Woolworth may be too far to reach by bullock cart or even by bicycle; the village radio may take the place of the English cinema. Or the social group may revolve around the tractor and the government agent. Moneylending may be removed from the hands of the banyas, who charge a usual rate of interest of 37½%, and become one of the functions of the village post office. Traveling film companies and radios will teach the peasants more remunerative ways of planting grain, and when the buffaloes have given place to the Diesel engine or the tractor, the first great change in village life will have occurred. A complex, closed, and hierarchic social order cannot take place at any speed above buffalo speed; even bicycle speed, by enlarging the number of available markets, has disrupted village life. Motorbuses are beginning to roar between the villages, and with motorbuses comes electric light. Under conditions of a purely agricultural civilization the fine passivity of Gandhi and his followers becomes tolerable and understandable—what happens when the pulse beat of the internal-combustion engine enters men's lives?

The transition from a rural economy to an industrial economy is nearly always disastrous—the jute mills that sprang up like mushrooms over Bengal suffered from the same characteristics that poisoned the one-night towns of the Middle West. No new cultural patterns were available. There were no temples, no orderly communities, no seasonal variations in the mushroom towns. The sacred trees and sacred gardens made way for the new retail shops, new factories, new tenements. The peasants had struggled with famine in their villages, but the industrial town offered no social advantages over the village community. In the bustees of Calcutta, made hideous by rabbit-warren architecture, stricken with disease, teeming with an overcrowded population, the filth of the houses thrown into the streets where the flies and vultures congregate through long summers, you are conscious of a sense of brooding insecurity and religious fanaticism that alone maintains men's strength to live; the rhythm of life is not the heartbeat but the tuberculous gasps of the starving who wander listlessly through the streets. The men are listless because they have no pleasures except sex, which is their only relaxation from an otherwise relentless struggle against the elements; they have no hope of living in a modicum of comfort, because they are continually in debt, and no hope of maintaining their health, because their overcrowded tenements are filled with the germs of disease. Cut off from the village, they have gone through a process of adaptation to industrial life that makes them bad villagers when they return. Caste and other social conditions make severance from the village a trial, but the same social conditions make it almost impossible for them to return to their homes. They live in utter squalor, absorbed in the mechanics of living till the next day, defeated from the beginning, in an atmosphere of hopelessness unknown elsewhere.

In 1931, 74 per cent of the population of Bombay lived crowded together in one-room tenement buildings. The population of all the large cities in India except Lucknow and Karachi has been continually increasing, with the result that conditions steadily become worse. Between 1931 and 1941 the population of Calcutta sprang from 1,160,000 to 2,109,000; during this time almost no building projects were undertaken, and the larger population was compelled to live in the same tenements that were inhabited by the smaller. Though the main density of population in India is only 246 persons per square mile, considerably less than that of Germany, Japan, England, Italy, or Java, the density of the population in Bombay and Calcutta is twice that of the most densely populated parts of Shanghai. In Bombay and Calcutta housing conditions have reached their ultimate worst. In the *Bombay Labour Gazette,* the official organ of the Bombay Government, we find such entries as this:

In one room on the second floor of a *chowl,* measuring some 12 by 15 feet, I found six families living. Six separate ovens on the floor proved this statement. On enquiry I ascertained that the actual number of adults and children living in this room were 30. Three out of six of the women living in the room were shortly expecting to be delivered. The atmosphere at night in the room filled with smoke from six ovens and other impurities would certainly physically handicap any woman and infant both before and after delivery. This was one of many such rooms I saw. In the rooms in the basement of the house conditions were worse. Here daylight with difficulty penetrated, sunlight never.

The result of overcrowding, during a rising tide of industrialization and in spite of the large increase of the city of Calcutta, has been a total decline in the proportion of industrial workers in cities —from 5.5 per cent in 1911 to 4.0 per cent in 1941. Calcutta and Bombay maintain their increasing industrial importance, but no other cities have their primacy; there is a trend back to the land. Several causes are responsible, including the gradual rise in the cost of living in cities as compared with villages, where the cost of living has always been low and it is possible to live by barter; in the villages there is comparatively little money exchange.

Just as the villages, founded upon the principles of caste, tend to break their traditional patterns under the impact of modern indus-trialization and modern ways of thinking, so the old Indian joint family system is slowly breaking down in the face of the advances of modern transportation. Transport is still cheap to a foreigner in India, but the wages of a village farmer are never sufficient to allow him to travel easily. If one or two members of the family escape to the towns, the whole system of the joint family, which always in-cluded a delicate balance of available forces, is disrupted. Elder sons tend to remain and look after the fields; it is the younger sons who disappear, taking with them some of the accumulated physical wealth of the village.

No one knows the origin of the joint family system. Theoretically, it was an extreme form of communism. By this system worship, food, and property were held in common and owned jointly; every member of the family had an unrestricted right to the common fund. Since the common fund represented capital, the sons of the family often married before they were self-supporting; their wives were supported by the family jointly. The waves of foreign invasion under the Moguls tended to dislocate the simplicities of the joint family system. Under a government at peace, the family could in-crease out of all proportion to the land sustaining it. With the com-ing of the Moguls cottage industries and rural handicrafts tended to grow obsolete, the days of the factories began, and there was nothing except farming and cloth spinning to keep the family together.

Family ties stretch far and wide in India; the most distant and underprivileged relation may find comfort and shelter under the joint family roof. In practice the poverty of the family makes this nearly impossible, and the rivalries between the members are often so acute that they live under a sense of perpetual frustration. The family system organized restraint, respect for elders, tenderness for the sick and maimed; but the strength of the chain depends on the weakest link, and too often the crowded life within the family walls led to a high infant mortality and the perpetuation of decadent superstitions. In theory the joint family system owed its physical basis to the presence of the oldest surviving member, who claimed the right of "dictating by love." But the oldest surviving member, though treated with immeasurable respect, may be, and often was, cantankerous and self-seeking. Feuds arose, as they arose inside the

Scottish clans. Worse still, there were developed in the younger members of the family an unyielding respect and devotion for the elders; equality had become impossible under so compact a system of privileges. Though no Indian would demand equality with the village elders, respect that verges on adoration is not a firm basis for democratic government. Notabilities are treated with almost regal dignity, all differences of village rank carefully calculated, the untouchables taking the most menial positions. Nehru said in 1924: "Your experience in Europe and America will not avail you in the least to find out what village system is native to the new India." What is certain is that no new system will succeed unless it takes root in the spontaneous grouping of the people themselves; but a modern industrial economy has little to offer the villagers except a violent uprooting. Nehru's conclusions in *The Discovery of India* are important:

The village, which used to be an organic and vital whole, became progressively a derelict area, just a collection of mud huts and odd individuals. But still the village holds together by some invisible link, and old memories revive. It could be easily possible to take advantage of these age-long traditions and to build up communal and cooperative concerns in the land and in small industry. The village can no longer be a self-contained economic unit, but it can well be a governmental and electoral unit. The village council, itself chosen by the adult men and women of the village, could form these electors. . . .

That communal and co-operative concerns are necessary to put new lifeblood into the Indian village remains undisputed; what is not so certain is whether the adoption of the Chinese hsien principle is a sufficient excuse for giving the village elders power. A million hsien exist in China, but the principles of election remain undemocratic—as in India the landowner has too great a power over the electorate. In the panchayat, the village council of five selected men who rule all village affairs, the servants are unrepresented, and though everyone may give his opinion, it is rare for the dissenting opinions of the villagers who are not members of the panchayat to be upheld. A kind of rough common justice exists in the panchayat courts, but it is still based on principles of aristocracy and paternalism. The panchayat requires a number of allies—the ballot box and a greater respect for the opinions of the least favored. The

government of the Indian village is at least more democratic than
the Chinese hsien; but no one can hope that by simply extending
the basis of the village system any advantages will come.

I have spoken to Indian students in Bombay who had just returned from an educational mission in the Indian villages. Asked
what their greatest adversary was, they answered simply: "The disease of aristocracy—everyone has his appointed place. We can't get
anywhere until this is broken down." I asked them what their
greatest potential friend was, expecting them to say "tractors" or
"education," but they answered: "Radios. If they all had radios,
then they wouldn't listen to the panchayats so often and obey them
so blindly."

Whatever the final solution may be, it is certain that the Indian
village will be too small a unit to possess effective electoral power.
The patriarchal and static social system will give place to a form
of regional collectivism, with state or regional insurance taking the
place of the family insurance that comes from the accumulated
responsibilities and rights of the joint family village. The male child,
with his first cry, became the joint heir of the family lands; in future he will become the joint heir of the productivity of the region.
Inevitably villages placed in the center of the region will prosper to
the disadvantage of those on the periphery. Where once a ford, a
sacred grove, a strange rock commanded the presence of an important market town, now the market town will arise because it is at
the intersection of motor roads. Tractors are already being used in
India; the time of the co-operative region cannot be far off. In the
solution of the collective problem India is already in advance of
China or Indonesia.

In the Punjab especially, remarkable co-operative experiments
have been pursued, largely as the result of the work of a devoted
Englishman, Sir Malcolm Darling. By 1940 India had 137,000 co-
operative societies with over 6,000,000 members and a working capital of 107 crores of rupees ($32,000,000). By land mortgage banks and
co-operative credit societies the peasants in these areas have been
able to restrict the uses of moneylenders, and with increasing social
education they tend to spend less money on the innumerable social
ceremonies that are still demanded from Hindus. Co-operative farming has at least one further advantage of inestimable significance;
land areas can be more easily consolidated (the Indian farmer may

have twenty or thirty small strips of land scattered in different places of the village), boundary disputes can be solved on a co-operative basis, irrigation can be arranged more fruitfully if the village land is held in the name of all the peasants acting together. By 1939 over a million acres of the Punjab had been consolidated; the land becomes a unit again, no longer the patchwork sheet with innumerable legal tailors sewing continually and haphazardly together. Ownership itself becomes part of a collective pride; the family is exchanged for the community, which demands the same loyalties. More important still, the community calls for vigorous leadership by younger men, and election on the basis of leadership supplants hereditary right. The modern tendency to assert rights at the expense of obligations cannot wholly succeed against the remnants of paternalism that will survive; the village archives, the village worship, the village hearths remain, but a greater unit overshadows them—the community working as one.

Co-operatives remain the peasants' only shield against exploitation and the tyranny of capital, his only school of self-government, his only source of real representation in the affairs of the nation, his only means of obtaining fair security for himself and his family. Gandhi would have preferred each man to plough his ten strips of land and weave his own khaddar cloth, but both are so uneconomical that they deprive the peasant of all chance of improving his condition. The panchayat will go. The regional co-operative government, elected by all the working peasants, will inevitably take its place; and though the elders remain, they will remain probably in the form of a senate, so that the village as well as the state is ruled by a bicameral legislature. It is not important that the village should become the government or electoral unit; far more important is it that it should form alliances with other villages. Nothing is more significant for the future of Asia than the rapid growth of co-operatives.

It is here that the various social evolutions of the Far East have their meeting place. The experience of one nation becomes useful to another, and the common tendency illustrates the developments of each. The republican Indonesian government announced its determination to introduce cooperative farming within three weeks of rising to power; a week after the abdication of the Emperor Bao Dai, Mr. Vo Nguyen Gap, the Minister of the Interior of the Viet

Nam Republic, announced that similar measures would be taken as soon as practicable. The theme of the co-operatives recurs continually in the agrarian reforms of the Chinese Communists. Liu Chien-chang, a successful co-operative director of a village south of Yenan, introduced four principles of co-operative marketing and farming that are famous throughout north China:

1. No individual's share is restricted, so long as every member has equal voting power. Leadership lies with the people as a whole, not with individuals.

2. There can be no discrimination against small merchants, because they are familiar with the human relations within the community and possess business knowledge essential to the prosperity of the co-operative. Co-operators should on no account work according to set plan but must understand the changing conditions of co-operative work.

3. Local people should be employed; every effort should be made to avoid introducing experienced people from outside. Frequent shifts should be avoided.

4. Wherever possible, co-operative selling prices should be below those of the market. Some co-operators argue that since a co-operative represents the interests of the people, a larger profit would mean a people's profit. These people have forgotten that the co-operative represents the instrument of the people, and since the people are the customers, co-operative dividends to the people from high profits are simply the people's money returned. Prices should therefore be as low as possible.

Though India offers special problems of its own, these principles have validity in India and elsewhere. Co-operatives are already successful and show signs of increasing success on farmlands with small industries; no one yet knows how to solve the problem of co-operative industries of a heavier kind. In China they have progressed stage by stage through co-operative salt wells, arsenals, and oil wells; but when the Communists captured Kalgan and Harbin, lack of experienced management prevented them from developing successful co-operative heavy industries, though manufacturing plants were at their disposal.

Few things are more certain than that the economic areas of Asia must be increased; the small farms are unproductive. The moon-shaped terraces of the Chinese farmers will go with the expanding productivity of better technical resources; and though the traveler in the airplane will suffer, for there is no country more beautiful from the air than China, each crescent tilled on the side of the mountains represents a drain on human resources. Chinese government officials have talked quite seriously of flattening large areas of China with atomic bombs—perhaps the only beneficial use to which the bombs can be put. Irrigation in India as in China has only started. Every province will need its TVA. The Sukkur Barrage in Sind, the Sutlej Valley project, the Mettur Dam, and the Tangabadra project in Madras give promise of opening up new fertile areas. Even in overpopulated Bengal only 67 per cent of the total cultivable area is under cultivation. A traveler leaving Calcutta for Delhi by train, after flying over China, is awe-stricken at the sight of vast tracts of uncultivated land stretching to the horizon. With the introduction of a controlled water supply in east Bengal, large areas of previously flooded marshland have been put to seed. When the land frontiers are increased, as they are by irrigation, there occurs an interval during which the race of population increase is stilled. Irrigation itself is an incentive to co-operative movements; in all the countries of the East a controlled irrigation system must be the first demand on the public purse. Though the Indonesians complain of the injustice of Dutch colonial rule, they complain more loudly that the Dutch were so lukewarm in their plans for irrigation, which alone could save the economy arising from a violently increasing population. By its barrages in Egypt and India, England has left a mark that cannot be expunged.

England failed in India, not so much by its indifference to the cry for independence, but because it tacitly acknowledged a social system that has lost its usefulness, and contrived nothing to put into its place. The vacuum created by the early colonial wars and the decay of the Mogul Empire was not filled; a social system continued by its own inertia. When Prakash Narain complains of the weakness of the Indian spirit—a weakness that Gandhi has done much to celebrate—he is acknowledging an internal defeat within the social system, for the physical weakness of the lower caste Hindus springs from the structural weaknesses of joint family rule. The responsibility lies with the religion of the people, which penetrates their lives more deeply than the British raj; but the raj possessed a moral responsibility to temper the extremes of religious bias. Unlike the proselytizing Spaniards, the British professed no interest in the Indian religious scene except in their abhorrence of thuggee, the Juggernaut, and the more cruel manifestations of the goddess Kali. "We could not make them eat cow meat," said Lord Minto, "and therefore we were forced to leave them alone." At this age and hour it seems insufficient reason; a colonizing empire cannot afford to leave vacuums alone.

It is not always pleasant to contemplate the picture of the Indian scene, with its communal clashes, its intensity of passions suddenly aroused, its fervor, and its fecund heat. In summer if you kick a stone, a million ants rush out; fecundity is in the smell of the air. There are moments when everything, including the Bombay architecture, has the appearance of being overripe. "We live," said Nehru, "on the verge of disaster continually. The Bengal famine, and all that followed it, were not tragic exceptions due to extraordinary and unlooked-for causes which could not be controlled or provided for. They were vivid, frightful pictures of India as she is." But he goes on:

Yet India today is one of the very few countries with the resources and capacity to stand on her own feet. Today probably the only such countries are the United States of America and Soviet Russia. China and India are potentially capable of joining that group, for each of them is compact and homogeneous and full of natural wealth, manpower and human skill and capacity; indeed India's potential industrial resources are probably even more varied than China's, and so also her exportable commodities which may be required for the imports she needs. No other country, taken apart from these four, is actually or potentially in such a position.

For China one might substitute Indonesia, which may be almost as full of natural wealth as India herself. Indian strength has not yet shown itself. A checkered and tragic history has not yet come to a necessary rebirth, but the implements of the modern world are to be found in the Indian soil, and there are brain and brawn enough to make India the third greatest power in the world.

Chapter 6

Protagonists in India

ONLY in India has the Asiatic revolt been complicated by religion. Indonesia is almost wholly Mohammedan, Burma Buddhist, in China three religions have failed to develop roots, Shintoism collapsed in Japan at the command of an American Episcopalian, Hinduism survives in Bali in spite of the proximity of the island to the vast island masses of Mohammedan Java and Sumatra. Except in India, where a peculiar chain of historic causes have been at work, the East is tolerant in religion and at the same time deeply religious. It is significant that while the French revolutionaries declared that "the state is based on the rights of man," Article 29 of the Constitution of the Indonesian Republic declares: "The fundamental principle of the Republic is that it is based on the service of divinity." Divinity remains, as it must in all agricultural tribes, unchanged or hardly changed by the impersonal terrors of industrialization or by the coming of revolutionary socialism.

Two angels with flaming swords stand guard over India. They face one another, brandishing their weapons, speaking different languages, encouraging their followers to different habits of mind, one hard as the sand of Mecca, the other fluid as the Ganges. It is inconceivable that any religions could be more opposed to one another than Hinduism and Mohammedanism. The Hindu eats pork, which the Mohammedan abominates, and worships the cow, which seems to the Mohammedan no more worthy of worship than the sheep. In their systems of family and communal organization, in their understanding of time and place, in their rituals and ceremonies and devotions, in their logic and food and clothes and most intimate habits and beliefs, it is unthinkable that they should be able to find reasons for compromise; yet nothing is more significant

76

for the future of India than that territories of compromise are being discovered.

It may be that there can be no final compromise in the abiding tenets of worship—the impulse of the Hindus toward tranquillity, seeing themselves like the river Ganges flowing into the quietness of the sea, and the Mohammedan impulse for action may be irreconcilable; but just as both possess the instinct for arduous pilgrimage, so both are capable of shearing off the more irreconcilable elements of their own religions. Moslem women are now not always heavily veiled. In spite of the precepts of the Koran they play sports, attend movies, travel alone, enter universities. I have heard Mahomed Ali Jinnah furiously denouncing the Hindus and pointing to the irreconcilable differences between the religions as the reasons for the necessity of Pakistan; then when I reminded him that during the communal riots educated Moslems and Hindus had gone out unarmed in an attempt to settle the differences, he became mellow and exclaimed: "Ah, this only shows you that we Indians are—" I have forgotten how he continued the sentence, and I have a feeling that it was never finished, but at least he had said "we Indians" on the day before his enemy was elected to power. When he attended the London Conference, he allowed himself to be photographed arm in arm with Jawaharlal Nehru. This did not prevent him from denouncing Nehru, but it is inconceivable that Stalin would allow himself to be photographed arm in arm with Franco.

Both Nehru and Jinnah were educated in England, a country where passions are rarely aroused. In India religious intolerance has been artificially encouraged. Even recently there were times when intolerance hardly existed. The conquering Mogul emperors married Rajput wives, who were Hindus. Less than ten years ago Gandhi and Jinnah were discussing how intolerance could be minimized. Increasing poverty, the war, deliberate provocations have sharpened the enmity between them, but on both sides of the conflict it is recognized that Mohammedanism came with a small band of conquerors, and considerably more than 95 per cent of the population is descended from Hindus. Jinnah may say that the word Hindustan is an invention of politicians; first, it is not true—it was invented by the Emperor Akbar; secondly, 90 per cent of the Moslems are of Hindu origin; thirdly, the country which we know as India has formed a loose federation of states since historical times. Undefinable, containing 222 vernaculars, divided into 563 states, with fantastic varieties of minor religions, India is not a continent but a state of mind, or rather two states of mind held in precarious balance, a vast land mass given over to schizophrenia.

The consequences need not always be disastrous; other countries —England, for example—contains racial groups so antipathetic to one another that it is hardly conceivable that they can combine under a single government. The descendants of Celts and Anglo-Saxons have had time to nourish their sense of community; the Hindus and the Mohammedans as opposing groups have only existed for four hundred years. The Indian Mutiny (which the Mohammedans were wrongly accused of instigating) and the problem of the succession of the Khalifat did more to sharpen their nascent opposition to the Hindus than any event prior to the second world war. Events outside India are mirrored on the sensitive Indian retina to an extent that can only be explained by a dangerous sensitivity; rancors, imaginary griefs, and the wildest excitement may be present at the same time as the most impressive serenity and detachment. It is necessary to insist on the subtle complexity of the Indian mind, trained by centuries of Sanscrit dialectics. The Indian lacks the casual tenderness toward the world of the Chinese; he is continually asking questions, stimulated by the vast heat of the Indian sun to incredible feats of intellectual daring. It is significant that the early epics describe heroes who gamble away their kingdoms at the throw of dice. The tradition has remained—daring is still one of the components of the Indian mind.

In January 1947, when Jawaharlal Nehru proclaimed the urgency of bringing the republic into being, he added: "We face a very great responsibility as the leaders of Asia." Four years previously, when Chiang Kai-shek was told about current talk in Chungking concerning the leadership of Asia, he replied that the question of leadership had never arisen—Asia would not be led, but would form its own institutions according to its own organic structure. But "the leadership of Asia" is far more than a catch phrase and represents a complexity of forces that are still only half understood. Long before he assumed power, Nehru issued invitations to the Asiatic states to a Pan-Asiatic conference in the spring of 1947. No hue and cry was raised; Wall Street remained unshaken. But simply by issuing the invitation, he had announced to the world the end of foreign domination and the beginning of the growth of an Asiatic concert of powers. It may still happen that an Asiatic bloc will be led by the Indian Congress Party, but it is far more likely to be led by the Indonesians, whose revolution was more successfully accomplished.

The newspaper gave no prominence to Nehru's invitation, even though it was the first physical sign of a completely new orientation of world affairs. An Asiatic concience had arisen. Education, the contacts derived from the war, a thousand influences have made the Asiatics increasingly conscious of one another during the last twenty years. The problems confronting the Asiatic states are basically similar; their traditions, their methods of agriculture, their systems of land tenure, their life expectancies, and even their rates of literacy are all approximately the same. Except for China and Indo-China, which were not invaded until the middle of the nineteenth century, they have felt the impact of the West for the same length of time; and though India and China have been industrialized to an extent unparalleled in other Asiatic countries the full strength of industrialization has not yet been felt. The Asiatics have a community of interests among themselves strong enough to suggest that an Asiatic federation, including India, Indonesia, Burma, Siam, Indo-China, and later China will come about much earlier than we imagine. There will be no reason why this Federation should not support a common army, a common fiscal policy, and foreign representation in common, a common parliament and a common Asiatic language and treaties held in common, and no barriers for trade. An Asiatic economy would be simpler to manage than a national economy. The hopes were vast, and in private conversation Nehru would suggest how necessary it was that India should take the lead, since she was not oppressed like China by unequal political philosophies, and being nearer to the West had greater opportunities. The symbolic gift from Indonesia of 500,000 tons of rice less than a year after the Japanese had surrendered augured well for a policy of mutual trust between the Asiatic states.

That Nehru should have been the first to develop the idea of a federation of Asiatic states does not surprise those who have met him. Mercurial, relentlessly logical, as little accustomed to compromise as Mahomed Ali Jinnah, given to occasional outbursts of inexplicable temper, a Brahman by birth and a student of the world's poetry by choice, he represents, like India herself, a fantastic combination of opposites. He shares with Mao Tse-tung and Soetan Shjarir a curious femininity and sensitivity; like them he is immersed in the habits of scholarship and has trained himself to a sense of profound self-dedication. A socialist but an aristocrat by birth, he has a real but guarded sympathy for people. He smiles easily but finds it difficult to suffer fools gladly. Now fifty-eight, he is casual and graceful, with the elasticity of mind of a much younger man, due probably to the Kashmiri toughness that has left him comparatively unharmed by the rigors of prison. He says openly that he is a desperately lonely man and finds himself most lonely when surrounded by Indian crowds, but like all essentially lonely men he has trained his mind to perform immense feats of concentration. The history of the world that he wrote in prison for his daughter suffers from a lack of necessary historical sources, but no one without an inexhaustible talent for doggedness could have performed the feat. He is as relentless with himself as he would like to be with the Indian people, saying that they must learn to work and build up the strength of the republic—the socialist objective must be obtained whatever the cost. Almost an agnostic, he would prefer—if the choice had to be made—to become a Buddhist, and he has always carried with him a photograph of the stone Buddha in Anaradhpura. He has a Buddhist sensitivity and a Buddhist delight in rigor, though he lacks Jinnah's fanatical desire to pursue an objective to the bitter end.

Physically, he is as changeable as Mao Tse-tung, who will resemble a schoolboy, a country vicar, a professor, and a workman at short intervals. Without the white Congress cap, his baldness and the fringe of snow-white hair suggest an amiable devil; there are moments when, wearing his cap, he resembles a university student or a professor in the junior common room. He has never sought to find a personal following and is dubious about the value of his popularity, inclined to believe that it is only one more legacy handed to him by his father, the celebrated Motilal Nehru. He has a loathing for the British sergeants who enjoyed beating up Hindus. For General Dwyer, who ordered the massacre at Amritsar and whom he overheard boasting of its success in a railway sleeper, he had nothing but shivering cold contempt; but the English soldier pleased him, and he said that he found himself happiest in the company of his own Kashmiri friends, but sometimes an English intellectual or an English private soldier would make him almost as happy. He insisted from the beginning, like Soetan Shjarir, that a passionate desire for independence must go hand in hand with a reasonable devotion to its immediate consequences—the building-up of a social democratic state. In spite of Congress's dependence upon Indian millionaires, he has never departed from his faith in socialism—a faith that he demonstrates at great length in his autobiography.

His attachment to Gandhi is almost as great as his attachment to his father; the most interesting pages of his autobiography describe the complexities of an attachment that gave greater strength to both men. There are elements in Gandhi's mind that he distrusted from the beginning—the almost peasant cunning of the older man made him unpredictable, liable to invent his logic as he went along, offering Solomon-like cures when simpler ones were at hand, as when, during the massacres of Hindus in Bengal, he suggested that the Hindu women would be wise if they poisoned themselves to avoid rape by Mohammedans. The practical wisdom of Gandhi delighted him; the theological wisdom was not always communicable, and sometimes seemed dubious. Gandhi had more faith in the innocence of the rich than Nehru, who could understand neither why the rich should be worshiped "for keeping their riches in trust for the people" nor why the poor should be worshiped because they are poor. Yet most of his life Nehru has lived under the shadow of his father or of Gandhi, and it was only at the end of the war that he emerged as a figure in his own right. Though he had been president of Congress three times, he was nearly sixty before he received great power.

The spectacle of organized religion fills him with horror. "No one can live without religion," Gandhi told him. Nehru set out with the firm conviction that at least he would try, but there are moments when doubt torments him and then like a cunning athletic Kim he follows the wandering path of Gandhi's guru, amazed by the delicacy and understanding the teacher, the resolve and the tenderness that are foreign to his own eclectic and more English philosophy. He has commented at length on his own lack of religious feeling. The strength of the denial suggests a deep-centered hesitancy; nothing he has written is so filled with religious feeling as his description of the death of his wife, Kamala, or the account of how, after his eighth imprisonment, he climbed the mountains of Kashmir. The world's tragedy haunts him. The greatest passages of *The Discovery of India* are concerned with the vision of the youth of the world now passed into industrial decay, with splendors that have vanished, with the ironies and overtones that enter when the first proud stimulus is passed. Quoting Pericles on the glory of Athens, he reflects that "the splendid eulogy for his beloved city was followed soon after by the city's fall, and a Spartan garrison occupied the Acropolis." It is not for nothing that he has attempted to model himself on the Buddha of Anaradhpura, once a city of half a million inhabitants, with royal treasuries and immense palaces, and now buried under creepers and vines. He knows that all history is tragic.

Somewhere there is unity, hope, a passion so deep that it is outside history altogether, a sense of dedication that includes the world's misery. He ends his autobiography with a gesture of socialist faith in a federated world, and if that is not possible, at least there may come about a federation of Asiatic states: India, China, Burma, Ceylon, Afghanistan, and Persia. Strangely enough, Indonesia—the first Asiatic country to express a valid community of interests with India—is omitted.

He has read widely. In his library in Bombay British White Papers are massed in confusion, but the works of modern English poets and novelists are carefully arranged on the shelves. T. E. Lawrence's *Seven Pillars of Wisdom* has been read closely, the wide margins filled with annotations; there are the complete works of D. H. Lawrence, Dylan Thomas, and W. H. Auden. In spite of prison, he has followed with prodigious care the renaissance of English literature between the two wars and quotes poetry widely in his own books and histories. Occasionally, a strange sentimentality appears in his quotations, as though for a moment the sharp mind had failed to bite. The swift prose style has a falling rhythm; a sense of tragedy and fatality pursues him even in the technical accomplishments of his prose which at its best has more color and life than Tagore's. Like Ernest Toller, whom he resembles to a quite extraordinary degree, he will say sometimes that imprisonment led to a life of contemplation, and nothing is more difficult than to pass from contemplation to action. He has described with glee the effect of an anonymous article he wrote on himself in the *Modern Review* of Calcutta, in which he opposed his own re-election. The intellectual Brahman suffers from a strange doubt of his own heroism—how can one be a hero and not be a fascist?

From the Far North to Cape Cormorin he has gone like some triumphant Caesar, leaving a trail of glory and a legend behind him. Is all this just a passing fantasy that amuses him . . . or is it his will to power that is driving him from crowd to crowd and making him whisper to himself, "I drew these tides of men into my hands and wrote my will across the sky in stars." *

What if the fancy turns? Men like Jawaharlal, with all their great capacity for great and good work, are unsafe in a democracy. He calls himself a democrat and socialist, and no doubt he does so in great earnestness . . . but a little twist and he might turn into a dictator. He might still use the language of democracy and socialism, but we all know how fascism has fattened on the language and then cast it away as useless lumber.

Jawaharlal cannot become a fascist. . . . He is too much an aristocrat for the crudity and vulgarity of fascism. His very face and voice tell us that. His face and voice are definitely private. . . . And yet he has all the makings of a dictator in him—vast popularity, a strong will, energy, pride . . . and with all his love of the crowd, an intolerance of others and a certain contempt for the weak and inefficient. His flashes of temper are well-known. His overwhelming desire to get things done, to sweep away all he dislikes and build anew, will hardly brook for long the slow processes of democracy. . . . His conceit is already formidable. We want no Caesars.

But the Hamlet he is prepared to conjure up does not occupy the stage for long; the miseries and rigors of the Indian peasant's life, seen through his own eyes and through the eyes of Gandhi, absorb him too often to allow him the luxuries of the "private face," a phrase that he borrowed from the poet W. H. Auden; and if everything else fails there is always the memory of the Far North, the Kashmir lakes and snows, from which he has come.

Socialism to Nehru does not spring entirely from the doctrines of Marxists and Fabians; it owes more than we are accustomed to realize to Gandhi's insistence on "right means." The study of Marx and Lenin influenced him profoundly, but the "revolution of the proletariat" and "the dictatorship of the proletariat" seemed meaningless in the vast primitive agricultural society of India. The tech-

* The quotation is from T. E. Lawrence's *Seven Pillars of Wisdom.*

niques of the West could not be adopted in India. He confesses that Marx "does not satisfy me completely, nor did it answer all the questions on my mind, and almost unawares a vague idealist approach would creep into my mind, something rather akin to the Vedanta approach." He constantly complains against the national prejudices of Marxists and socialists, remembering that Marx complained with the same bitterness against the dangers of a purely national socialism. For Nehru there are no frontiers except poverty of the body and of the mind. He complained that European socialism rarely dealt with the problems of nationalism, colonial administration or native rural economy. It was not only that the principles of socialism could not be adequately transferred to India in their present form, but he wanted to find their natural expression arising from rural economies already in existence. In India, where the villagers are ruled by the landed proprietors who held their land by hereditary right, there exists no communalistic ownership as in many districts of Indonesia. The complex village is society in its most feudalistic form, with its hierarchies and near serfs arranged in watertight descending order; the panchayat or representative council is itself nearly always hereditary, the headman an office created and protected by government, the owners of the village fund the proprietors themselves. Socialism entered India, not through the village communities, but through the trade unions, and then only among industrial workers, until the founding of the Kisan Sabha (All-India Peasant Union) as late as 1936. In a country of 390,000,000, the trade unions have a membership of only 600,000, and the Indian peasants remain for the most part unorganized.

Faced with such backwardness, Nehru could only insist on the necessity of economic socialism to give them greater rights. In his presidential address to the Indian National Congress at Lucknow in April 1936 he admitted that the power of Congress stemmed from its desire to complete independence, but like Soetan Shjarir later, he viewed independence as only a step toward a democratic socialist state. The end was socialism, the means national independence. For the first time he gave his unalloyed allegiance to socialism:

I am convinced that the only key to the solution of the world's problems and of India's problems lies in socialism, and, when I use this word, I do so not in a vague humanitarian way but in the scientific economic sense. Socialism is, however, something more than an economic doctrine; it is a philosophy of life, and as such also it appeals to me. I see no way of ending the poverty, the vast unemployment, the degradation and sub- jection of the Indian people except through socialism. That involves vast and revolutionary changes in our political and social structure, the ending of vested interests in land and industry, as well as the feudal and aristo- cratic Indian states system. That means the end of private property, ex- cept in a restricted sense, and the replacement of the present profit system by a higher ideal of co-operative service. It means ultimately a change in our instincts and habits and desires. In short it means a new civilization, radically different from our present capitalist order. . . . I do not know how or when this new order will come to India. I imagine that every country will fashion it after its own way, and fit it in with the national genius of the place. But the essential basis of that order must remain, and be a link in the world order that will emerge out of the present chaos.

Socialism is thus for me not merely an economic doctrine which I favor; it is a vital creed which I hold with all my head and heart. I work for Indian independence because the nationalist in me cannot tolerate alien domination; I work for it even more because for me it is the inevi- table step to social and economic change. I should like the Congress to become a socialist organization and join hands with the other forces in the world which are working for the new civilization. But I realize that the majority in the Congress, as it is constituted today, may not be pre- pared to go so far. We are a nationalist organization, and we think and work on the nationalist plane. It is evident enough now that this is too narrow even for the limited objective of political independence, and so we talk of the masses and their economic needs. But still most of us hesitate, because of our nationalist backgrounds, to take a step which might frighten away some vested interests. Most of those interests are already ranged against us, and we can expect little from them except opposition even in the political struggle.

It was the most important statement he had made on the future of the future government of India. He was not prepared at that time to force the issue, and he lamented that Congress by failing to encourage khaddar (homespun cloth) was no longer in direct con- tact with the village masses—there were checks and feints in the inner organizations of Congress that appear between the lines of his speech—but in insisting on socialism, he was discovering a method that would enable Congress, if it followed him, to main- tain its power among the broad masses of the people. What is sur- prising is not that his faith should resemble so much, even to its details, the faith announced by Mao Tse-tung in *New Democracy* and by Soetan Shjarir in *Indonesia's Fight,* but that he should have stated it so openly at a time when independence was not even in sight.

The presidential speech of 1936 is cardinal to an understanding of Nehru's own policy and foreshadows his insistence that the princes must surrender their power. He said it was neither "dignified nor becoming" that the rulers should depend upon the external authority of Great Britain. The appeal to their dignity was subtly addressed, not to the princes themselves, but to the Indian masses, who could be forwarned in time against the validity of the acts of state, the protocols, and the theories of paramountcy that would remain even when a republic of India had been proclaimed. It was unthinkable that a republic could be founded as long as it included native states under British paramountcy. The states occupied more than two thirds of the land area of India, and were inhabited by nearly a third of the population, living in various stages of feudal authority. In the same speech Nehru proposed a collective affiliation of trade unions and peasant organizations. The proposal was not relished by the right-wing "High Command" but remained as part of the Congress election platform without opposition. Nehru had stolen some of the thunder from Jaya Prakash Narain's Socialist Party, founded in 1934.

The tug of war between the "High Command" and the moderate socialists continued, with Nehru holding a precarious balance somewhere left of center. Two years later the Bombay Industrial Disputes Act had imposed under Congress sponsorship a four-month period when no strikes could take place. Nehru's star seemed to be in the wane. He had refused to follow Gandhi into the wilderness after Gandhi's dramatic resignation from Congress at midnight on October 28, 1934, the socialists found him too lukewarm and the "High Command" found him too revolutionary; but he remained partly as a symbol of Congress continuity, partly for the respect in which his father was held, and partly for his own qualities. His power stemmed from a complexity of causes; and his precarious balance became increasingly insecure while Congress itself became more complex.

Nothing could be more erroneous than to imagine that Congress was a coherent, homogeneous organization. It was continually faced

with rebellion from within. It represented huge and sometimes irreconcilable forces; it included saintly Mahatma Gandhi and near
communists, factory managers, coolies, and millionaires. Yet it
represented the most efficiently representative body in India. To a
degree equaled only in China, its policies were brought about not
by individual persons but by the conflicting impacts of personalities.
Argument was continual; Congress remained healthy for this reason, unlike the Moslem League, which, demanding as Gandhi
sometimes demanded overriding powers and a common policy to
be obeyed blindly, showed from the beginning its lack of argumen-
tative health and its obedience to pressure groups. Nehru was a
whole pressure group in himself, his popularity so widespread that
it was becoming dangerous, but the power of Congress was greater
than that of its most influential members. Health remained; its
policies, endlessly debated, retained their complex overtones even
when they were passed as resolutions, and though Nehru and
Gandhi remained to a quite extraordinary degree representatives of
Congress policy to the outside world, they would have been the last
to maintain that they represented Congress at all—they were members and liable to the same treatment as the rest.

In this sense Congress was democratic. Nehru himself had little
patience with the complicated urgencies of debate—he had said himself that only a hairbreadth divided him from the potential dictator
—but he learned to understand the necessity of debate. His arguments were couched in tones that demanded analysis from others
more experienced in analysis, and in Congress debates the aureole
that surrounded him in public, the ceaseless tribute he received
from the peasants, the implacable determination of so many Indians
that he should be regarded as a god—all these disappeared. Gandhi
could speak as though he were voicing the intentions of the Almighty; Nehru, the Brahman Kashmiri, could only voice the intentions of the people and his own ceaseless intellectual debate with
himself. The private debate became public when he announced furiously in the spring of 1939:

"We laid down further our line of action in the event of world
war breaking out. It was for the people of India to determine
whether India would join a war or not, and any decision imposed
upon us by the British would be resisted."

Like Nehru, Mahomed Ali Jinnah comes from rich parents, studied law in England, entered politics through Congress, and thrived on the complexities of the Indian scene. There are moments when Jinnah gives the appearance of a much older and thwarted Nehru. It is characteristic of him that he approves of the title that the Moslems have given him: *Quad e Azam,* which means The Great Leader. In his elegance, his fierceness (which is not ferocity), his implacable opposition to argument, the tautness of his sprung mind, and his bitter contempt for his enemies, he crystallizes like Chiang Kai-shek a world that has already passed from the scene. He lives heroically, fighting heart disease and tuberculosis—his doctors gave him a year to live ten years ago—assisted by the single weapon of his impervious will. He has none of Nehru's charm, which repels him. He looks like a skeleton, but it would be a mistake to believe that his smile is insincere or that his bitterness is cynicism. More complex even than Nehru, he represents forces so incurably mixed together that it is better to regard him as a sphinx than to pretend that the springs of his action can be easily disclosed. Though he is leader of the Indian Moslems, he is not an orthodox Moslem; he shaves his beard, lives in an entirely western style, dresses impeccably in western clothes, and flaunted Moslem law and tradition by marrying a Parsi woman. His gestures are aristocratic, his house in Bombay is one of the richest in a city of palaces, yet he represents 93,000,000 poor Moslem farmers. Though he thunders for Pakistan, until recently he was known as the ambassador of Hindu-Moslem unity; and though he excoriates Congress, he was for long one of its principal supporters, and the public hall of Congress headquarters in Bombay is still named after him. His earliest sympathies were for democracy and against British rule, but at the present time, though publicly refusing any allegiance to British rule, he knows that the Moslem League will be at the mercy of the Indian Congress once the British are removed. With a trained lawyer's mind and infinite complexity, with grace and vindictiveness, he still takes delight in inventing simple and dangerous slogans that are the denial of all his training, and even of his understanding. As he has grown older, he has become more dramatic, simpler, borrowing much from his chief assistant, Liaquat Ali Khan, the broad-shouldered son of a nawab who controls the Moslem League executive. The process of growth seems to be reversed, and the chief initiator of Moslem-Hindu amity has become the chief dissenter.

His appeal stems from various factors—his unyielding contempt for his enemies (he will introduce at a first meeting the debating point that Moslems eat cows, which the Hindus worship), his intellectual stamina, the loyalty of his followers (who would follow him if he ordered them to capture New Delhi or Moscow), his sensitive understanding of the problems confronting the Moslem minority, and his indefatigable delight in ceremonies. When he travels, he is received everywhere as a king, whereas Nehru is likely to be received as a crown prince. Though his smile resembles the gleam on the handles of a coffin, he is more human than his detractors have ever suggested; and it is not his fault that his secretary, through whom most foreign correspondents are compelled to interview him, is more proud than the Quad e Azam himself. There are many things to be said in his favor. He is a supreme (though rare) controversialist. He has refused all proferred titles. His letters to Gandhi show that the argument was not always in Gandhi's favor—he asked for definitions where none were provided. He refused to co-operate with non-co-operation on the grounds that it was basically self-defeating—nothing has happened since the Nagpur session in 1920 to suggest that he was misled, and the Republic of India was not brought about by non-co-operation, but by the growing weakness of British power and the emergence of a British Labour Party. He is incorruptible and hardheaded, and if politics is a game, he plays it superbly and dangerously. When the communal riots broke out in August 1946, he was the first to inveigh against the communalists on both sides, but he continued to make inflammatory remarks that stirred the Moslems to frenzy. He sees himself as the presidential successor to the Khalifat, and would like to assist into being a huge domination of Moslem power stretching from Morocco to the Philippines. Obsessed by the problems raised by the Moslem minority, he will say one moment that "British rule is maintained by British bayonets, and Hindu rule by Hindu knives," and the next moment he will talk of the possiblities of peace between all three sides, all bitterness forgotten. He is changeable always, the lawyer's razor-keen mind sharpening on the irreconcilable elements of the Indian scene.

But sharpness is a dangerous weapon, as he knows to his own

cost; he has gained privileges and renown through sheer force of intellect, but the weapon is double-edged and sometimes spins in the air without purpose. Though Nehru has devoted three pages to Jinnah in *The Discovery of India,* he has failed completely to come to grips with the man and concludes lamely enough: "It took Mr. Jinnah a long time to realize that what he had stood for throughout a fairly long life was nonsensical." Jinnah can answer that if it is nonsense, at least there are simplicities to the Moslem religion that are denied to the Hindus. In spite of Jinnah's Hindu ancestry—like all converts to a new nationalism he displays the extremes of a nationalist temperament—he represents to an almost fantastic degree the feudal virtues and vices that are the legacy of Mogul rule.

It is in his recent benediction to Pakistan that Jinnah has become most incredible. Pakistan has been so much referred to in recent years that we are sometimes inclined to believe that it represents an age-old and legendary desire of Indian Moslems. In fact, it was born in 1933 in the brain of an Indian Moslem, Chaudhary Rahmat Ali, whose address is 16 Montague Road, Cambridge, England. The word Pakistan means "the land of the pure," but according to Chaudhary Rahmat Ali the movement was named Pakistan because it included the first letters of the names of the federation of Moslem states that he hoped to bring into being—Punjab, Afghanistan, Kashmir, and Sind. By the resolution of the Moslem League, passed in Lahore in March 1940, the names of the states are not given, but it was resolved that Pakistan should include the areas "in which the Moslems are numerically in the majority, as in the north-eastern and western zones of India" and that they should be grouped to constitute "independent states." To those who were familiar with the Danzig corridor nothing could be more calculated to displease, for the new "independent states" included three large areas that were not contiguous and could only function together by means of corridors. Pakistan has never been accurately defined, though it appears to include the Northwest Frontier, Punjab, Sind, British Balukistan, Assam and Bengal, Kashmir, and the Sikh state of Patiala. In all these groupings except Assam (which is claimed for reasons that were never made clear) Moslems are predominant. Unfortunately for the peace of India, the Hindu minorities in these regions are as vocal as the Moslem minorities in other regions. The plan has not been formed as a concrete proposal for the preservation of Moslem independence in India but was wider and more revolutionary associations. The strength of Pakistan lies in its irrationality and the mystical faith in a Moslem empire that is conjured up by the spectacle of India acting as a bridge between the Islamic worlds of East and West.

Fiercely dogmatic, insistent on feudal virtues, the Islamic faith in the West searches for a passage to the East. Beyond India eastward the intensity of faith declines until in Indonesia it has become part of an accepted code of behavior, no longer the urgent proselytizing creed of the Middle East. In Indonesia Islam has been tempered by animism, laziness, the quick Malay intelligence, which does not concern itself with extremes. Even in Cairo there is little of the urgency that Islam manifests in India, where it is sharpened by conflict with a Hindu majority, each side openly despising the habits, customs, and morals of the other. Pakistan—as a dream of world empire—could only have sprung from India.

In conversation Jinnah rarely elaborates on his schemes of empire, but the Moslem League has published at length its view on the Moslem belt stretching from Morocco to the Philippines. In *Pakistan and Muslim India,* to which Mr. Jinnah contributed a foreword, the plan of a federal empire is explained in its misleading simplicity:

1. A federation of Arab states including Saudi Arabia, Yemen, Oman, Kuwait.
2. A federation of Syrian states including Trans-jordan, Palestine, Syria, Lebanon, Latakia, Jebel Druse.
3. The Sudan shall come under the Egyptian government.
4. Tunis, Tripoli and Algeria to be declared an independent state ruled by a single Bey.
5. Morocco to be restored to independence, and to include the Riff and Rio del Oro.
6. Abyssinia, Eritrea and Somaliland to form an independent state under Moslem rule.
7. Russian and Chinese Turkestan to be similarly incorporated and placed under Muslim rule.
8. Afghanistan to be offered an outlet to the sea; the north-western Indian states to be incorporated with Afghanistan.
9. Punjab, Sind, the Northwest Frontier and Kashmir to form an independent state.

10. Another state to be formed out of Eastern Bengal and the Muslim area of Assam.
11. The four western provinces of China to be incorporated into a single state, separate from the Chinese Republic.
12. Indonesia, together with the Malay Peninsula, to form an independent Muslim federation.
13. Albania, Azerbaijan, Daghestan and Circassia to form independent states.
14. A Muslim federation in Africa to be formed from the states south of the Sahara, including Nigeria, French Sudan, the Gold Coast, Togoland, Sierra Leone, Ivory Coast, Senegal, Liberia and the Chad Valley.

This plan has some attractive elements, notably its simplicity; a vast Moslem federation stretching down the center of Africa and across southern Europe and central Asia, forming a gigantic T. Unhappily, there is very little real possibility that it can be brought about, and its significance lies chiefly in the fact that the proposal has been made at a time when the bonds connecting the Moslem states, except in the Middle East, have become less secure than ever.

Yet the Moslems remain in India a consistent force, deriving their strength from the remote past and the still more remote future. Some kind of federation of Moslem states remains possible as long as the Middle East encourages the movement and grows wealthy on oil; but it will be looser than the confederation that Jinnah passionately upholds, and its growth will become increasingly difficult during the present stage of the Asiatic revolution, where social stresses cut directly across all religious stresses. The story of Indonesian independence was for a long while the story of Serakat Islam; but though Islam remains powerful in Indonesia, it was not Islam that brought about the revolt against the Dutch. As more and more Moslem students became educated in universities, and the excesses of purdah are restrained, and new social organizations find a place among the Moslem Indians, the strength of the purely religious movement will grow weaker. Jinnah, a past master at swimming against the tide, will find that even visions of Pakistan are unavailing.

Pakistan did not arise solely as a result of the vision of a Mohammedan empire; it grew inevitably as a result of the tensions between

Congress and the Moslem League. Congress cannot be entirely condoned in its attitude toward Jinnah and the Moslem League— Nehru's attempts to explain Jinnah away spring from a fundamental unawareness of the Moslem character, which demands privilege and honor as the Hindu character demands paternalism and a variety of gods. To the Moslems all Moslems are equal below Allah; their abhorrence of caste restrictions is greater even than that of the British, who have caste restrictions of their own. The course of recent history, by which the Moslems were given far more than their deserved proportional representation by the process of "weightage," has weakened their case; as a minority, protected by law, under a Moslem president of India, they would possess more effective power than if they insisted on an equality of representation and threatened always to use force. Jinnah claims in conversation that the Moslems are the warrior guards of India. The majority of the soldiers in the revolutionary Indian National Army were Sikhs, who belong to a religion closely akin to Hinduism. The Moslem League, by refusing to define completely the boundaries of Pakistan, stating that the boundaries will be decided by " a plebiscite of Moslem populations only," have further weakened their case; nor have they offered any suggestions about how the boundaries, once demarcated, would be kept peaceful. Pakistan is not so much a solution as a state of mind bordering, not on hysteria, but upon an unattainable dream of past empires. Economic necessity demands a federal India divided into five or perhaps six self-governing federations on the model of the American states; the portfolios of foreign affairs, reconstructions, co-operatives, war, and national finance cannot be divided between Pakistan and Hindu India without serious dislocation of the national economy.

I once asked Mahomed Ali Jinnah whether there was any message he cared to give to the Western peoples. Looking more stern than ever, he answered: "There is only one message to give to the West —that is, that they pay the least possible attention to Indian affairs, and let us settle the issues ourselves." I suggested that that would mean a solution by force, a ten-year civil war, with both sides inadequately armed, and it seemed to me that the civil war would never be decisive, for no other nations would assist either side. There would not be, for example, American aid to the Hindus or the Moslems on the scale of American aid to the Kuomintang. He answered: "We have spiritual weapons." Strangest of all the strange talks I had in India were these words of an English-trained Moslem lawyer speaking in the tongue of Gandhi.

But the war will not be settled on spiritual terms, for there is no means in the modern world by which spiritual sources can compromise; the mere effort toward compromise sharpens their differences and reveals their weaknesses. "Punjabi" has written a widely read book called *Confederacy of India,* which suggests that the Islamic revolution has passed beyond the stage of a local Indian conflict, and must be seen in world terms. "It would be impossible for us to maintain for long in an un-Islamic world our ideal Islamic state. As such we shall have to advocate world revolution on Islamic lines." If, in the new outlook of Indian Moslems, Mr. Jinnah is to take the place of the Japanese emperor, nothing could be more disheartening for the future of Islam's relations with the Western world. But the die is not yet cast. The real importance of the struggle in India lies in its fertile breadth of unattainable ambitions. There is no merit in the struggle except in as far as it sharpens differences and brings them into the open. The British, seeing that most of their warnings are fulfilled, have achieved the glory of Cassandra, whose most dread warnings went unheard. In India itself confusion and shame envelop the educated classes, who see no reason for a conflict that has lost all meaning.

One solution remains: the rise of education among the Moslems. Radio, irrigation, sanitation, village co-operatives answer the needs of the modern peasant more completely than religion. It is significant that at the Pan-Asiatic Conference, called by Nehru in the spring of 1947, the Moslem League held aloof, though representatives from the Moslem states of the Near East arrived. The British may accept Pakistan in fear of civil war. Geographically and historically partition is meaningless, and most particularly meaningless at the present time when the tendancy is toward confederations of states in larger groupings; and the Moslems would have greater opportunities in a federal India than in an India implacably divided forever.

Chapter 7

The Rise of Congress

FOR over fifty years the party known as the Indian National Congress has directed the Indian Nationalist movement, but in its earliest days it asked for nothing more than better relations between government and the people of India. An Englishman, Allan Octavian Hume, founded the party on the day when he wrote a letter under four headings to the graduates of Calcutta University, calling on fifty men to form an organization to encourage closer relations between Indians and the India Office. He asked for a permanent delegate to England "who would represent to our rulers the true state of the country and who would agitate Indian questions." More important was the second demand: he asked that suitable means should be adopted for imparting political education. The third demand was characteristic of the times: national trades and industry must be encouraged, and he suggested that prizes, certificates, and testimonials should be awarded to the inventors of new methods in engineering and authors of treatises. It was an age of testimonials, and neither Hume nor the Indians with whom he hammered out the plan of an Indian Congress had sufficient experience to know how industry should be encouraged. The fourth and last of the demands was almost as important as the second: he asked that means should be adopted for the creation of good feeling between the different religions of India. The history of Congress has been the history of these four demands, to which more recently there had been added the demand for complete independence.

The first Congress brought together the outstanding Indians of the time, and included Dayanand Saraswati, who had recently founded *Arya Swaraj,* a party which believed in the principles of the ancient vedas and had close links with Mrs. Annie Besant's theosophy. It is easy to imagine these early champions of Indian self-government as cranks, but nothing could be further from the truth; they were hardheaded men, trying to look into the future and to find a method of escape from the unruly domination of British power. Gandhi came later, bringing with him ideas that were foreign to the earliest members of Congress, but even in the earliest meetings men spoke as they spoke now, their aims were the same and their methods, though quieter, followed the same ends. At the second meeting of Congress, which five hundred delegates attended, the venerable Raja Rampal Singh declared: "We are deeply grateful to government for all the good it has done for us, but we cannot be grateful to it when it is, no matter with what best of intentions, doing us a terrible and irreparable injury. We cannot be grateful to it for degrading our natures, for systematically crushing out of all martial spirit, for converting a race of soldiers and heroes into a timid flock of quill-driving sheep." Almost the same words were to be used nearly seventy years later by Jawaharlal Nehru and Prakash Narain.

The first Congress was presided over by a Hindu, the second by a Parsi, the third by a Moslem. Three Congresses have been presided over by Englishmen. Since the Congress of 1907, the first at which Gandhi attended, the ideas of Gandhi have been growing increasingly powerful. Congress had begun as an act of protest; it became in time the machinery by which the protest was affirmed. In its growth it differed hardly at all from the growth of all the other nationalist parties of Asia, which have begun as study circles, attended chiefly by educators and businessmen, and grown into vast organizations dominated by the inevitable party bosses. The educators and the businessmen remain—they are still the two most powerful elements in Congress.

Allan Octavian Hume made four demands, but implicit in them was the demand made by Raja Rampal Singh—that the Indians be given back their arms. The Indian Arms Act of 1878 deprived all Indians of the right to bear arms "of any description whatsoever except under a license and to the extent permitted thereby." The British Government was caught in a dilemma. It dared not employ Indian officers in the army, and it had no knowledge of how, under the government of India, intelligent young Indians should be employed. There were no openings outside the professions, and these were limited, by the caste system, by pride, and by lack of opportunity, to medicine, law, banking, and commerce. "The timid flock of quill-driving sheep" became a drug on the market, and B.A. (Calcutta) was the sign of a lost generation which had no stimulus for reforming the country and no capacity to carry out reforms even if the stimulus existed. The British were to learn too late that national pride, once taken from a people, festers; they lose their initiative and hope to survive. Even at that time the situation might have been saved by sending the young bachelors of arts into the villages, where they could teach modern applications of agriculture and reading and writing to the uneducated villagers, but the B.A.'s thought in terms of private practice and had little reason to return to the poverty-stricken villages. The vicious circle continued. Without arms, without employment, attempting to ape the British, the young Indians found themselves caught in the net which Shjarir has described in his articles; they could neither turn backward or forward, and they were to remain lost until the moment came when their resentment against the West was modified by the invasion of new ideas, new possibilities of a marriage between East and West, a marriage that could only take place against the background "of the universality of the values." This background was provided by Gandhi.

The rise of Congress has been the rise of Gandhi. No one else has achieved such power over the Indian masses or combined in himself so many of the Indian contradictions. He behaved at times with the intransigency of an emperor, and at other times with the cunning and even the brutality of a witch doctor, but it is more than ever necessary that we should understand him, as we must understand Mao Tse-tung, Chiang Kai-shek, Nehru, Jinnah, and Shjarir.

It is not easy for anyone to understand the influence of Gandhi if he has no sympathy with the doctrines of Tolstoy, Thoreau, and Ruskin. Very early in his life Gandhi swore an oath "to keep away from women and from animal food and to live as purely as possible." In doing this he was doing no more than an act of penance, since he was deeply conscious of the sin he had committed in leaving India without the blessing of his clan. Penance has been his symbol throughout his life; in his repeated acts of penance he has most closely identified himself with the Indian people, who have proclaimed the necessity of sacrifices since the earliest times.* But the penance that Gandhi has been performing ever since he left England after taking his law degree has been on an almost universal scale. From the beginning he has regarded himself as a scapegoat, consciously manipulating the forces of history so that the disgrace and the punishment wherever possible should fall on him.

Soetan Shjarir analyzed the strange meeting of East and West as taking place in two phases: one of absolute recoil, the other of absolute acceptance against the background of the universality of values. Gandhi's position is halfway between these two extremes. He rejects Western science and Western medicine, with angry contempt. Determined to reduce life to its utmost simplicities, he can see no need for what he calls the terrible mysticism of Western science. Over a large part of his life he has done everything within his power to destroy the machine while placating the great industrialists who were erecting machines all over India. The contradictions have never been completely resolved, but the great virtue of Gandhi was that he stated the contradiction in his own life, and was therefore a far more typical figure than anyone else within Congress. His ideal state would be the anarchist state, with every small village possessing complete economic independence. He has no sympathy with theoretical socialism, and his paternalism is not always to be distinguished from Chiang Kai-shek's. His doctrine of nonviolence (ahimsa) may have seemed remote from practical politics; Gandhi alone is responsible for its success, and it is significant that he prefers to call it a religion rather than a doctrine. "The religion of nonviolence," he said, during the first mass experiments in 1921, "is not meant merely for the rishis and the saints—I want to prove that it is meant for the common people as well." He proved his thesis abundantly, but as time passed he would increasingly give a temporary benediction to those like Prakash Narain and Subhas Chandra Bose who employed violence in all its forms.

To understand Gandhi it is necessary to understand the idea of penance and to accept as the basis of his deepest thoughts that the enslavement of India was due to some wrong committed by Indians themselves. Gandhi has announced the proposition several times,

*In March 1947 Gandhi announced what is probably, according to old Indian customs, the supreme act of penance of his life when he took his granddaughter to bed with him in an effort to try himself to the uttermost.

suggesting that the guilt is his own and that of all those who think and behave as he does; but though the psychological basis of his attacks against British power are clear enough, it is not necessary to accept them at their full value. Instinctively, with a formal distrust of all Western logic, he had come to a conclusion that Nehru achieved by a more purely utilitarian logic. Writing to his daughter Indira from prison, Nehru said:

We had to ask ourselves how freedom was to be obtained? Methods of mere protest and begging, which Congress had so far followed with more or less vehemence, were not only undignified for a people, but were also futile and ineffective. Never in history had such methods succeeded. History indeed showed us that peoples and classes that were enslaved had won their freedom through violent rebellion and insurrection.

This was the moment when Gandhi put forward his program of non-violent non-co-operation. He taught us to rely on ourselves and build up our own strength. He made us shed the fear that crushed us, and we began to look people in the face and speak out our minds fully and frankly.

Was it this teaching that won the masses, or was it the character of the man who resembled to an almost unbelievable degree the legendary *bapu,* the father of all men, the ruler of the panchayat, the unmoving center of the whirlwind? Gandhi's charm must not be underestimated. He would explain it himself by saying that since he had almost no sensuality, he was provided with a spiritual force that could be felt. It would be absurd to question this claim, which is believed throughout India and China; those who have met him have been conscious of a spiritual strength that he can use as he pleases. Indians have said that this is precisely the danger, because the spiritual strength is absolute, but his use of it is sometimes dubious. He speaks with authority, as Socrates spoke, but like Socrates he is capable of minor errors, and sometimes the daimons forget to warn.

Under Gandhi's leadership Congress became the largest national party in India, and only in Bengal, where the revolutionary fiber is strongest, was its hold weak. It was Gandhi who insisted that Congress members should have a badge, a uniform, and perform their daily act of penance in common. The badge was the cloth cap, the uniform was the simple khaddar skirt, and the daily act of penance was two hours of spinning. Spinning had begun as an attempt to employ the unemployed; it ended by becoming the largest single threat against British investments in India and the greatest factor in producing a sense of community among Congress members. Of all the dramatic events in Gandhi's life—he had renounced poverty, renounced his not inconsiderable fortune, renounced sex, renounced his law practice, and spent so many years in prison that he confessed he had never been able to count them—the most dramatic renunciation of all was the renunciation of modern technology through the spinning wheel. The movement was perhaps inevitable—a step back in order to step two paces forward, for the spinning wheel gave India an opening into the textile market that it had never possessed before. The charkha, the motionless spinning wheel that appears in the center of the Congress flag, was a greater adventure than the march to the coast in 1921, when he set out to disobey the government edict on the gathering of salt and the paying of salt taxes.

With Nehru, Gandhi's relations have been those of the untiring father, confidant, and adviser, yet at times their relations have been strained. Nehru cannot understand Gandhi's complete devotion to the Indian people, which includes the princes and paupers alike; Nehru cannot always conceal his intellectual horror of Gandhi's anarchism, his assumption of the scapegoat, his unhesitating opposition to socialism. "The Ramarajya of my dreams," Gandhi said to a meeting of businessmen in the United Provinces in 1934, "ensures the rights alike of prince and pauper," and he continued: "You may be sure that I shall throw the whole weight of my influence in preventing a class war. Supposing there is an attempt unjustly to deprive you of your property, you will find me fighting on your side. Our Socialism or Communism should be based on nonviolence and on the harmonious co-operation of labor and capital." To Nehru such a statement could only be meaningless. Gandhi is the supreme opportunist whose impulses belong to the common impulses of the people; but in the broadest possible sense he represents the traditional rather than the present. Of the socialists he said in the same year that he addressed the businessmen in the United Provinces: "If they gain ascendancy in the Congress, as they well may, I cannot remain in Congresss." Nehru could say of him: "On almost everything on earth I differ from him, yet he is invaluable and I follow him." Gandhi announced publicly in January 1942 that he regarded

Nehru as his successor, though at that time the differences between them could not have been greater.

Gandhi remains a puzzling phenomenon, but one explanation has not hitherto been advanced. The anarchist, who speaks so significantly of chaos as the time when God takes India into his hands, is always a pronounced fatalist. The fate of India, not its destiny, has been his preoccupation from the earliest years. When he led the march from Ahmadabad to Dandi on March 12, 1930, he announced: "I am out to destroy the system of government. We are not out to kill anybody, but is it our dharma [duty] that the curse of this government should be blotted out." Duty and fate became reconciled; he saw each in terms of the other, and there are long passages in his writings that approximate to the chapters of Chiang Kai-shek on the virtues of the sages. The value of Gandhi does not lie in his love of tradition; his chief importance lies in the fact that he has refashioned the most ancient traditions and breathed new light and life into the people. The old peasant wisdom moves by deliberate impulses and sees clearly where others see blindly. Long speeches in Congress, voluminous reports, all these are meaningless to him, because he understands that all problems are basically simple, and the most complex problems must be solved cleanly. Nehru would not have thought of the salt march as a protest against the British government refusal to grant dominion status; it is much more likely that he would have thought of strikes, which he approves ("they are powerful weapons, the only real weapons in the hands of labor, but they must be cherished and preserved and used in an organized and disciplined way with effect when necessity arises") and which have their place in his concept of socialism. But the organization of an all-India strike, with its incalculably complex problems of communication, was unnecessary—seventy-one ragged volunteers accompanied Gandhi from Ahmadabad to Dandi, and wrote their page on history.

Gandhi's clearheadedness remains; it is this which endears him to the people—the capacity to seek into the heart of a problem and report what he has seen. Talking to Louis Fischer he said: "Your President talks about the Four Freedoms—do they include the freedom to be free?" Such remarks endear him to the people, for the whole problem is gathered up in eight words, *and there are no other problems.* It is precisely here that the danger lies: his own solutions tend to shadow all other possible solutions, and since they are rarely arrived at by any processes of logic, they remain arbitrary solutions. The old peasant stamina and the peasant reasoning have usually saved him from making the greatest errors; it is doubtful whether they have always saved him from gross mistakes.

From the beginning the attitude of Congress toward the paramount power had been one of an attempted reconciliation. Hatred for Britain exists, but it is tempered by a desire to obtain freedom without violence. Subhas Chandra Bose, who later raised an Indian National Army in Singapore was striving against the current; there were sound historic reasons for attempting a peaceful solution. Gandhi's mystical belief in the potentialities of men given over to peace, which derives from classical authority, can be explained in practical terms, as Nehru explained them at the Lahore Conference:

Violence too often brings reaction and demoralization in its train, and in our country especially it may lead to disruption. It is perfectly true that organized violence rules the world today, and it may be that we could profit by its use. But we have not the material nor the training for organized violence, and individual or sporadic violence is a counsel of despair. The great majority of us, I take it, judge the issue not on moral but on practical grounds, and if we reject the way of violence it is because it promises no substantial results. Any great movement for liberation must necessarily be a mass movement, and a mass movement must essentially be peaceful, except in terms of organized revolt.

Yet Gandhi's horror of violence can sometimes be as arbitrary as his delight in ahimsa. In 1922, shortly after his release from prison, Gandhi approved of a civil disobedience campaign in the small district of Bardoli, which has a population of 87,000. It was a typical center, neither less nor more important than others. Suddenly he learned that in the little village of Chauri Chaura in the United Provinces there had been a clash between the police and a crowd of peasants, which ended when the peasants burned down the police station and killed several policemen. Gandhi summoned a special meeting of the Congress Working Committee at Bardoli on February 12, 1922, and called off the whole campaign because of "the inhuman conduct of the mob at Chauri Chaura." In spite of the protests of Motilal Nehru, the campaign was called off. Taken to its logical extreme, no civil disobedience campaign could have been possible as long as murders were committed in India.

Since 1920 Gandhi has led Congress; he still leads it, though he takes no part in the discussions. The role of elder statesman suits him perfectly. Nearly eighty, this canny anarchist, with the deep sense of guilt and the still deeper belief in the peasant of India, contrives to weigh the balance between the new and the old. He is not always successful, for he has little sympathy with the future, and toward all modern inventions he has something of the attitude of the Wreckers:

> *Around and around we all will stand*
> *And sternly swear we will.*
> *We'll break the shears and windows,*
> *And set fire to the tazzling mill.*

He remains the arbiter rather than the precursor of the Indian revolution, for even if Indian independence is gained peacefully, there will be a tazzling mill still to be faced. The man who believed in nonviolence has been responsible for a violent outbreak of nationalism; the man who most hated technological progress has been most responsible for its adoption. And whatever kind of revolution still lies before India, some of the complexities and contradictions inherent in Gandhi will remain, to make the anguish greater but the final acceptance easier. It is significant of the man that when his bodily health was almost negligible, he should have taken part in a walking tour in an attempt to bring the Moslem and Hindu factions together. Those who have been to India cannot believe the fable that once he dies revolution will break out; like Sun Yat-sen's his legend will be stronger after death than in life.

Twice he has brought the revolution almost within sight. At the Lahore Congress convened in December 1929 it was Gandhi who was responsible for the adoption of a program of *Purna swaraj*—complete independence, and for the Congress authorization that "whenever we deem fit, we shall launch upon a demonstration of civil disobedience including the nonpayment of taxes." The almost innocuous words were filled with revolutionary overtones. It was due to him that during the meeting of the All-India Congress, at the stroke of midnight on December 31, 1929, the flag of Indian independence—three horizontal strips of red, white, and green—was unfurled, and the Declaration of Independence was read:

> We believe it is the inalienable right of the Indian people, as of every other people, to have freedom and enjoy the fruits of their toil so that they may have full opportunities for growth. We believe also that if any government deprives a people of their rights and oppresses them, the people have a further right to alter it and abolish it. The British Government in India has not only deprived the Indian people of their freedom, but has ruined India economically, politically and culturally and spiritually. We believe therefore that we must sever the British connection and obtain *purna swaraj*.

What is characteristic of this declaration is its dissimilarities to the American Declaration of Independence, the insistence on growth, and the enjoyment of the fruits of toil. Yet the revolt of 1929 was short-lived in spite of the civil disobedience campaign that opened in full strength almost immediately afterward. It was twelve years later before open rebellion took place, and Gandhi's position in the revolt is so confused that even the British White Paper, which makes debating points of nearly every issue, finds it difficult to pin the blame on him. Gandhi uses words according to a purely personal interpretation; it is not the usage of a confused mind but of a mind that sees things always in personal terms.

As the war swept over the Far East, Gandhi seems to have suffered from a feverish distaste for the British and Japanese alike, seeing no difference in the predatory instincts of conquerors. The most turbulent of all Congress meetings was held, and at this meeting Gandhi spoke openly of revolt, but no one knows whether he meant spiritual revolt or physical revolt, and 60,000 people were arrested because he used a term that was not communicable to his adherents. There are semantics in revolution as there are in the conduct of daily affairs; once again Gandhi was caught in a dilemma of his own making. In 1942 there broke out the last and the most bitter revolt since the Indian Mutiny.

Chapter 8

The Revolt of India

I N this new revolt nonviolence was jettisoned—not completely but so nearly completely that it made little difference. It was not the organized revolt of the people, nor was it as carefully manipulated as the British thought at the time, but for the first time since the Indian Mutiny a concerted effort was made to disrupt British power.

No revolt could have taken place under less hopeful auspices. Congress was divided on the main issues; both Nehru and Rajagopalacharia found faults with the main thesis of Gandhi, for if the Indian people revolted against the British in the middle of a world war, Japan would only fill the vacuum, demanding the same airdromes, strategic points, and supplies that had been denied to the British. Gandhi had called for an "unarmed revolt against British rule." He said: "I have not asked the British to hand over India to the Congress Party or the Hindus. Let them entrust India to God, or in modern parlance to anarchy. Then all parties will fight one another like dogs, or will, when real responsibility forces them, come to a reasonable agreement. I shall expect nonviolence to arise out of chaos." Nehru could ask whether nonviolence was the only thing that rose out of chaos, and whether there were advantages in chaos in favor of the Japanese.

The previous "Quit India" resolution had been inspired more by a sense of mounting frustration than by a reasoned argument of revolutionary policy. The dilemma, which had haunted Congress through the previous twenty years, remained. Gandhi said at the press conference at Wardha, after the Working Committee had passed the resolution of July 14, 1942: "There is no room left for the proposal of withdrawal or negotiation. There is no question of one more chance. After all it is open rebellion." Gandhi has since denied that he used these last words, but there seems to be no doubt that he used words at least equally inflammatory, though by "open rebellion" he still may have meant passive rebellion. The British interpreted the words in another sense. Other forces were at work that made the limits between violence and nonviolence purely theoretical.

The revolt of India in the summer of 1942 was not the careful elaboration of a concerted plan, though the socialist wing of Congress issued manifestoes, and Gandhi himself, in a last message to the Indian people before his imprisonment, gave a curiously double-edged interpretation to nonviolence. All weapons except violence were to be encouraged. "Every man is free to go to the fullest length under ahimsa by complete deadlock, strikes, and all other nonviolent means. Satyagrahis should go out to die and not to live. It is only when individuals go out to see and face death that the nation will survive. Do or die!" But all this was exhortation; it was not a planned uprising, though from the point of view of the Congress leaders an unplanned uprising possessed advantages, the temper of the country could be more readily understood, and even a partial success would put an end to the sense of frustration that dogged the Indians everywhere, seeing imperial powers on all sides of them, the British to their minds no better than the Japanese, and the Germans only a little worse. On those hot, heavy days of summer the frustration seemed illimitable. None could hope that Great Britain would win the war for many years. What was surprising was not so much the air of defeatism that hung over Congress, but that no one in this largely agricultural country had pondered the inevitable effect of the huge reserves of American industry on the fate of the Allies. Once again Congress was looking at the map of the countries bordering the Indian Ocean, not the map of the whole world.

Though the revolt has been justified by Indian leaders, there was no reason for justifying it—it had the same validity as the Revolution of Independence in America, or the French Revolution. What it lacked was a concise plan of operations or any practical means of assuming power. There was the British Army in India, and the Japanese Army on the borders; no revolutionary government-in-being (and at this moment Congress already possessed a revolutionary government-in-being) could hope to win against such overwhelming odds both inside and outside the country. The better counsel would have been to delay the revolt at least till they were in touch with the Indian National Army, or to wait till the end of the war.

Partly, the frustration arose from the long imperial reign of Lord Linlithgow, who possessed few talents of administration and held himself in rigorous aloofness from the seething quarrels of the country. The legacy of a hundred and fifty years of British rule had also to be accounted for, but more important than either of these was the growing political consciousness of the Indians, who found themselves for the first time in a situation where they were conscious of their own strength and almost powerless to use it. No one had ever before invoked a revolution by nonviolence. Even the socialist wing of Congress, the most politically mature, could not give better advice on the technique of the revolt than to insist that all actions should be interlocked: "None of our activities should be regarded as independent; all must be subordinated to mass action" —and that no physical harm should come to anybody in the conflict: "None of our activities should be such as to endanger life, whether Indian or British, and warnings to this effect should be given." It was a strange revolution that specified the absence of force; and though force was used on both sides later, and atrocities were committed by both sides, there is little reason to doubt that Congress sincerely believed that a show of nonviolent strength might have led to a situation in which Britain would surrender many of her rights. On both sides, in the British White Paper and in the apologies of the Indian leaders, there is a specious air of special pleading, neither prepared to accept responsibility. This would not be so unwelcome if it had not already appeared clear that India was determined upon at least one major right—the right to rule the country by means of an interim government "subject only to the maintenance of the present war policy and international relations." This demand, made by Rajagopalacharia on August 5, only two days before the All-India Congress Committee was due to meet in Bombay, represented a demand that might have won the approval of a British government less perturbed by events in Europe. In London Sir Stafford Cripps, speaking for the war cabinet, repeated that a complete change in government was impossible; the door was closed for Indian representation in wartime. For the Indians, frustrated beyond belief, only one course remained—a show of force. The long series of conversations had come to an end with a final explosion of bitterness, and on August 7 Nehru said: "The fact is patent to me that the British Government, and for certain the Government of India, think the Indian National Congress to be the Enemy Number One."

Reading these statements long after the revolt petered out, one is amazed by the intolerance of both sides. Of all the actions of the British Government during the war, none was so disingenuous as the refusal to allow India political control.

When at last the revolt broke out, it was sporadic, unorganized, localized during the first two weeks to the Central Provinces, Bihar, and the United Provinces, where the socialist wing of Congress was strongest. Railway stations and post offices were burned; trains were derailed; strikes (hartals) spread through Punjab; in the large steel city of Jamshedpur the strikers remained away from work for a fortnight. In Ahmadabad, the largest textile center in India, a strike continued for three months, but in Cawnpore there was no strike at all. The university students, to whom the socialists issued a special appeal, came out *en bloc* and disappeared into the countryside, forming roving bands of agitators; but without knowledge of revolutionary technique and without any possibility of communicating with whatever headquarters there were, they failed to awaken the nonviolent revolt for which Gandhi had hoped. The people were sullen. Small gangs of professional robbers and murderers appeared to take advantage of the crisis—they were to appear again in August 1946 during the communal crisis. Churchill had stated that never in the history of India had there been so many soldiers in India under arms as at that time. "It was a foolish and inopportune challenge," Nehru was to write later, "for all the organized and armed forces were on the other side." But at least the challenge had been made, and in parts of Bengal and the United Provinces the revolutionary spirit blew strongly. In Bihar two Canadian airmen were killed after a forced landing. It became clear that other elements besides nationalism were entering the scene. Sometimes the Indian peasants seemed to be destroying railways and police stations out of the same deep sense of frustration that made the Wreckers destroy the machines in the early nineteenth century. The picture of India at the time is one of overwhelming frustration and insecurity; the leaders in prison, all hope of independence—even comparative independence—lost. No one has studied the phenomenon of mass frustration, but there are good grounds for believing that it is at the root of innumerable political rivalries. In India, in that baking August, mass frustration may have reached its limit—beyond that there was nothing except sullen, distressful acquiescence.

The British Government announced that up to September 22, 721 persons had been killed, 1,219 injured, 258 railway stations had been destroyed, out of 550 post offices attacked 50 had been completely destroyed and over 200 seriously damaged, and 210 government buildings had been destroyed or attacked. It was not strange that the railways and post offices should be destroyed, for they represented in the interior villages the centers of British influence; what was strange was that they were destroyed deliberately, under the orders of the socialist students, when by preserving posts and communications the revolt could theoretically have achieved greater results.

The figures published by both sides are not trustworthy. It was to the advantage of the British to claim that the destruction was small, unrepresentative, and un-co-ordinated. In fact, the revolt had been co-ordinated as much as possible. The Moslems could point with pride to the fact that the disturbances were greater where Moslem ministries were absent, for the same reason that the Moslems pointedly remained quiet when four years later communal riots broke out where the Moslems were more numerous. The proportions meant little. All that could be said with certainty was that a desperate effort had been made. It had been quashed, but the disease remained. After the riots were over, Prakash Narain, leader of the Socialists, issued a statement that was more mportant for its omissions than for what it said:

There was not sufficient organization of the national revolutionary forces that could function and give effective aid to the mighty forces which were released. The Congress, though a great organization, was not attuned to the pitch to which the revolution was to rise. The lack of organization was so considerable that even important Congressmen were not aware of the progress of the revolt, and until late in the course of the rising it remained a matter of debate in many Congress quarters whether what the people were doing was really in accordance with the Congress program.

After the first phase of the rising was over, there was no future program placed before the people. After they had completely destroyed the British raj in their areas, the people considered their task fulfilled, and went back to their homes, not knowing what more to do. Nor was it their fault. The failure was ours; we should have supplied them with a program for the next phase. When this was not done, the revolt came to a standstill and the phase of the ebb began.

The revolt inside India was over; almost simultaneously, through the Indian National Army, another revolt of Indians was to take place outside India, with the same results—lack of organization, distrust, difficulties of communication—and in both the failure lay in the lack of practical knowledge on the part of the combatants. Neither revolt was glorious; for months afterward Indians were to complain bitterly of the lack of leadership.

Knowledge of the revolt in India was heavily censored by the British Government. The first information of any extended rebellion came from Mr. Churchill's speech in Parliament in which he said: "It is fortunate, indeed, that the Congress Party had no influence whatever with the martial races, on whom the defense of India apart from British forces largely depends." No statement could have been more mistaken; the surrendered Indian soldiers at Singapore were at that time still forming their Indian National Army under the slogan "Forward to Delhi" under the leadership of a former president of Congress.

The full story of the Indian National Army has not yet been revealed, though enough to form a picture of the army's growth, its dissensions, and final collapse came out in the trial at the Red Fort in Delhi of some of its captured officers.

The fall of Singapore was the greatest known disaster to British arms, but India and Australia suffered more heavily than Great Britain. Sixty thousand Australian soldiers surrendered when the pipe line from Johore was cut, and with them went an estimated twenty-five thousand Sikh soldiers. The Australians, together with some British troops, were sent to build the railway in Siam; two days after the surrender the Japanese marched the Indians to Ferrar Park and called upon them to form an army of liberation to take part in a frontal attack on the mainland of India. British officers were immediately removed from their command; in their place a certain Captain Mohan Singh was given full authority to organize a new army on Japanese lines.

The formation of the new army was brought about slowly. As in Nanking, the Japanese suffered from a curious complex of ferocious superiority. Indian women from the coolie lines of the rubber estates were molested and raped; Indian soldiers were given servants' quarters and treated like menials. Riots broke out; the tall Sikhs found it difficult to obey orders from the small Japanese officers who were nervous in the presence of the Indians. Indians who refused to join the Indian National Army were punished—their food allowance restricted, their quarters taken away from them. In some cases they were thrown naked on the mud floors of prisons, where the ants bit them and they went mad. If the Japanese had acted with more restraint a formidable fighting force might have been brought into being. The history of the Indian National Army was one of continual friction, from the highest levels to the least important sepoy. There had been far more cohesion in the Indian Mutiny. From the very beginning the Japanese seem to have suspected that the Indians, who would form a national army for the liberation of India, would do their best to prevent the Japanese from taking a foothold once an occupation had begun. By March 1944 Captain Shah Nawaz Khan, one of the leaders of the Indian National Army, could write in his diary that Indian soldiers were being used by the Japanese almost exclusively as laborers. He added bluntly: "I wonder what is going to be the outcome of all this one-sided coprosperity." He need not have wondered. The friction that existed almost from the beginning had its origin in the whole history of the Japanese campaign in the East—the Japanese were not liberators, in spite of their professed claims. At about the same time Soekarno was writing secretly to Amir Sjarifoedin: "This cannot continue. Either we must have full independence, or we must wage a war against the Japanese which may last for centuries."

It was necessary to find a leader. The leader was forthcoming in Subhas Chandra Bose, who had been president of Congress in 1938–39 but was compelled to resign and give place to Rajendra Prasad in May 1939 largely as a result of the pressure of the group surrounding Gandhi. Both Gandhi and Nehru seem to have distrusted him for his delight in his own powers of domination and for the strange streak of fascism that remained with him to the end. He was a man who inclined easily to drama, brilliant, sensitive, full of a kind of brooding desire for supremacy and turmoil, never happier than when he was fighting alone. At sixteen he ran away from home and wandered among the foothills of the Himalayas; later he took a B.A. with honors at Cambridge and passed fourth in the examination for the Indian Civil Service, though he never entered the service. He was elected mayor of Calcutta in 1930 while serving a prison sentence in Burma. Thereafter his rise to power was continuous, though he was frequently in prison, and before he died he had spent nearly fourteen of his forty-eight years in jail. In July 1940 he was arrested under the Defence of India Act, but in December he was released on account of his health. On January 26, 1941, he disappeared mysteriously from his home. Afterward his frequent appearances and reappearances became one of the more curious facets of the Far Eastern scene.

It is doubtful whether he actually reached Germany. One of his friends has since written a book in which he describes how Bose simply disguised himself as a coolie and proceeded through northern India, Afghanistan, and Russia, where he was flown to Germany. No other evidence has been brought forward. He spoke over the Berlin radio, calling upon the Indians to rise against Great Britain, but there is no reason why he should not have transmitted his speech by phonograph records from Japan, yet his sympathies from the beginning seem to have been more in favor of the Germans than the Japanese—while he was president of Congress he had sent a small group of Congress doctors to join the Chinese Communists, who were then fighting against the Japanese. His voice was heard over Radio Saigon, and later from Tokyo. On November 17, 1941, Radio Tokyo announced that he had signed a pact with Germany "to send an army to free India," but the pact might just as easily have been signed at the Germany Embassy in Tokyo. Mystery surrounds all his movements until the October day in 1943 when, wearing an ill-fitting Japanese major general's uniform, he made a proclamation from the town hall of Singapore calling upon the Indians to unite against the British. He had arrived in Singapore in July or August. Immediately he had been faced with problems of organization and the discontent of the Indian soldiers. The

Indian National Army had come formally into existence on September 1, but it was a month later before all the mechanical details of its operations with the Japanese had been worked out. Promises had been made on both sides, and as a final inducement Tojo promised that the Andaman and Nicobar Islands, renamed Shahid and Swaraj, would be transferred to the provisional government of a free India. The promise was never kept: the Andaman and Nicobar Islands remained under Japanese sovereignty till their surrender to Admiral Mountbatten at the end of the war.

To the members of his cabinet, Bose explained that the Provisional Government of the Azad Hind (Free India) differed from all previous governments—its function and composition were of a unique kind, its main and only task until the Indian people could elect a new government was to form the fighting organization that would launch the last war against the British on Indian soil. Only four ministers were appointed—finance, publicity, women's organizations, and one minister without portfolio. For himself he assumed the role of president (netaji) and commander in chief of the Indian National Army. He had never previously commanded armies. In fact, the formation of a military government of this kind was by no means unique: Dr. Sun Yat-sen had assumed the same powers and suffered the same reverses. In spite of his plea that historically he was simply following the inevitable line taken by national revolutions in the past—he quoted the examples of Ireland, Masaryk's provisional government in Washington, and Mustapha Kemal's provisional government in Anatolia—the speech that he delivered from Singapore town hall was more convincing as one more illustration of the frustration from which India suffered than as a defense of his own assumption of power. Nearly all the leaders of Congress were in jail; Bose's speech did at least represent the feelings of a considerable number of Indians. Like all the important recent speeches of revolt in the Far East it looked back to the American War of Independence and the past freedoms enjoyed by his countrymen, sometimes employing terms taken from French and American sources. He said:

After our defeat at the hands of the British in 1757 in Bengal, the Indian people still fought an uninterrupted series of hard and bitter battles over a stretch of a hundred years. Fighting their last war as free men under the flag of Bahadur Shah in 1857, they were then forcibly disarmed by the British and lay prostrate until the birth of the Indian National Congress, when there came a new awakening. From 1885 until the end of the First World War the Indian people in their endeavor to recover their lost liberty attempted all possible means to dispel British rule by strikes and nonviolence and even by terrorism, sabotage, and armed rebellion; but all these failed, and in 1920, haunted by their sense of failure and groping for a new method, Mahatma Gandhi came forward with new doctrines of nonviolence and civil disobedience.

For two decades thereafter the Indian people went through a phase of intense patriotic activity. The message of freedom was carried to every Indian home. Through personal example, people were taught to suffer, to sacrifice, and to die in the cause of freedom. From the center to the remotest regions people were knit together into one political organization.

Now that the dawn of freedom is at hand, it is the duty of the Indian people to set up a provisional government of their own, and to launch the last struggle under the banner of that government. But with all the Indian leaders in prison and the people at home totally disarmed, it is not possible to set up a provisional government within India or to launch an armed struggle under the aegis of that government. It is therefore the duty of the Indian Independence League in East Asia, supported by all patriotic Indians at home and abroad, to undertake the task of setting up a provisional government of Free India and to conduct a last fight for freedom with the help of the Army of Liberation organized by the League.

The Provisional Government is entitled to, and hereby claims, the allegiance of every Indian. It guarantees religious liberty, as well as equal rights and equal opportunities to all its citizens. It declares its firm resolve to pursue the happiness and prosperity of the whole nation and all its parts, cherishing all the children of the nation equally and transcending all the differences cunningly fostered by an alien government in the past.

In the name of God, in the name of bygone generations in the past who have welded the Indian people into one nation, and in the name of the dead heroes who have bequeathed to us a tradition of heroism and self-sacrifice, we call upon the Indian people to rally round our banner and to strike for India's freedom. We call upon them to launch the final struggle against the British and all their allies in India and to prosecute the struggle with valor and perseverance and with full faith in final victory until the enemy is expelled from Indian soil, and the Indian people are once again a free nation.

It is difficult to understand how a man who could quote almost textually the American Declaration of Independence could see an effective alliance between the Indian National Army and the Japanese. He seems to have been overwhelmed by the size of his army, forgetting that though ten thousand soldiers on a parade ground appear invincible, they form only a small number in terms of modern battles. In October he ordered that three regiments in Singapore should be named after Gandhi, Nehru, and Maulana Abul Kalam Azad—all three of whom in varying degrees were convinced pacifists. Difficulties began from the beginning. In December Captain Mohan Singh, who had addressed the Indians at Ferrar Park and assumed the original command, was placed under arrest by the Japanese. Small revolts occurred. A mass meeting at Port Swettenham broke up; the offending Indians were punished. Bose was invited to Tokyo. He remained a few weeks longer in Malaya and then set up his headquarters in Burma. The Indian National Army was approaching India.

It was a year before his Indian National Government was recognized by Tokyo, but once the Japanese recognized it, Germany, Italy, Thailand, the Philippines, Croatia, Manchuria, and Burma followed. At the trial that took place after the war at the Red Fort, one of Bose's lieutenants is reported to have complained bitterly in a speech to his soldiers: "Our fight is for the freedom and well-being of India, and not for the benefit of the Japanese. When we reach India and if we notice any Japanese maltreating our women, he should be at first warned by word of mouth not to do so, and if he continues to do so, then we are at liberty to use force, and we must shoot." The war, which had begun with surrender, seemed likely to end the same way. Distrust for the Japanese increased; and the Indian soldiers began to ask themselves what they would do when they reached the Burma front and found themselves fighting against their brothers. Captain Shah Nawaz related that when they were fighting in the Chin hills, he knew that his own brother was fighting opposite him. He had been torn helplessly between loyalty toward the Indian Army and a free India, for his father had served the Army for over thirty years and of his clan more than eighty had born arms for the King. His diary, which was put forward as evidence, shows the increasing strain of the conflict within him. On July 7, 1944, he wrote that he was surrounded by Indian soldiers dying of starvation, left to their own resources by the Japanese, and a week later he wrote that his men were dying like flies, some were committing suicide and the Japanese were giving no help.

As commander in chief of the Indian National Army and president of the Free Indian Government, Bose enjoyed considerable fame in the areas under Japanese occupation. In November 1943 he visited Nanking, flying from Tokyo to attend the Greater East Asia Conference and meeting Wang Ching-wei. Two months later he flew from Singapore to Burma, where he inspected troops and was received by the Burmese "puppet" Ba Maw and Renzo Sawada, Japanese ambassador to the Burmese government. On January 23 his forty-seventh birthday was celebrated in all the capitals of Japanese-occupied territory. He is known to have visited Indonesia. In January 1944 he reappeared again in Nanking, toasted Wang Ching-wei, and broadcast on a transmission beamed to Chungking urging Chiang Kai-shek to fight the British and Americans "since all promises of assistance from America and Britain are illusory." On November 1 he was received by Shigemitzu, and two days later he spoke at the Hibaya Hall in Meiji Park to a vast concourse of Japanese soldiers. But his difficulties were only beginning; he objected strongly to the terms in which Japanese broadcasts were made for India, and he recognized that the Indians, who were detested by the Burmese, who knew them only as moneylenders, would face hard struggles in Burma. Reports were coming through that his armies were disobedient and surrendered rapidly to the British, who were beginning their long-planned efforts to drive the Japanese out of north Burma. For a short while the Indian National Army had penetrated Indian soil, and the Indian National Government was already in existence in a small territory of Manipur and Bishevpur comprising perhaps 1,500 square miles. The government, though it lacked ministers, possessed a treasury of thirty-five lacs of rupees and was in touch with the branch of the Free Indian Army organized by Prakash Narain in Assam and Bengal. But the end was not far off. During the Japanese retreat, the Indian National Army, without resources, hated by the Burmese and despised by the Japanese, wandered into the forests or surrendered to the incoming tides of British and Indian troops, its hour of glory over and its leadership bankrupt. In 1942 Vichy radio broadcast a mysterious message to the effect that Bose had died in an airplane crash. On August 19, 1945, immediately after the surrender, he died in an airplane accident off Taihoku, Formosa, together with his chief lieutenant Haribur Rahman. The announcement was made four days later by Tokyo radio in the short interval between the surrender and the landing of American troops.

Subhas Chandra Bose represented during his tempestuous life a more dynamic struggle than Gandhi had been willing to practice. Among university students and some soldiers he had a wide following; but the publication of his book, *Our Struggle,* alienated him from the more liberal elements in the Congress, and the title of the book bore too close a resemblance to *Mein Kampf* to make him entirely trustworthy. After his death his name became a legend. It was widely believed, even by Gandhi, that he was not dead but hiding, and it was said that he would appear from some Indian village when the time came. A messianic aureole surrounded his name. "I admire his courage and patriotism," wrote Gandhi, "but I have no belief in the method he adopted. The people of India cannot obtain freedom by the sword." The legend remained; the son and brother of lawyers, president of Congress, president of the Bengal Provincial Congress Committee, he was the first to assume the title of netaji and commander in chief of an Indian Nationalist Army, and the first Indian commoner to command a standing army.

Two Indian revolts occurred; one inside Indian territory, the other along the road that led from Singapore to Manipur. Neither was successful; they failed for the same causes, the violence of the same dilemma making them impracticable from the beginning. Though Bose possessed great intellectual talents, he possessed none of the qualities of a military leader; he was easily flattered, and he suffered even more than the Congress leaders from a blind and passionate hatred of foreign rule. His importance lay in the fact that he was a precursor of Indian power, and to a greater degree than Prakash Narain, he symbolized the awakened strength of the Indian people. The two revolts complemented one another, but they occurred at the same time only by accident—Bose himself complained that he possessed no knowledge of what had happened in August 1942 till long afterward. Communications were as difficult for the Indians outside India as for those in the interior. Foraging parties from the Azad Hind Fauj found themselves easily entrapped when they attempted to enter the territory of India proper. The Indian Army remained loyal to the Crown, and the frustration of the people had endured so long that they no longer had the strength or the inclination to fight. In his book *The Discovery of India* Jawarharlal Nehru entitled the chapter in which he discusses the seething months of 1942 simply "Frustration." Under such conditions, Nehru said, revolution seemed almost impossible, and even incomprehensible. The dilemma remained; it was to remain for a long time after the war.

Passions that have been aroused do not die suddenly; they linger and change their shape and become less virulent at the same time that they become overlaid with a sense of helpless abandonment, so that they are liable to burst out suddenly and capriciously, beyond any domination of reason. Almost unconsciously the British had played on the Indians' weakest nerve.

The sense of frustration, which had only increased during a hundred years of alien rule, was allied to the physical weakness of the people who suffered between 1943 and 1944 the greatest famine that had been known to India. In 1942 Bengal had been one of the countries where the revolt was put down most heavily—the Bengalese, like the Cantonese, have a strong reputation for rebellion. Sir John Woodhead, presiding over the official Famine Relief Inquiry, computed that as a direct result of the famine and the pestilences that followed in its train a million and a half had died. The figure was as exact as he could determine, but did not include figures from other provinces, equally affected, and other figures approaching four or five million over the whole of India are likely to be true. The famine had arisen as a result of a host of causes, notably hoarding and the transfer of grain to feed the armies. both of which were causes of the famine in Hunan during the following year. It was a famine that could have been prevented; so too, under a wiser administration, the rebellions could have been prevented. A wiser British policy, a greater degree of understanding of the problems facing the Indian peasantry, popular suffrage, a determined agrarian reform, greater trust in the Indian leaders—with these there might have been no necessity for those continual and turgid imprisonments of Indian leaders that made British rule the arbitrary endowment of a few men in the India Office in Whitehall.

The tragedy of India lay not only in the sense of frustration and the poverty of the Indian people, but in a gradual withering of the historical roots of the occupation. The Government of India Act in 1833 had declared that no native of India should "by reason only of his religion, place of birth, descent, colour, or any of them, be disabled from holding any place or employment in the said Company." If this act had been faithfully kept, the disastrous consequences of the last fifty years would not have followed. Just as Chiang Kaishek, almost singlehanded, was responsible for the growth of the Communist party in China, so the behavior of the British viceroys was largely responsible for the growth of nationalism in India. With the appearance of the Indian National Army in Singapore, India had a fighting force outside India for the first time since the end of the Srivijaya Empire. The armed power of Asia was still small, but it is significant that it was in Burma, where so many of the Asiatic cultures meet, that American-trained Chinese troops met British-trained Indian troops, and fought each other.

Wrote Jawaharlal Nehru:

The very thing India lacked the modern West possessed and possessed to excess. It had the dynamic outlook. It was engrossed in the changing world, caring little for ultimate principles, the unchanging, the universal. It paid little attention to duties and obligations, and emphasized rights. It was active, aggressive, acquisitive, seeking power and domination, living in the present and ignoring the future consequences of its actions. Because it was dynamic and full of life, it was progressive, but the life was a fevered one and the temperature kept on rising progressively.

Few things were certain in the confused maelstrom of Indian political life, but there were signs that the Indians were beginning to emphasize their rights; and their two short-lived revolts spoke of a time, when they, too, would be active, aggressive, and acquisitive. The revolts were on a small scale, but they announced the beginning of the end.

Chapter 9

New Blood

GANDHI, Nehru, and Jinnah held the stage, but they were not always the chief protagonists. The complex forces of India met in these three men, who became in the eyes of Indians almost indistinguishable from gods, and like gods they were credited with a full knowledge of all that was happening in India. Gandhi, writing his editorials in *Harijan* or spinning in his ashram, maintained a vast correspondence. Jinnah and Nawabzab Liaquat Ali Khan ruled the Moslems from the quiet water-cooled chambers of their marble palaces in Delhi and Bombay. Nehru, living in his sister's house in Bombay or wandering restlessly over the countryside alone, seemed to be in continual contact with the people; yet age and education and something of the Brahman pride kept him from ever completely revealing himself to the peasants. A mirror walked, faithfully reproducing the surrounding scene but rarely absorbing it. Again and again in his own writings he complains of the glaze through which he saw everything. Brilliant and inconsistent, tortured by self-doubts, always shut off from the world, yet least shut off when he was in prison, he complains bitterly of the hero worship he receives, and can see no reason for it except that he is evidently "like a stone thrown up on the shore, which reveals the existence of the riches in the sea." He was surprised and resentful when he found that pictures were being reproduced of himself and his wife, Kamala Nehru, with the inscription "the perfect marriage." It had not been a perfect marriage—Nehru wondered whether any such marriage had ever occurred—and seeing these pictures, he became more and more distrustful of the self-glorification that grew from his political associations and his imprisonment. He was on intimate terms with Gandhi. Gandhi had stated openly that he re-

garded Nehru as his successor, but was the fiat of Ghandi alone to
rule the Indian scene? Other protagonists were arising. No one
could foresee who would inherit Gandhi's rule.

The leader of the socialist bloc in Congress was Jaya Prakash
Narain, who was born to a minor police-court official in 1904. He
lived in a Bihar village till he was eighteen, and then drifted uncer-
tainly to Calcutta. "This was the first time," he said, "that I ever
saw a motorcar—I simply had not dreamed that such things existed.
But then I discovered bigger things even than tramcars and motorcars." He lived for a while in the seething workers' quarters and
was caught up in the non-co-operation movement. When the movement ebbed, he decided to be a university professor, began studying
biology in his spare time, and decided to go to America. Before sailing, he had married Parbhavati, the daughter of a Bihar politician,
who joined Gandhi's ashram shortly afterward, waiting for him to
return with his B.Sc. He arrived in California in October 1922. He
worked on a fruit farm, earning forty cents an hour by picking the
bad fruit from the baskets in a community of California Sikhs. He
studied at Berkeley for a month, then went to Iowa State University,
where tuition fees were cheaper, working by taking odd jobs. In all
he attended five American universities, worked as a packer in a jam
factory, became a mechanic in an iron foundry and a waiter in so
many restaurants that he soon lost count. "I was diligent—this is all
that can be said profitably about me in that time. I did not have any
bearings, but I did know how people sweated their lives out." In the
end he took his master's degree in sociology almost on the same day
that he received his membership card of the American Communist
Party.

Though he still called himself a communist when he returned to
India, no one at that time took his communism seriously. His wife
joined him when he returned to Bihar, and his connections with
Gandhi became closer. He organized the Bihar Socialist Party and
at the same time vigorously attacked the communists for setting up
splinter trade unions; Nehru invited him to set up a Labour Research Department of the Indian National Congress. In the Civil
Disobedience Campaign of 1932-33 he was thrown into prison. Released at the end of 1933, he began to form small bodies of Congress
shock troops who would assume the responsibility of leading the
revolution. He addressed university students, peasants, communists,

and socialists wherever they could be found—he had found his place at last as an organizer, but he was swinging increasingly away from Gandhi, continually protesting against the interference in Congress affairs of the Indian industrialists, but reserving his chief wrath for the British raj. He spoke quietly, in a strained voice; when the speeches were over, he usually disappeared into hiding. In May 1940 he was imprisoned again at Deoli jail, where he continued to direct the organization of the "antiwar freedom movement" by sending messages through his wife Parbhavati. The Congress Socialist Party never revealed its membership, but it was known to be spreading, and never more quickly than when its director was in jail. He had contemplated ever since his return from America the formation of "socialist storm troops." In the long year before the Wardha Declaration the "storm troopers" were coming out into the open—the revolt that eventually occurred was largely due to his organizers.

In 1942 he was transferred to Haziribagh Prison, where it was thought he would be safer. His importance was increasing because it was generally becoming known that he approved of socialists acquiring funds by all available methods, including robbery. One night in November he climbed over the wall and disappeared into Nepal, where he summoned a meeting in the forests and formed the only branch on Indian soil of Subhas Chandra Bose's Japanese sponsored Indian National Army, which had as it symbol three arrows—Freedom, Bread, One Nation. For this he incurred the enmity of the Indian Communist Party, which had consistently attacked Bose from the beginning. The Indian National Army in Nepal had only one engagement to its credit. When Prakash Narain was himself arrested by the Nepalese government, they stormed the prison and released him. He continued to make fiery speeches until he reached Lahore, where he was arrested by British police. He remained there until Gandhi begged his release from Lord Wavell "as an earnest of Britain's intentions to quit India."

Gandhi's position toward the users of violence was never made clear; he wrote in a long series of letters to Puran Chand Joshi, the leader of the Indian Communist Party, remonstrating with him on the means to which the Communists were dedicated; he said of Subhas Chandra Bose that "he was the spirit of liberty in an unfree world." Of Prakash Narain he said, after insisting that he could not offer his blessing on the means employed: "In this matter I am like someone who watches the incoming tide. Many things will be swept ashore, and among them there will be some with sharp edges."

Talking to Indians during the communal demonstrations in 1946 I was told: "One should have not too much faith in the leaders of the herd. They are like the old elephants, who have fought for a long time; they are given the powers to lead; but their tusks are blunted. Somewhere among the elephants following them are some with sharper tusks. So far, they may still be hidden."

Prakash Narain's tusks were sharper than any of the others. He had assumed full credit for the small successes of the August rising. He was offered the presidency of Congress, but refused it, growing increasingly critical, not only of the "Old Guard," which had accepted the Constituent Assembly, with the Viceroy and British troops still in India, but of all other parties. Offered membership on the Congress Working Committee, he accepted "only in the interests of solidarity," retaining the right to attack whomever he pleased. Very often his attacks were directed bluntly at Nehru; the Kashmiri and the Bihari had little in common. He warned the Indians to prepare for "an active campaign against the British." He seemed, like so many extremists at the time, concerned at the thought that India might be offered freedom without bloodshed. But the growth of the Moslem League in importance made him cautious. He still insisted that the Moslem League itself was a kind of trick thrown into the pool at the last minute by the British. He believed that all the parties in India, the Moslem League, the Hindu Mahasabha, the princes, the big businessmen and even the communists, were attempting to prolong British rule. Together with Sarat Chandra Bose, the brother of the Netaji, he resigned from the Congress Working Committee.

His explanation of the defeat of the August rising was a document of considerable power. In August 1943 he elaborated on the main cause of the defeat:

"An ancient nation like ours, with all its glorious achievements, not the least among them its survival through the ages, should have possessed more self-confidence. But while our people have faith in the least potent of things, from stones to tombstones, they have no faith in themselves and know not their own strength."

As a summary of a situation, it left much to be desired, but it demonstrated the springs of his action. Three and a half years later he told the students and faculty of Benares University:

"In the coming fight Congress will not have the same objects as in past struggles. Congress workers will not go to jail. Instead, they will have strength enough this time to do the arresting themselves. When the revolution starts, out strategy will be to capture all Government offices and institutions and establish a People's Raj. British governors and pro-British officials should be jailed."

The theme of India's unawakened strength recurs continually in his speeches; it is not calculated to be so successful as the more mystical and more urgent themes of Gandhi. He is almost alone among the Congress leaders in having been educated in America; American forthrightness does not always pay dividends in a country where mysticism is still a mark of honor. At the Congress meeting in December 1946, Prakash Narain and Mrs. Aruna Asaf Ali both attempted to attack the older members of Congress. Mrs. Ali pointed at the leaders and said: "All of you without exception are attempting to lead the country to the brink of ruin. You are too old and too senile for the contest." The party leader, Sirdar Vallabhbhai Patel, answered: "The horse which has pulled the cart for sixty years now finds a dog, wagging its tail, running alongside. But it's not pulling the cart." But though the answer was greeted with cheers, no one doubted that this was not the final answer.

The Socialist Party had grown slowly along lines directly opposed to Congress, though it was included within Congress. The weight of the large manufacturers, the mysticism of Gandhi that tends to cover every decision with a syncretic and Biblical tinge of paternalism, the studied legalism of Nehru—all of these provided an excuse for more direct action. The communists were too small and ineffectual, in spite of Joshi's work among the peasant *kisans,* to provide the "direct action" that seemed so often to be necessary. "I am a sociologist and an anthropologist, and I am sick of dealing with lawyers," Prakash Narain once said. He was also, to an extent unsurpassed in India, a revolutionary leader, though he had failed.

The "Old Guard" of Congress remains in power; dominated largely by Patel, Nehru, and Rajagopalacharia. Though Patel is sick, and there have been continual rumors of his impending resignation, control of the party machinery remains largely in his hands. His friendship with Ghandyash Das Birla, the most powerful of the industrial magnates, was not always calculated to delight the younger members of Congress, who saw a surrender by Congress to big business as an extraordinary *volte-face;* in different degrees and with different arguments Narain and Joshi, the leader of the small Indian Communist Party, have assailed his position, only to be quelled by the authority of the much older man. Patel, at seventy-two, has an air of authority so complete that even Nehru looks like a young sophomore in comparison. He speaks roughly and bluntly, in Gujarati, without gestures, numbing his listeners with the cold sobriety of his arguments, in which neither mysticism nor idealism have any place. He likes to quote figures, his memory for them so complete that Gandhi, whose mathematics is woolly, has said that, "'in all matters concerning the arithmetic of our movement I have full confidence in Patel." Unfortunately, Patel has assumed over the years something of the aspect of an *éminence grise,* with little sympathy for labor reforms and less sympathy for the strident young members of Congress who demand them. It would be a mistake to conclude that Patel is a reactionary party boss to be compared with party bosses in China. The Congress lives only by its support from the peasants, and though it tends occasionally to move away from them, the reasons are nearly always concerned with the peculiar atmosphere of Gandhi's mystical doctrines and the double-edged nature of nearly all Gandhi's weapons. While Gandhi remains alive, purna swaraj (complete self-government) will never be obtained by revolutionary force—the doctrine against violence is too strong. When Gandhi spoke of the chaos he envisaged as a result of the removal of the British raj, he was not speaking in terms of anything more horrible than a governmental vacuum. If Gandhi dies, Patel will take his place, following as far as he can the doctrines he has imbibed, but possessing a far greater knowledge of actual circumstances than Gandhi ever possessed.

The settlement of the communal issue still remains the most important item on the agenda of the party leaders, who may sometimes be assumed to have accentuated communal differences. Indian politicians are not celebrated for the mildness of their speeches—a sharp-cutting brain combined with indignation and a ferocious desire for equal status with the outside world tend to make most speeches unguarded. Nehru's violent fits of temper are well-known and generally excused; Gandhi has been known to fly into quiet passions; Narain will sometimes make speeches that sound like incitements to the lowest passions. What is surprising is that this violence is often calculated, on the theory that the Indian masses are so plunged in poverty and despair that only extreme language will awaken them. The theory explains the curious calm with which both Nehru and Jinnah received the news of the communal risings in August 1946—neither could entirely believe them. It was only weeks later that official machinery was put into operation to try to prevent them from spreading. The most significant event of those days in August was not the communal rising itself, but the efforts by both Mohammedans and Indians to try to heal the wounds on an unpolitical plane. Small bands of middle-class and educated Indians put themselves in danger by attempting to mediate between the conflicting parties; often they were schoolmasters, government employees, small tradesmen. As in China, there was an increasing belief that political problems could not be solved by political action; the moderates hoped at least that they could give an example. As in China, too, there was a dearth of political talent. The old names were revered, but there were very few new names to take their places. Neither Gandhi nor Patel nor Rajagopalacharia could be expected to last for many years more; Jinnah, suffering from a weak heart, tuberculosis, and at least two more diseases, was already a walking ghost, living on the sheer energy of his will. No one could contemplate with any real hope an India ruled by the conflicting wills of Nehru and Liaquat Ali Khan, Jinnah's second in command, for though both have been lawyers, the differences between them are extreme. Liaquat Ali Khan, who has the manners of a feudal emperor and whose father is a nawab, a man with an enormous capacity for work and an intense belief in Islam, has none of Nehru's subtlety, and little of Nehru's vision. His belief in Pakistan is so firm that he is prepared to assume that he has possessed it all his life; his hatred of the Hindus goes deeper than Jinnah's, and he has never been known to attempt a communal settlement on the basis of compromise. Heavily built, with great shoulders—he was a good football player—he swings into his speeches in the manner of a bishop commanding his flock, the voice low and charged with emotion. He can convince you for half an hour; half an hour later the subtleties and the special pleading begin to lose their charm. Unlike Nehru, who is torn between a devouring interest in life and a still more devouring interest in theory, Liaquat Ali Khan deals only in the subtleties of power. More than anyone else on the Indian scene, he seems to be remote both from life and from theory.

The young are often surprisingly young. Puran Chand Joshi, the son of a schoolmaster in Almora Province, was already the leader of the Indian Communist Party at twenty-nine. Arrested during the Meerut Conspiracy case he was sentenced to five years imprisonment. He became a law student at Allahabad University, where he was acknowledged even by his enemies to be the best student of the year. In 1934 when the Communist party was declared illegal, he went underground. But when Russia entered the war he placed his considerable literary gifts at the service of the war against Japan. Unlike Congress, he believed that the Indian National Army was a fatal invention, whose consequences could not but be disastrous.

Other leaders proliferated. No one can foretell who will be the masters of the Indian scene within the next ten years. Only one thing is certain—the old influences will remain, the old courses of conduct will be followed, and while Gandhi lives his tremendous shadow will hide the light of the young.

Chapter 10

The Rulers and the Ruled

IN an essay written more than twenty years ago, the Chinese poet Kuo Mo-jo wrote: "What the devil is the use of studying medicine? You can kill parasites and germs, but how can you kill the loathsome social system that breeds them? It is comparatively easy to give the rich a dose of Epsom salts for their stomach troubles, but when you see the poor run down by motorcars and armed soldiers slaughtering thousands of your fellow countrymen —there's nothing a doctor can do? Fraternity? Humanity? If you have a clear conscience and don't sneeze, you become a saint. And how can I become a saint?" Generalissimo Chiang Kai-shek would answer: "Nothing is easier than to become a saint—all you have to do is to adopt the Confucian principles."

Of all the characters thrown up by the Asiatic revolt, the least complex and the most anachronistic is the character of the Generalissimo. It has been possible to prophesy his actions at almost all points of his activity. Tall for a Chinese, with deep-set brown-gold eyes, a high forehead, and indrawn lips, he resembles almost a caricature of the ancient unbending scholar, remote from life, urged by deep principles, confused and heartbroken in the world, and with no instinct for the understanding of people, and considerable impatience for their foibles. He claims with perhaps half a million other Chinese to be descended from the great scholar-soldier Duke Wen, who founded the imperial Chou dynasty three thousand years ago; he has greater claim to descent from the Ming princes who escaped south at the end of the dynasty. Born among the volcanic hills and pine forests of Chekiang, not far from Ningpo, where there were vast foreign trading interests at the time of the T'ang dynasty, he is almost certainly not of entire Chinese descent, and

like the Soong family he may have considerable Malay or Arab
blood. Though his claim for imperial descent is considerably
stronger than H. H. Kung's claim to be descended from the philosopher Confucius, his intellectual descent from the philosophers
and conquerors of the Chou dynasty cannot be questioned; like
Mussolini he belongs to the family of the anachronistic *condottiere,*
but unlike Mussolini he has forged out of the ancient and dying
principles of a China that no longer exists certain intellectual pre-
occupations that give him considerable authority. Almost plain-
tively, in founding the New Life Movement, he attempted to give
currency to the virtues of the old soldier-scholars, and he seems to
be incapable of understanding that these virtues, however worthy,
must be succeeded by virtues representing the present time. There
can be no greater misunderstanding than to believe that Chiang
Kai-shek represents modern China; he represents the tradition that
died when a barrel of gunpowder exploded in the Russian concession
in Hankow in November 1911.

Like the old scholars he is given to sudden angers, deep loyalties
to friends, a sense of command, a belief in his own incorruptibility.
He will sometimes forgive his enemies if they are soldiers, because
he believes, like Marshal Pétain, in the community of soldiers; but
he is unyielding in his hatred for those who disagree with his fundamental thesis that Chinese life must return to its ancient vigorous
ritualistic worship of the Confucian virtues. Because he is almost
wholly ignorant of the West (he has visited Russia and India for
brief periods, but otherwise he has never been beyond China or
Japan), he could write in *China's Destiny:*

> Our ancient Chinese ethical system is the embodiment of a detailed
> and profound investigation of the way in which mankind and society
> are bound together. Although social organization evolves unceasingly,
> the following are the unchangeable rules of social life: the way of fathers
> and sons, husbands and wives, elder and younger brothers, and friends;
> the order of the upper and lower, superiors and inferiors, men and
> women, the old and the young; and the principles of mutual assistance
> among neighbors and in illness.

There is no evidence that he has thought in sociological terms
more widely than this. Unlike Sun Yat-sen, who was inclined to
believe that the faults of the Chinese derive from their essential

anarchism, he believes that the Chinese are essentially faultless when they subscribe to the Confucian virtues, but they have been demoralized by their contacts with the West. Repeatedly in *China's Destiny,* which was published in 1943, at the time when America was rushing its supplies of arms and ammunition to China by the most difficult routes, he excoriates America and Britain for their unequal treaties and their failure to understand the Chinese character. He has little knowledge of modern warfare, though he was able to foresee in 1934 that future wars might take place underground; the tunnel warfare of the Communists when fighting against the Japanese and the Kuomintang proved that his last guess was right. But faced with the imponderables of modern war, he knew less than any American GI, and his errors during the war sprang from fantastic ignorance and inefficiency of command. A prince of the Chou dynasty, three thousand years old, was rocketed into a war where the most devastating tools of modern mechanization were being employed, and it is not surprising that his armies, attempting to obey his confused orders, were underfed and misled, tactically incapable of following up the advantages they possessed in manpower and mobility. To the very end of the war Chiang Kai-shek was daily consulting the epigrams on war written by Sun Tzu twenty-five hundred years ago to demonstrate how one wins battles with spears and swords.

The faults were inevitable, but greater resilience of mind might have enabled him to avoid the harsher features of a disciplined yet unruly temper of mind. The personal discipline, which he learned when for three years he joined a Japanese army group with the rank of second-class private, remains. Every morning, for half an hour after waking, he will stand in solitary meditation by an open window. He refuses to drink tea or wine, and has regulated his meals and his habits to split-second routine. A miserable childhood has left its mark on him. At the age of fifty, on the eve of the Japanese invasion, he broadcast a message to the nation. It might have been expected that he would speak at great length of the resources of the country and the possibility of invasion; instead, he spoke of his great love for his Buddhist-Confucian mother, who had taught him that loyalty was the greatest of all virtues. The same word was invoked when he was arrested in Sian by orders of Chiang Hsueh-liang, who would have killed him if the Communists in Yenan had not insisted on his release, believing that General Ho Ying-chin would have made peace with the Japanese if Chiang Kai-shek was dead. Yet though he publicly forgave Chang Hsueh-liang, his hatred for the Communists remained, neurotic in the intensity of its unappeasable and relentless fury, which stems from the faith he possesses in Confucian doctrine. The superiors and inferiors, men and women, the old and the young—all must have their due place in the hierarchy of power; he cannot understand that other forces are at work which give power to elected representatives, and to them only.

He was a man with many gifts, but the supreme gifts of statesmanship were denied to him. As a symbol of dogged resistance only did he possess a kind of perfection, and a noble simplicity. Between 1937 and 1939 he represented to an unprecedented degree the symbolic unity of the Chinese people against Japanese aggression, but he himself never led the nation—the nation led him. Because he squandered so much of the strength of the Chinese armies in hunting down the Communists, he must assume the responsibility for the initial defeats of the Chinese Army.

His simplicity is complex. In April 1946 he summoned his old adversary General Feng Yu-hsiang, the "Christian General," into his presence. He complained of lumbago, sudden pains of the heart, restlessness, and ill temper. General Feng, whom he addressed as *ko-ko,* or elder brother, sympathized with him and suggested pointedly that he should have a rest.

"Then who would follow me?" Chiang Kai-shek answered. "There is no one I can trust sufficiently to carry out my wishes."

On the way across the Yangtze river, General Feng sang the ode which appears in the first chapter of the great military epic *The Three Kingdoms,* where power is shown to be as fleeting as the clouds, "and only the clouds are still and remain." The Generalissimo wept. In all this he was betraying his Confucian character—extreme sensibility and extreme rigor; but it has not yet occurred to him that it is for the Chinese people, not for him, to choose its representative leader. He has never been elected to office by the people. Under the system of political tutelage, by which all rights were taken from the people and China was ruled by a military junta, even the administrators of the hsien, the small county unit, were chosen by the government.

He suffered abundantly in his youth. His father, a poor salt merchant and corn chandler, left debts. His mother, taking courage from her own strict village upbringing, imbued him with the task of recouping the family fortunes. He was never well fed, and even later, when he went on a scholarship to Japan, studied in the military school, and joined the Japanese Army, the hunger remained:

During the first fortnight after I joined the artillery group, I was so hungry that I could hardly work during the day. In the evening we were allowed to buy biscuits at the barracks, but these too were limited in quantity and you could only buy two or three biscuits at a time. The biscuits were so hard that no one would have given them a second thought at home, yet we ate them with passionate enjoyment. After a fortnight the hunger left me, and in three weeks I no longer needed the biscuits. No life could have been harder than the life we led. Older soldiers bullied younger soldiers. We had to wash their clothes, brush their boots, mend their clothes. If we did not obey them immediately, we were beaten.

When he talks to students, he will often refer to the hardships of his own youth, yet somehow, by constant repetition, these hardships seem to have faded into a remorseless pageant of heroic endurance. No one has denied his physical courage, but his own account of the episode in Sian, which he carefully edited, shows that he hid in a cave after escaping from his headquarters in his nightshirt, and only after considerable inner conflict did he decide to show himself to the enemy. He wanted a martyr's death. He did not want to die as the result of a chance shot in a cave. He recorded the conversation he had when he was imprisoned in an unheated and unfurnished room in Sian. The record shows internal evidence of being almost wholly true, but it is impossible not to believe that he has inserted occasionally words that he wished he had said. He said to Chang Hsueh-liang:

I am your superior, and you are a rebel. According to military discipline and the law of the land, you as a rebel deserve not only reprimand but punishment. My head may be cut off, my body mutilated, but I must preserve the honor of the Chinese race, and must uphold law and order. If I allow the honor of the 400,000,000 people whom I represent to be degraded by accepting any demands in order to save my own life, we should lose our national existence. Do you think that by using force you can expect me to surrender to rebels? Today you have lethal weapons; I have none, but instead I am armed with the principles of righteousness.

These are my weapons of defense. With these I must defend the honor of the people I represent, and with these I must be the faithful follower of our late leader. I shall do nothing to betray the trust imposed upon me by the martyrs of the revolution. I shall not bring shame and dishonor to this world, to the memory of my parents or to my nation. You, young man, do you think you can make me submissive by force? You mistake my firm stand on the principles of law and order for obstinacy. If you are a brave man, kill me; if not, confess your sins and let me go.

No passage in any of his multitudinous speeches is so revealing; here he reveals the springs of his character and of the peculiar mysticism by which he has his being. When he speaks of righteousness, he deliberately employs the old Chinese concept of li. When he speaks of being beheaded and his mutilated body shown to the populace, he is speaking the language of the old princes of the Chou dynasty who suffered in this way. The accents of the *Spring and Autumn Annals* are everywhere, and almost one overhears the voice of the celebrated Prince T'ung, who wrote to a neighboring lord, with a present of a flute: "A soldier who fights in three campaigns perishes, and this is my third campaign. Farewell, my lord, I shall not see you again." There is a curious brazen chivalry in his desire for martyrdom, but the logic defies analysis, for he claimed death as the representative of 400,000,000 who had never elected him, at a time when popular will desired that he should take measures against the Japanese—up to that moment he had agreed to all the Japanese claims and was filling the prisons with students and soldiers who wanted immediate war with Japan. He has said himself: "I am happiest in the camp," and during the whole of the negotiations at Sian he behaved as a captive general rather than as a captive political leader.

Like Confucius, Chiang Kai-shek is obsessed by trivialities. Confucius elaborated at great length on the minutiae of deportment and behavior, where mats should be placed, how food should be eaten, how a man should worship, sleep, eat, and ride in a chariot. All life is reduced to an arid code under the Confucian system—a code which has considerable meaning in an orderly feudal society but lacks meaning entirely under the complexities of modern civilization. He gave orders in Chungking that ricksha coolies should button their shirts, and he has been known to send telegrams to the front before an engagement to remind the high command that soldiers should go to battle with their faces washed. Passing a motor-car with its door swinging wide open in Chungking, he ordered his own car to stop, walked across the road, waited for five minutes until the owner of the car returned, then slapped him across the face. The owner of the car was an officer. He was later court-martialed and ordered to pay a fine "for dereliction of his duty to the public." On another occasion he discovered that conscripts were being roped together and held in barracks where they were dying of starvation. The general in command of conscription was executed the following year, but convicts could still be seen roped together in villages remote from the capital. As the years passed, he began to realize that his orders were rarely carried out, but he continued to believe the reports that were sent to him by his trusted generals, though their accounts of victories were rarely as simple as their fabricated maps. He, who sincerely hated inefficiency, was cursed with inefficient commanders and armies that dragged themselves wearily to battle and out of battle again.

He read omnivorously, but though he understands English, he has never acquired the patience or the time to read English books —his secretaries are continually busy with the translations of leading articles. During the war he ordered the translation of Machiavelli's *The Prince,* Hitler's *Mein Kampf,* and large extracts from Churchill's *Marlborough.* His favorite reading continued to be the *Analects* of Confucius, the mysterious *Book of Changes* compiled by his ancestor Duke Wen, Mencius, and the writings of Tseng Kuo-fan, the general who put down with the help of foreign advisers the Taiping rebellion. He has identified himself with Tseng Kuo-fan and continually quotes from the moral utterances of the great imperial viceroy. A few of Chiang Kai-shek's letters to his children have been published. It is significant that the majority of them are filled with moral precepts. After quoting from the family letters of Tseng Kuo-fan, who urged that all human physical functions should be carried out at definite hours of the day, he wrote to his elder son, Ching-kuo:

You are always falling sick and have no regular time for meals and sleep; this will be a great obstacle for your career. In future I hope you will very often read the suggestion of Tseng Kuo-fan on study and health, and you should be especially careful to put them into practice without negligence.

The tone of pious exhortation is continuous; he rarely gives way to corrigible enthusiasms, yet he is possessed of a deep-seated and curiously mystical belief in China. In his speeches he talks continually of "the sons of the Yellow Emperor," meaning the Chinese race, and "the white sun in the blue sky," meaning the Kuomintang flag with its twelve-pointed star. Chinese calligraphists, accustomed to telling character from handwriting, have observed that he writes with vigor and impatience, modeling his handwriting on the Han dynasty bronzes, but the brush slips too often, and he has no authentic sense of form. Nearly all Chinese statesmen are accustomed to writing verses, but the only verses that he is known to have written by his own unaided effort date back to his school days. Literally translated they read:

> *See how the hill is abundant with bamboos:*
> *They can produce coolness on summer days.*

His prose style is diffuse and repetitive; his delight in hammering in a few cardinal ideas does not necessarily represent the dialectician's insistence—there are probably very few basic ideas that his mind can play with. There are pages in *China's Destiny* so diffuse that they almost baffle translation. He is obsessed by certain words like "state," "unification," "the three principles of the people." Once in a lecture he quoted the old saying: "The honor of the country must be avenged if it takes a hundred generations." He commented ponderously: "That is to say that the honor of the country must still be avenged even though it may be in the hundredth generation." As often in Chinese argument he omits connecting links, bare statement is followed by bare statement, and the bare hypotheses, mounting upon one another, have the effect of the cumulative events of a tragic drama. To explain the necessity of crushing the Communists before he could send his armies against the Japanese, he said:

One of the conditions of our future resistance against the invader is unification. After unification has succeeded, our strength can be concentrated. After the concentration of our strength, one portion of it is capable of doing ten times more work. If there is no unification and the country is divided, the effort to achieve something will be increased twofold. In this case the nation will eventually be destroyed. This is the difference between a modern state and barbarism. It concerns the preservation and destruction of the nation. I hope you will pay particular attention to this matter.

During the war while in Chungking he lived in a house called "The Eagle's Nest." Reminded that this was also the name of Hitler's house in Berchtesgaden, he explained that there was considerable difference between the two houses—his own was furnished with Spartan simplicity. He exalts the Spartan virtues and has a particular fondness for the more Spartan heroes, including the Sung dynasty general Yo Fei, who as a child had carved in red irons on his back the solemn injunction: "Loyalty to the Emperor under all circumstances." He believes himself truly loyal to the empire, and sometimes he will describe himself, like the most ancient emperors of all, as "the loneliest one," half believing that he is the intercessor between the Chinese Heaven and the Chinese people. He berated his general staff in 1943 for preparing in his honor three bronze tripods—the traditional gift in the Chou dynasty for the emperor after great victories. In his refusal he said that "such a gift is not only inappropriate to the spirit of the time, but suggests that my generals are wanting in respect for the great emperors of the past." Nineteen forty-three was the year of his greatest defeats.

He has a passion for acting secretively and mysteriously; hence his passion for his private airplane, which allows him to disappear and arrive at any place without notice. Unfortunately, since he is himself the government, official papers cannot always follow him, and at crucial moments he is apt to be far from the capital. His secret police, largely under the command of cadets from the Whampoa Academy, which he founded with Dr. Sun Yet-sen in 1924, is exceedingly powerful and complicated. Based on the Russian NKVD, it operates within wide limits beyond the law; neither the president of the Control Yuan nor the president of the Legislative Yuan have power to alter its decisions. In conversation with the venerable Dr. Yu Yu-jen, the president of the Control Yuan, I have heard him say: "I am ashamed—every day more ashamed of the secret police." Dr. Sun Fo, the son of the founder of the Republic, merely opened his arms wide apart and exclaimed: "What can I do —the Government will not obey the laws?" Since every Yuan can impose its own laws by orders in council, which amount to fiats, it has been necessary to appoint a special committee to assemble and codify the laws of the different departments of the government. Unfortunately, only too often the laws of one department are in direct opposition to the laws of another.

From his authoritarian heights the Generalissimo is incapable of understanding not only the foibles but also the sufferings of others. There are only three recorded times when he is known to have given way to deep grief—once after the success of the northern march in 1927, when he paid his respects and uttered a vow at the mausoleum of Dr. Sun Yat-sen at White Cloud Temple outside Peking, once at the death of President Roosevelt, and once at the death of General Tai Li, the commander in chief of his secret police, who died in an airplane crash near Nanking in April 1946. It did not occur to him that grief for General Tai Li was incompatible with grief for President Roosevelt. His poker face remained on the day the Pacific war ended—once again he had obeyed the injunction of Confucius that the scholar-soldier should not show signs of emotion.

His moral strength arises from a complete sense of dedication and loyalty to the Chinese empire. In this he resembles any Japanese soldier. His simplicity, his love of intrigue, his immaculate uniforms, his contempt for the masses spring from a mystical belief in his own righteousness as the successor of the imperial dynastic rulers. He openly confessed in the journal he wrote after his capture in Sian that the phrase "the people's verdict" meant nothing to him. Chang Hsueh-liang insisted that he should follow an eight-point program, of which the first point was that the Nanking Government should be reorganized to include all parties. Chang Hsueh-liang insisted that this was "the people's verdict." The Generalissimo answered: "When I heard the words 'the people's verdict,' I realized that this was a malicious plot to kill me by using the mob as an excuse." *

Unlike any of the other government leaders, he possesses extraordinary dramatic power. He can enter a room and by his mere appearance electrify the whole audience. Partly this power comes from the brilliance of the very clear and deep-set eyes, partly it comes from his sheer air of authority. Under his spell it is hardly possible to dissent from his opinions, and commanding generals are known to have sworn an oath that they will fight for their own opinions

* *A Fortnight in Sian,* the Generalissimo's record of his captivity in Sian, was produced in a special edition in flowered silk binding, with an introduction by Dr. Leighton Stuart of Yenching University.

only to find that they are powerless in his presence. He will keep soldiers standing in the sun for four or five hours while he delivers, in a high piercing voice, employing a harsh Chekiang accent that is hardly intelligible to the majority of them, an address on the single theme of "unification." If a soldier faints, he will be publicly reprimanded. He is too apt to forget that in his own youth his body was weak, and that not all men have his dedication to a single idea.

Like all actors, he suffers from the aftereffects of relentless self-projection. Sleeplessness, and sometimes remorse, follows. There are days when, suffering from lumbago, with a splitting headache, unable to concentrate on the rising mass of papers on his desk, his temper becomes ferocious, and the injunctions of Confucius have been disobeyed. Like Hitler, he has been known to strike high officers with a riding whip. Unlike Hitler, he will perform even this act of childish heat with considerable dignity.

Unlike the great scholar-soldiers of the past, he did not grow up in the calm atmosphere of the court. He learned intrigue the hard way. He claims to have made an important contribution to the revolutionary cause in 1911, when almost singlehanded he attacked the yamen at Hangchow, but under the revolutionary government he was given no high post; he was asked to be content with a minor administrative post in Chekiang, an offer that he refused bluntly, deciding to dedicate himself to the reform of the revolutionary army. He wrote editorials on the nature of Chinese strategy in a journal called *The Military Voice*. At no time under Dr. Sun Yat-sen did he receive posts other than purely military ones, with the result that problems of government are still baffling to him—he prefers to settle issues by the sword, or by prompt decisions, and is impatient of evidence. He is apt to make decisions without pondering the possibilities of error; the inner voice speaks a little too promptly, and as he grows older, he becomes increasingly impatient of the fumblings of others who see issues with all their complexities. He will pose as an authority on Biblical criticism, sewerage, nursing homes, the tasks of a newspaper editor, at a single meeting, passing from one question to another with the air of an oracle. When Dr. John Wu was ordered to prepare a new translation of the Bible, problems arose that the Generalissimo solved with commendable promptness. His Methodism is deeply-seated; it is not strange that of all the variants of the Christian religion, he should have chosen the one that would have most appealed in its intransigency to Confucius. Dogmatic at all times, incapable of seeing his own errors, only too sharp-sighted in observing the errors of others, he forgets his prevailing miseries in contemplating the self-righteousness of the Lord God of Hosts, on whom he has modeled himself closely. It is inconceivable that he should have understood the tenderness of Christ.

The early photographs show him strong-jawed, with a full face, thick lips, and unruly hair, but by the age of twenty-six the photographs have subtly changed; the eyes become darker, there are small lines round the eyelids, there is a drawn hungry look on the adult face. His friendship for Chen Chi-mei, who was later assassinated, drew him into the world of intrigue, the secret societies with their complex and poisonous ramifications through the economy of China. On Chen Chi-mei's assassination, he adopted the two nephews, Chen Li-fu and Chen Ko-fu as his own nephews, with disastrous results in the war years; except for a short interval after 1935, they were given vast secret powers in the organization of the Kuomintang. Between them Chen Li-fu and Chen Ko-fu organized the internal unity and the external policy of the Kuomintang; they were the heart of the Kuomintang's physical body, of which the Generalissimo was never more than the titular head, exercising the supreme functions of direction and acting as the personification of party rule, ruthlessly incapable of the detailed work to which the Chen brothers, by their religious devotion to their uncle, were dedicated. It is significant that when Chiang Kai-shek first met Chen Chi-mei in Japan in 1908, Chen was studying the Japanese secret police methods. As the Kuomintang increased in power after the northern march of 1927 it became increasingly a party, not of the people, but of the secret police, and the prisons were continually filled to overflowing. If Sun Yat-sen made the greatest mistake of all in allowing the executive to transgress over the functions of the judiciary, and in introducing the fantastically disdainful system of military tutelage over a people whose culture was perhaps the greatest in the world, Chiang Kai-shek made a mistake of hardly less consequence—in 1927 he proscribed the parties of the left, with the result that they were compelled to exist underground, and therefore to become more powerful. Almost single-handed he brought the Communist party into being. By his remorseless efforts to exterminate them, he was responsible for their growth. If he had been more balanced and co-operative the great split would never have occurred.

He had a real hatred for Japanese violence, and his radio message to the Japanese people after the rape of Nanking was a model of reasonable appeal. But he could not understand some of the sturdy American officers who came to Chungking, and he would compare them unfavorably in their deportment to the Japanese generals he had known. In 1927, when the Japanese were still threatening Manchuria, he visited Japan and met his former Japanese commander, General Himatsu, to whom he presented a typical Confucian scroll: "Not to fall short of the teacher's instruction," signing it with his full name—Chiang Chung-chen.* On the advice of General von Seekt he introduced the German goose step into the Chinese Army, which still parades like the Potsdam grenadiers, to the amusement of American soldiers and the bafflement of Chinese villagers. In the first number of *The Military Voice* he deplored that the Chinese armies were not trained with the punctilio of German soldiers.

There is a sense in which his allegiances to Japan, Germany, and the feudal dynasty of Chou at the beginning of Chinese recorded history are far greater than his allegiances to the present Chinese race. He would be the last to admit it, but no summary of his character can fail to conclude that he is unrepresentative of our times. His strength does not come from the tolerant Chinese but from the rigid intolerance and simplicity of his character. In the most complete sense he is a "great man," but it is only recently that he has begun to recognize that absolute power includes an infinite capacity of self-deception. He is the ruler of 300,000,000 Chinese.

In the winter of 1920 a young Hunanese, who had been an assistant librarian in Peking University, wandered over southern Hunan and Kiangsi. He carried no arms. He wore rice-straw sandals, baggy white trousers, a thick blue padded cotton coat, and a sun helmet. He was swarthy and broad-shouldered, like nearly all Hunanese, and he had a passion for eating red peppers. He carried in his pocket a history of the American War of Independence and the *Story of*

---

* The name given to him by his mother at the age of eighteen, meaning "balanced justice." Chiang Chieh-chih (in Cantonese, Kai-shek), meaning "between stones," is his courtesy name.

the Three Kingdoms, an immense epic written to celebrate the quarrels of frontier dynasties in southwestern China. Occasionally, sitting on a stone by the roadside, he would write a poem on a slip of paper, then slowly crunch it into a ball and throw it in a rice field. He was twenty-two. There was not yet a price on his head, for he was still unknown. He was Mao Tse-tung, who is now the elected ruler of an estimated 100,000,000 Chinese.

He was a man who had already enjoyed a distinguished scholarly record in Hunan. He had read omnivorously, entering the public library at Changsha as soon as it opened and refusing to leave until it was closed. He had been given a scholarship, and when the provincial soldiers attempted to take over his school for barracks, he had been in command of the defense. At the age of fourteen his friend Hsiao San had given him a book in Chinese that recorded the histories of Napoleon, Washington, Wellington, Lincoln, and a host of other military and political figures. He had returned the book the next morning with a single comment: "The Chinese must have heroes like these." Heroism had burned into him. He was determined to be one of two things—either a scholar or a hero, and if possible he would be both. Because the province of Hunan has produced the majority of the scholar-soldiers known to Chinese history, this decision was not quite so unprecedented as it might appear—there were perhaps hundreds of thousands of other young students obsessed with the same enthusiasms.

His father was a poor peasant and a retired soldier who lived in the town of Hsiang-tan on the immense blue sweeping stretch of the Hsiang River, where the red cliffs come down to the shore, and huge white-sailed sampans float all day, and ringed cormorants dive for fish. The Hunanese are naturally rebellious, and they have never entirely become absorbed into the fabric of Chinese government—the indigenous Miao tribesmen live close to them, and their blood is mixed. Of his family Mao Tse-tung says that he remembers nothing except that he was occasionally beaten by his father, a strict Confucian. Almost nothing is known of his mother, and when asked whether he knows anything of his forebears, he will shrug his shoulders, saying that the Hunanese are a mixture of all races and the country has been devastated so often that nearly all family tablets are lost.

When I saw him in June 1946 he gave an impression of extraordinary quietness and serenity. He wore a thick woolen Sun Yat-sen uniform, his blue-black hair was brushed straight back, very long and glistening; and wearing steel-rimmed spectacles, he resembled a country vicar. He had no mannerisms. When he entered the room, you were not conscious that he was there, there was no display of electric power, he talked softly in a quiet feminine voice, making the gentle gestures of a scholar.

His first wife had been executed by Ho Chien, once governor of Hunan, and one of his children had been lost during the Long March in Kweichow; every effort to find the child had failed. He had an attractive second wife and a daughter. He lived in a small hut overlooking the Yen River and shadowed by the baked loess cliffs; and against this landscape the son of a farmer seemed perfectly at ease, talking freely with the peasants, without guards, working late into the night and waking late in the morning. Edgar Snow has recounted how at a meeting with Lin Piao, Mao Tse-tung took off his trousers before he studied the maps on the wall one hot summer's day. If there had been peasant roughnesses in his youth, they seemed to have totally disappeared; he was growing older—he is now fifty-four, ten years younger than Chu Teh, the commander in chief of the Eighth Route Army, and there is a settled sadness in his features in repose. Yet like all the other Chinese Communist leaders he has a curious ingrown air; for more than ten years he has lived in the valley of Yenan, which is parched in summer and flooded in winter, and something of that barren landscape has entered his soul.

In Yenan you notice maps of China; you very rarely see maps of the world. Once you have flown there, it is difficult to believe that the rest of the world exists. There are almost no houses—two small streets of shops, a large bank, the government auditorium, and for the rest men live in caves supported by wooden beams. The caves are whitewashed, cool in summer, not too cold in winter, reached by steps cut out of the loess soil. Except for an occasional red blanket or a saddlecloth embroidered with Persian roses, you see no colors except green and yellow. Pears, grapes, dates, tomatoes, and potatoes grow in abundance; the winter wheat climbs on the shallow hills. There are no graveyards or burial mounds, for people are buried among the rocky shadows of the hills, and if you look down at Yenan from the hills, you see only the empty valley and perhaps a solitary rider coming from a distant battlefield to report to General Chu Teh at his headquarters; which is a large date garden. The empty valley is the capital of the Communist empire.

Mao Tse-tung fits into the background of Yenan as Chiang Kai-shek fits into the background of Nanking, with its parades, motorcars, and immense acquisitions of unearned wealth. Mao represents the peasant strength of the country; but he is a man of many disguises. He has been scholar, poet, military leader, revolutionary, trade union organizer, librarian, newspaper editor; he was once secretary to Hu Han-ming, and he was said to be in Chiang Kai-shek's counsels until Chiang Kai-shek brought the revolution to an end in 1927. He has never been arrested and has never been out of China, though his knowledge of foreign affairs is partly derived from the innumerable other Chinese Communist leaders who studied abroad—mostly in France. He reads English nearly as well as he reads Chinese. He used to smoke sixty cigarettes a day, growing his own tobacco in his backyard, but under doctor's orders he now smokes hardly at all, and he is no longer allowed to eat red peppers. Mellowed by the years, he remains intransigent toward the Kuomintang, utterly incapable of forgetting or forgiving the massacre of the left wing in the years following 1927, remembering the death of his wife as Lenin remembered the execution of his brother. Asked why he did not order the assassination of Chiang Kai-shek, he said: "Assassination leads nowhere. Why should I? He represents a system, and it is much more likely that he will be assassinated by his own men." Though he is physically strong—when he was young he liked wandering over the Hunanese plains, shirtless in the rain, and deliberately toughened himself—he nearly died four times during the Long March and suffered from complete nervous prostration in April 1946 when General Yeh Ting and nearly a score of other Communist leaders were killed in an air crash near Yenan. Like Chiang Kai-shek he drinks little; unlike the Generalissimo, he has no fixed routine of life and is prepared to accommodate himself to whatever routine fits best with his friends. Again like the Generalissimo he is capable of making endless speeches—the whole text of his book *New Democracy* was originally delivered as a speech, lasting eight hours. He still writes poetry and has recently collected his poems in a private edition called *Wind Sand Poems,* but the edition is so private that only his most intimate friends have seen it.

The poems follow the ancient classical tradition. In speeches to writers he will insist that the classical tradition is outworn, and no one should be encouraged to write in the old medium, excusing himself by saying that he is approaching old age and was brought up under a tradition different to theirs. His favorite modern poet is an old Yunnanese revolutionary called K'e Chung-ping, who models his verses on the style of folk ballads. Only three of Mao Tse-tung's poems have been smuggled out of China. The most impressive is a long poem called "The Snow," describing his journey by airplane to Chungking in October 1945. It was the first time he had even been in an airplane, and he describes with extraordinary accuracy the vision of China seen from the pilot's cabin. In another poem, written toward the end of the Long March, when the Communists were still thinking of reaching the Great Wall in an effort to offer resistance to the Japanese, his feelings for the Generalissimo, the Kuomintang, the Japanese, all of which he hated equally, are summed up in the last line:

> *The sky is high, the clouds are winnowing,*
> *I gaze southward at the wild geese disappearing over the*
> *horizon.*
> *I count on my fingers—a distance of 20,000 li—*
> *I say we are not heroes if we do not reach the Great Wall.*
> *Standing on the highest peak of Six Mountains,*
> *The red flag streaming in the west wind,*
> *Today with a long rope in my hand,*
> *I wonder how soon we can bind up the monster.*

This is not essentially a poem against the Generalissimo—the Japanese were more monstrous than the Kuomintang; unlike Li Li-san, Mao Tse-tung was continually obsessed with the necessity of destroying the Japanese invasion—a task more urgent than forming a Marxist state on Chinese soil. During the Long March Li Li-san insisted that the Communist armies should remain in Chinese Turkestan. Mao Tse-tung, who had been expelled from the Comintern, saw no reason why he should attempt to set up, in the comparative seclusion of a frontier province, a model state existing in a vacuum; it was necessary that the Japanese should be destroyed first —the day of the Kuomintang could wait. In this he reversed the policy of Chiang Kai-shek, who insisted that the danger from the Chinese Communists was greater than the danger from Japan.

Life in Yenan is incredibly unlike life in Soviet Russia. Almost none of the major plans introduced by Soviet Russia have been incorporated in Communist-held China. There are no Five-Year-Plans, no collectivization programs, no heavily regimented bureaucracy, no vast hordes of political prisoners in prison camps, no effort to proscribe books—the most widely read book after Mao Tse-tung's own *New Democracy* and *Coalition Government* was the Generalissimo's *China's Destiny,* which was continually being reprinted in Yenan. The text was unchanged, but a considerable number of notes suggesting the falsity of the Generalissimo's argument was added. There were, however, labor heroes—I could find no other importations from Soviet Russia—but even the nature of the labor hero had changed. A Stakhanovite receives a large cash reward; in Communist-held China he receives a rosette nearly eighteen inches in diameter.

Nothing could be more erroneous than to maintain that the Chinese Communists are simply agrarian reformers; they form a political party, backed by a large army, and though they have little hope of achieving supreme power, they will continue to prolong the armed conflict until they have received political satisfaction. They will not lay down their arms lightly—too many of them have seen their friends murdered by the Kuomintang secret police to believe in the Generalissimo's good intentions. The whole theory of Kuomintang government, based upon military tutelage and the enormous concentration of power in the hands of the chief executive, is a denial of the basic rights of the Chinese people; the Generalissimo's repeated offers of constitutional government are suspect, because he retains in addition to the armed forces of the Kuomintang a vast organization of secret police, and because his almost hysterical opposition to labor movements has not changed with the times. The prisons are still full, the secret police is widespread, the liberal elements are still being continually threatened. Under such a system, offers of constitutional government, even if well intentioned, are deprived of force by past history, and the continual postponement of constitutional government—it was postponed seven times between 1936 and 1946—do not augur well for collaboration. One solution to the conflict, dramatically offered on the last day of his ill-fated journey to China, was offered by General Marshall when he declared:

The salvation of the situation, as I see it, would be the assumption of leadership by the liberals in the government and in the minority parties, a splendid group of men, but who as yet lack the political power to exercise a controlling influence. Successful action on their part under the leadership of Generalissimo Chiang Kai-shek would, I believe, lead to unity through good government.

In fact, the National Assembly has adopted a democratic constitution. It remains to be seen to what extent the government will give substance to the form by a genuine welcome of all groups actively to share in the responsibility of government. The amount of representation accorded to liberals and to non-Kuomintang members will be significant. If the termination of one-party rule is to be a reality, the Kuomintang should cease to receive financial support from the government.

By implication, General Marshall would seem to have insisted that government should be neutral, neither Kuomintang nor Communist, a government of the talents, which would accord well with the traditional history of China. Unfortunately, the long tradition of scholar-politicians has broken. With few exceptions the Chinese professors are not democratic; their sufferings during the years of inflation and exile in southern universities have made them either lukewarm or incapable of refusing the advantages of political position. On the rare occasions when eminent scholars have taken political positions, they have rarely shown themselves to advantage; while those whose leanings are toward a democratic state are still terrorized by the secret police. For the moment the only effort toward a solution that has any likelihood of success would be the retirement from the scene of the aging Generalissimo and perhaps of the leading Communists, whose intransigency and bitterness make any compromise impossible.

Yet there are good grounds for believing that the intolerance of the Kuomintang leaders is even greater than that of the Communists. Innumerable high positions on the Kuomintang side are held by military officers whose wealth and dignity depends upon the survival of the Kuomintang regime. The Communists claim that the Kuomintang is dependent upon support from only three classes: the banks, the landowners, and the military, adding that the secret societies are in close touch with all of them. The claim is not unfounded, and there is considerable evidence that the Kuomintang Party, which obtained power by force of arms and without the encumbrance of elections, is maintained by groups that act consistently against the social revolution. American assistance to the Kuomintang during the closing stages of the war, and during the civil war, only inflamed their belief that the Kuomintang was prepared to seek help wherever there were opportunities of destroying the social revolution, for though they respected General Marshall and were prepared to believe that he was doing his utmost to prevent the civil war, it was not difficult for them to see a new orientation of American policy against Soviet Russia; and if it was necessary for them to choose between Russia and the United States, they would choose Russia. Yet they were careful never to make the choice. They were Chinese first, and Communists afterward. Also, because the liberal elements had not yet risen from among the people in any force, they remained the only party that systematically put the social revolution into practice.

The achievements of the Communists in agrarian reform should not be underestimated. The Kuomintang failed dismally to improve the lot of the peasants. Elections were never held, all governors were government appointees, and if they refused to obey the orders of the Supreme Military Council, they were overthrown by force. The governor of Yunnan, General Lung Yun, was ordered in September 1945 to send his armies to Indo-China. During their absence troops of the Fifth Army from Honan and Hunan surrounded his capital in Kunming, he was ordered to surrender, and his garrison troops were savagely butchered during five days of civil war. The reason was simple: the Yunnanese government was comparatively democratic and had done much to aid the fortunes of the growing Democratic League, then still in its infancy, by giving protection to Dr. Lo Lung-chi and refusing to allow the Central Government to maintain its secret police in the province of Yunnan in any force. The three greatest universities of North China were then living in exile just outside the city walls. Two months after the civil war, in December 1945, the new Kuomintang government did its utmost to suppress the students, fired over their heads at mass meetings, threatened both professors and students, and finally ordered a small massacre in order to demonstrate its power. The culprits, who were known, were never arrested, though some three months later they were quietly removed from their posts, under the pressure of popular opinion.

The record of the Kuomintang is not impressive. Dr. Sun Fo has shown that under no conditions did his father, Dr. Sun Yat-sen, envisage a government by military junta. He said to me in April 1946: "If the Kuomintang continues at present along the same lines as it has been moving in the past, there will be nothing at all to show for my father's work. My father believed first in the livelihood of the people—the Kuomintang has produced no laws which suggests that it wants to help them along the path of livelihood. On the contrary, the Kuomintang government deliberately takes no cognizance of law. The secret prisons are a sufficient proof, since we have the law of habeas corpus on our statute books."

In one sense the Communists suffer from the same disease as the Kuomintang. A closely organized party, with an adequate propaganda machine, and an army estimated at ten million soldiers excluding village guards, who are often unarmed, it tends to consider itself as a power in being, and the puritanical faith of its followers makes it impatient of wider issues. Mao Tse-tung has continually warned the Communists against dogmatism, but dogmatism survives. There is something incestuous in those hundreds of thousands of small armed village groups determined to defend their principles to the last, never mingling with the world outside, just as there is something incestuous in the Kuomintang groups, who huddle together for comfort against the growing power of the villages. In the last instance, the battle between the Communists and the Kuomintang is a battle between the towns and the villages, between centralization and decentralization. It is necessary that we should realize that the power of the Communists cannot die, that from every dead Chinese Communist a hundred spring up, and that power in China is not measured in guns but in manpower, and in the rate of increase of manpower. By this argument, the decline of the Kuomintang is inevitable, unless it is completely reorganized.

Mao Tse-tung's *Coalition Government* made in 1942 the same suggestions made by General Marshall five years later. He called for a government of all parties, an army under purely military leadership, the introduction of long-overdue reforms in social policy, the abandonment of the secret police and the introduction of the secret ballot.

Our starting point [he wrote] is to serve the Chinese people earnestly and wholeheartedly, and never to be severed from the people; to set out always from the point of view of serving the people's interests, not serving the interests of a small group or oneself; to give equal responsibility to the people and the guiding organization. Experience during the last twenty years has taught us that all tasks, policies and methods that were correct corresponded to the demands of the people at that definite time and place, and all that were incorrect were separate from the people's will.

The book is impressive because it demonstrates the necessity of armed union between the Kuomintang and the Communists against the Japanese, and prophesied in considerable detail the course of the civil war that would break out at the end of hostilities. Trained as a historian, Mao could see cleanly and dispassionately the course of events as well as the necessary changes in the form of government that bring about unity. The People's Consultative Council, which met in October 1945, seemed at the time to offer hope that the two parties would be reconciled on the basis that the more liberal representatives in the center, without party ties, would have a preponderance of power. The honeymoon ended in February 1946 when the Kuomintang threw out the propositions made by the People's Consultative Council, and made demands on the Communists that they were unable to fulfill. The onus of responsibility rests considerably on the Kuomintang for failing to accept these propositions. But at least one thing had been accomplished—Mao Tse-tung's *Coalition Government* and the proposals of the conference differed so little that the way was clear for any future reforms toward constitutional government. In their own territory the Communists balked at taking too great a share of power; they instituted a method by which they should never have a claim for more than one-third share in the representation. If the Kuomintang could have been induced to follow a similar policy, the present mishaps might have been avoided.

The method of the Communists was removed from rigid bureaucracy. The popular will, expressed through the village councils, determined the course of government policy. Social democracy relies on the government to express the popular will, not its own will. To prove that popular will may sometimes be in advance of government, Mao wrote in *Coalition Government*:

Our comrades must not think that what is unintelligible to us is also unintelligible to the masses. Very often the masses stride ahead of us, and want urgently to advance forward, while our comrades do not act as leaders of the broad masses, but on the contrary reflect the opinion of some backward interests. Every comrade should be made to comprehend that the highest criterion of all our statements and activities is whether they correspond to the highest interests of the broadest masses, and whether they are supported by the broadest masses. Every comrade should be taught to comprehend that as long as we rely on the people, firmly believing in the infinite creative power of the people, then we may be able to overcome all difficulties, no matter how serious they are, and no enemy will be able to overwhelm us, but will be overwhelmed by us.

This was not essentially the policy that was pursued in the early days of the Communist revolution in China; it was a policy hammered out of war against the Japanese, when it was necessary, if north China should survive that *all the people* should take part in a common battle against the invader. The Kuomintang failed to unite the people in the south, or even to awaken their political consciousness; the Chinese Communists succeeded. The incontrovertible evidence would suggest that the party which is aware of the social revolution has better claims to represent the people than the party which, in the words of the son of the Father of the Republic, "has failed to make itself a living issue." Just before the celebrated march to the north in 1927, Chiang Kai-shek said: "My aim is to be a person remembered in history." Mao Tse-tung, with a deeper knowledge of history, wrote in *Coalition Government* a statement of the aspirations of the Chinese people:

People must understand that no matter how tortuous the path may be, the independence and liberation of the Chinese people will be realized, and the time for it is already at hand. The great aspirations of countless martyrs during the last 100 years must be fulfilled *by our generation*. Whoever desires to prevent these aspirations from being translated into fact, that man will fail.

Chapter 11

The Kuomintang

WHEN Sun Yat-sen died in March 1925, his body was taken within the boundaries of the Imperial City in Peking, draped in the colors of the Republic, and on a wooden tablet above his head there was inscribed in gold letters the most famous words of his will: "The Revolution is not yet accomplished." In talking of the revolution before his death Sun Yat-sen had shown signs of despair. For a long while he had refused to make a will, and the version that is recited all over Kuomintang China on Monday morning ceremonies was not written by him but by Wang Ching-wei, who was later to become the puppet president under the Japanese, governing from Nanking. In one sense the will was a pure fabrication. Asked whether he approved of the will, he made a motion of assent with his hands, but no reported conversations are known that show that he took any active interest in it or recognized the importance that would be attached to it. The original draft of the will was written by Wang Ching-wei on February 24. On the evening of March 11, Sun Yat-sen summoned his wife, in whom he had full confidence, and with her help added his signature at the bottom of the will. At that moment he was blind, speechless, and choking for breath. He died the next day.

The will in its final form read:

I have devoted forty years to the work of the national revolution with the aim of securing for China a position of freedom and independence. After forty years of experience I am profoundly convinced that in order to achieve this aim, we must call up the masses of the people and unite with those people of the world who will treat us on terms of equality and who will struggle together with us.

The Revolution is not yet accomplished. All my comrades should work unceasingly according to the *General Principles of Reconstruction,* the *Outline of Reconstruction, The Three Principles of the People* written by me, and the declaration issued by the First National Congress of the Kuomintang, until this aim is achieved. The convocation of the People's Assembly and the abolition of the unequal treaties that I have advocated recently must be carried out with the least possible delay. This is what I wished to call your attention to.

In this will eight major theses are recommended as the future policy of the Kuomintang; of those eight theses one has been put into practice—the unequal treaties were abolished by America and Great Britain in February 1942—and even the greatest admirers of the Kuomintang cannot point to the successful accomplishment of any of the others. The will, which is regarded as a sacrosanct document, has not been obeyed for reasons of high Kuomintang policy; nor could it be obeyed, since the assumption of dictatorship by Generalissimo Chiang Kai-shek in 1927 destroyed the basis upon which the revolution could be successfully carried out. Though there are grounds for believing that the document was fabricated in the sense that Dr. Sun Yat-sen took no conscious part in assembling it in its final form, no doubt remained in the minds of those who were by his bed that he would have written such a will if he could. He had said these words, or words very like them in the past; * he had made the hazardous journey to Peking in the desperate hope that a national assembly, representing all parties and all warlords, could be brought into being; and for months previously he had looked forward to a time when a national assembly could be convened. In his mind, the last hope for peace lay precisely in the convocation of representatives from all the five nations that comprise China. Even his last words, uttered a few minutes before his death, "Peace—save China," were concerned with the national assembly. Until 1946 no national assembly was ever convened, though delegates had been chosen by the Kuomintang in 1936. When the time came for the Assembly to come into being, the Communists protested that representation upon the basis of a choice made arbitrarily in 1936 could have no validity at the present time, and refused, perhaps wrongly, to take part.

Even if the Kuomintang Party was to lose its power overnight,

* An account of the events leading up to the signing of the will is given in Stephen Chen and Robert Payne: *Sun Yat-sen, A Portrait,* 1946.

the significance of the will would remain. Dr. Sun Yat-sen would have objected to the use that has been made of it. The Monday morning ceremonies at Kuomintang headquarters, where the will is read out as though it provided the rubric for a form of ceremonial mass, would have been distasteful to him; but it was to the credit of Wang Ching-wei that he was capable of seizing at the last possible moment a motive for the revolution. The will provides, in effect, a series of commands. The revolutionaries are ordered to accomplish certain aims "with the least possible delay." That they did not accomplish them would suggest that though the will was employed as a kind of oriflamme, the intentions of his successors differed from the intentions of the Father of the Republic.

Dr. Sun Yat-sen had no very great command of sociology or economics. The famous Three Principles of the People, which he delivered as lectures in Canton, were never completed and suffered from the inevitable defects that occur in all political manifestoes written at a time of crisis. Though there are brilliant passages in the book, it consists largely of generalized statements, apothegms, anecdotes, and purely hypothetical arguments; in this it follows the pattern of most Chinese theoretical works written until recently. The book is not a scholar's carefully considered and objective account of the forces at work and the necessary cures for a dying economy; on a broad basis it suggests three undefined remedies for the situation in China as it existed at the time. Under nationalism two separate ideas are understood: that China should be a sovereign power and the five nations (Chinese, Mongol, Manchu, Tibetan, and Mohammedan) comprising modern China should have some form of sovereignty, never completely defined; a similar confusion exists in Chiang Kai-shek's *China's Destiny*. Under democracy, Dr. Sun Yat-sen insisted that government should stem from the elective powers of the smallest political unit—the county—and at the same time he insisted that to the traditional Western forms of government two more should be added—the traditional imperial prerogatives of examining students for government service and of obedience to censorship; and these should have final powers and the ministers should rank equally with the ministers in whom were placed the charges of the executive, the legislatures, and the judiciary. Dr. Sun Yat-sen attached far-reaching importance to what he called "the Five-power constitution," and it is mentioned in his will; but the complete collapse of the Control Yuan during the war, and the absence of any fair examinations for recruitment into the civil service, showed that the innovations were never taken seriously. "I have no powers whatsoever," said Dr. Yu Yu-jen, the Minister of the Control Yuan in April 1946. There had been a time when Dr. Sun Yat-sen seemed to regard the Control Yuan as the greatest of all depositories of power. The last and most important of the Three Principles was Livelihood. He taught that the land must be evenly distributed among the tillers of the soil, the abuses of capital must be restrained, and the economic life of the country must be deliberately directed along socialist lines. By demanding "Livelihood" Sun Yat-sen became the implicit Kuomintang spokesman for the agrarian revolution and an even balance between industry and agriculture. Insisting on the necessity of an industrial revolution in the same breath that he insisted on the necessity of an agricultural revolution, he was demonstrating the theoretical possibility of both revolutions existing at the same time—a purely agrarian revolution could hardly hope to be succesful in a country of undeveloped industrial resources. The two revolutions were to ride abreast, each helping the other.

But Dr. Sun Yat-sen, though he possessed a prodigious knowledge of railways—after his resignation from the presidency in 1912, he made a prolonged study of railway administration—knew little of the problems of industry; his book on the industrial reconstruction of China, with its blueprints of vast new ports and still vaster mineral exploitation, was as academic and theoretical as the similar blueprint with which Generalissimo Chiang Kai-shek completes his study of industrial reorganization in *China's Destiny*. A Chinese mind, trained on the Confucian classics, cannot easily conform to an understanding of the interlocking complexities of industry. "The scope of Dr. Sun Yat-sen's industrial plan far surpasses that of the T'ang and Han dynasties," Chiang Kai-shek writes in *China's Destiny*, forgetting that no comparisons are possible or desirable. He continues, after moral exhortations: "The scope, the plans, the determination and ability to carry them through should be derived from the lessons of five thousand years of Chinese history, and should be determined in the light of China's geographical situation and the evolution of the world situation. As to practical application, it should proceed from small to large-scale tasks, and from what is near at hand to what is distant." The uneasy, theoretical, and jejune basis may be disarming to scholars; it is terrifying to people who are actively concerned with the social and industrial reconstruction of China. The sacred words thrown pell-mell on the page accumulate overtones—one realizes dimly that this is Confucius himself attempting vainly to speak about a world of machines. Only once does Chiang Kai-shek come to grips with the subject. This is when he says: "We must adopt a planned economy and social legislation to secure the livelihood and survival of every citizen, and it is imperative that we eventually accomplish the objective of transforming capital into state capital, and transform all enjoyment into enjoyment for the masses." It is difficult to understand how such a policy differs in theory from socialism, but no social legislation has been introduced during twenty years of Kuomintang leadership along these lines, and it is significant that this is the only time that he uses the word livelihood in *China's Dynasty*. One would have considerably more faith in this announcement if it were not immediately followed by a fantastic enumeration of the machines of various kinds which should be built according to a ten-year plan.

"The heart of Chinese economy lies in its industrialization," says Chiang Kai-shek. The statement is incontrovertible, but the mechanisms by which a rural economy is transformed into an industrial economy are complex; and the mere enunciation of figures is not always helpful. Significantly, railways are placed first. Of an optimum 140,000 kilometers, he insists that the goal for the ensuing ten years should be 20,000 kilometers—the optimum will only be reached in seventy years. A million and a half kilometers of highways must be constructed, of which a quarter of a million must be built in ten years. The ultimate goal of harborage is stated to be 186,000,000 tons clearance, of which 100,000,000 tons clearance are to be built in ten years. It is clear that harbors are more significant under this plan than railways or roads.

The fantastic, almost meaningless list continues through seven pages of the Chinese text. An optimum mercantile fleet of 14,000,000 tons is followed by:

Power generators	40,000,000 h.p.
Tooling machines	4,500,000
Other machines	7,000,000

Electric power (hydroelectric)	20,000,000 watts
Telegraph lines	36,000,000 kilometers
Wireless stations	3,000
Telephones	9,000,000
Receiving sets	18,000,000
Civil airplanes	120,000
Houses	50,000,000
Cotton spindles	10,000,000
Annual output of coal	150,000,000 tons

The amazing list includes the number of students in different branches of learning, the amount of asphalt to be manufactured (in one edition of *China's Destiny* this is computed as 288,000 tons and in the revised edition the figures become 751,000 tons), the amount of copper, lead, zinc, caustic soda, nitric acid, rubber tires, hydrochloric acid, sugar, salt, wheat, beans. No explanation of how the figures were arrived at is given, and in proof that the plan will succeed, Chiang Kai-shek offers a statement that Dr. Sun Yat-sen made to him on the battlefield of San Ho Pa in 1918: "Japan's population and territory are eight to ten times smaller than China's; therefore a project that takes Japan eight to ten years to finish would require only one or two years in China." Chiang Kai-shek confessed that in the military academy at Poatingfu he found "mathematics exceedingly difficult."

It is necessary to insist that the ten-year plan follows, except in its dimensions and larger inaccuracies, the statements previously made by Dr. Sun Yat-sen. The chichés of the former book are repeated within the later book, and the Generalissimo quotes with approval the statement from the *Programme of National Reconstruction*:

The people's livelihood occupies the place of primary importance in reconstruction. In regard to the four great requirements of food, clothing, shelter and movement for the people of the entire country, the Government should endeavor in co-operation with the people to develop agriculture to provide sufficient food for the people, to develop textiles to provide sufficient clothing for the people, to construct large-scale housing to provide the people with comfortable dwellings, and to keep roads and canals in good condition to facilitate peoples' movement.

In China, such statements continually repeated may have the sopo-
rific power of national hymns, but they are not calculated to
advance the cause of industrial progress. Dr. Sun Yat-sen had said
that "the government should endeavor in co-operation with the
people to develop agriculture," but there is nothing in *China's
Destiny* that points to the significance of industrial and agricultural
co-operatives. The plan is not meaningless, but more than any other
plan it suggests the spiritual bankruptcy of the Confucians faced
with the nascent industrialism of China.

The Generalissimo has paid considerable attention to the railways
and harbors; problems concerning the balance between agriculture
and industry are not studied. Yet the most pressing problem facing
the new industrial China is how this balance can be brought about.
It clearly cannot come about through unrestricted free trade. Future
historians may regard the opening of Shanghai to unrestricted foreign imports as disastrous—on a rising black market competition
between Chinese goods and foreign goods became impossible. In
1936 Professor Chen Tai-sen of Tsinghua University wrote in Dr.
Hu Shih's *Independent Critic*:

> We must be clear in our minds whether the extension of roads and
> railways is desirable. If they serve only to accelerate the import of foreign
> goods to the interior, thereby draining and exhausting more rapidly than
> ever before the financial resources of the hinterland, we may well ask
> that they should not be extended. The theoretical advantages of improved
> communications can be realized only if Chinese industries in the coastal
> regions and agriculture, forestry and mining in the interior are progres-
> sively developed at the same time.

Professor Chen Tai-sen, a close friend of Dr. Chang Hsi-jo, represented here the belief held in all academic circles in China throughout the war that the problem of balanced economies was the most
critical problem that China had to face. What is surprising is not
that the Generalissimo, following Dr. Sun Yat-sen, has omitted any
reference to the problem, but that he should be so singularly un-
aware at all other times that the problem existed.

The strange doctrines of *China's Destiny,* written by a man who
is obsessed with a Pelagian occupation in Human Depravity that
can be cured only by a reversion to the pure fountain of Confucius,
have now become the Bible of Kuomintang China. In a long chapter

the Generalissimo bitterly attacks the West, which is responsible for all the plagues, floods, military defeats, and terrors that have afflicted China since the Opium War of 1842. Though modern science is considered to be necessary, the Chinese student is advised to read the writings of the Emperor Yu and Kuang Chu rather than the digests of the latest scientific studies in soil fertility, and to consult the *Book of Rites,* written two and a half millenniums ago, for information on grain storage. He says airily that the Emperor Yu was the first and greatest economist who has ever appeared in China or in the world; still more airily he pleads that all modern systems of economics are either immature copies of Chinese originals or basically wrongheaded. He begins an astonishing chapter on landholding, in which no conclusions are drawn except that in ancient times a man was allowed to possess five mu of land (about an acre) for his house and a hundred mu for his farm, with the statement: "The production of farmers depends upon the land." The book is not characterized by excessive helpfulness in dealing with modern problems.

Yet the book is required reading, and it would be a singularly brave man who would deny that the greater part of it is acceptable to his followers. Immature, vicious in its attacks on the West, restrained in its anger against the Communists, written according to the old principle of joining quotations from the classics into a pattern of accusation against modern progress, it represents the dying protest of an ancient feudal civilization whose roots are lost in the past. Astonishing fallacies remain: it is simply not true, for example, that "our numerous national humiliations of the past all resulted from the fact that we debased ourselves and scorned our own cultural heritage." The protest is made, and the gauntlet is thrown down. Unable to see the world in terms of political and economic development, he theorizes in terms of the most ancient philosophers of all, and finds among them a sense of refuge. He had always possessed a belief in the existence of the mythical Yellow Emperor. Now he introduces the Yellow Emperor as a fact of considerable importance to explain the common origin of the Manchus and the Tibetans. It is as if a British prime minister urged the common origin of the Celts, the Goidels, and the Saxons by appealing to Adam.

It is not impossible to imagine that sustenance for modern theories of sociology could be found in ancient Chinese texts; what is surprising in Chiang Kai-shek's book is that the most famous text of all is omitted—the text that emphasizes that the ruler owes his "mandate from Heaven" to the acquiescence and trust of the people. More than any other figure in the book, there occurs the great patriarchal dignitary, the Emperor Yu, with whom Chiang Kai-shek would appear to have identified himself. The mythological background is overwhelming. He employs something of the technique of Adolf Hitler, capitalizing upon the unequal treaties in the same way that Hitler capitalized on another unequal treaty. Strange, too, in a man who appeals so much to the ancients is his contempt for scholars in Chinese universities, who are excoriated in a passage so bewildering that it should be quoted in full:

From 1911 to the Nationalist revolution, academic traditions underwent changes in unison with the changes in academic teaching, and all the ideologies of the nations of the world, such as Liberalism, Nationalism, Communism and Anarchism, were subject to examination. If we look at them closely, we may observe that although a large degree of progressiveness was diffused in the social structure, a tradition of genuineness, sincerity, stability and honesty failed to materialize. *Scholars did not seek truth through practical effort.* Some concentrated on thinking without learning, closing their eyes to facts, and engaging in hollow discourse and setting up rival schools of thought. Others learned without thinking, uncritically selecting a theory here and there. Those that admired westernization abandoned China's own culture in favor of allegiance to foreign theories. Those that upheld the national culture reverted to an isolated chauvinism. The scholars were careless and irresponsible in their lectures, uncritically echoing the popular trend in order to court favor with the people. Their concept of "liberty" was based on their own selfish desires, while their theory of "democracy" was based on their desire to advance their own material interests. Observance of the law was regarded as humiliating, and resistance to orders as clever. They took advantage of the ignorance of youth and called themselves "teachers of youth." They wantonly spread superficial propaganda and called themselves "academic torch bearers." The ultimate consequences were turmoil in the state and the decline of the nation to the point of extinction. While such trends existed, it was difficult to find many persons who accepted the principle that the rise and fall of the state was the responsibility of every individual. Such being the condition of education and academic teaching, the attempt to reform social and political customs was as futile as climbing a tree to look for fish.

In any other context the passage would be amusing, but no country in the Far East depends for its fulfillment so much as China on its young students and professors, nor has any country a longer tradition of teaching. He says that education as it existed was leading to disaster and suggests the alternative that "every teacher should develop his sense of duty and strengthen his sense of responsibility and focus education on the concept of statehood, and place the ideology of nationalism before everything else." But the failure of the Kuomintang derived from the fact that it focused its policy precisely on the conception of nationalism to the exclusion of the remaining two principles of Sun Yat-sen—democracy and livelihood.

The book was written in the autumn of 1942. On its publication in the spring of 1943, in spite of the great shortage of paper in Szechwan, two hundred printings were issued; all university students and government officials were ordered to buy copies, and soldiers were ordered to read it, or have it read to them, whereupon they were asked to make critical commentaries in their notebooks. Prizes were offered for the best criticisms, and there arose inevitably a competition upon the part of soldiers and some students to defend its most poignant theory that all China's ills were due to the incursions of the West. For the first time millions of Chinese became acquainted with a complete and one-sided account of foreign imperialism. Extraterritoriality, the 5-per-cent tariff, inland navigation, concessions, foreign garrisons, indemnities, spheres of influence, the partition of China, the leasing of territories, and the grants of railroads, use of harbors, and fishing rights—the list is impressive enough, but no gratitude is offered to the survivors of the imperial dynasty who fought against foreign impositions, and even the Boxers, for whom he might be expected to have some sympathy, are characterized as "stupid and stubborn." One would have thought stubbornness might be a virtue, and that something might be said in favor of the reformers like Kang Yu-wei, who is dismissed as a member of a conservative clique. Stranger still, the second edition of *China's Destiny* pointedly omits the original slogan of Dr. Sun Yat-sen's first political party—the slogan that did more to overthrow the Manchus than the rising in Wuchang: "Drive out the Manchus, recover the territory of China, establish a people's state and equalize land rights." Chiang Kai-shek includes only the two opening statements, relating to the Manchus and the territorial integrity of China, thus reducing the original impetus of the revolutionaries to one of nationalism only.

The ulterior purpose of his attempt to exaggerate the evil effects of foreign domination appears more clearly in the long, labored, and hesitant chapters in which he recounts the Kuomintang's revolutionary struggle and final success in abolishing the unequal treaties. The Kuomintang is identified with China, and the abolishing of the unequal treaties must be considered a success, not so much for the Chinese people who had fought against and deserved the removal of, the treaties, as for the party that was in power at the time when they were removed, the party that "bases its principles on universal justice, its motives on absolute sincerity and its spirit on the ancient virtues of the nation." He emphasizes that the grant of equal treaties was given to the Kuomintang rather than to the Communists, and that the purpose of the revolution is still not accomplished, because the people are not yet conscious of their national equality with other nations. He insists that the removal of the treaties is only one more reason why every man in China should be armed, and every student placed under suspicion. His fear of the students is manifested in a hundred places; they are only less dangerous than the professors who have so sedulously mistaught them. Only the utmost rigidity and control, and their indoctrination with the principles of the Three Principles of the People, will save them from being susceptible to outside influence, for "like a piece of paper they can be painted red, black, gray or yellow." What is necessary is that the people's three-hundred-year tradition of cowardice and despair shall be broken; it will be broken only by "rebirth in self-endeavor" and a ten-year industrial plan.

While the book was being written in the autumn of 1942, the Chinese government under Chiang Kai-shek's orders issued decrees ordering all workers to join labor unions. The government appointed the secretaries of the labor unions. Legislation was passed providing for a twelve-hour day and one day's rest in every two weeks. Strikes had already been outlawed by the National Mobilization Act of May 5, 1942. Unions were further warned that "any actions disturbing social security were to be punished to the full extent of the law." The pattern was repeating itself. Nothing in the attitude of the government toward the workers and the peasants had changed. Not only was the war not being fought vigorously— a task that was left to the American and British forces in the Pacific and Indian Oceans—but it became clear that the government was employing its reserves to build up a machine for pursuing civil war. *China's Destiny,* like Hitler's *Mein Kampf,* was a factual blueprint of the intentions of its author, who refuses to allow the Communists or any other parties to enter the government unless they accept the conditions he authorizes: full and instantaneous subjection to party rule, and to the wisdom of the course he has mapped out for the nation. The liberal tradition of the West is castigated; in its place he elevates the Confucian power-state in the hour of its final triumph. His vision of China is one with vast industrial resources on the coast, collective farms where the farmers are trained by military officers in the intervals of farming and breeding, enormous concentrations of financial power and prisons for students and professors who refuse to come within the orbit of his power. A trained Hitler *Jugend* with unspecified but sacrosanct privileges will form that part of the police force which is not already included in the army. The teaching of Western economics will be banned; personal loyalty to the Generalissimo will be encouraged; no attention will be paid to a balanced economy or the problem of liquidating the Chinese Army after a long war—the soldiers will presumably be still under arms, their resources of manpower lost to the nation except in so far as they are valuable in "mopping-up operations." In this strange chaotic book he has announced the future program of the party he controls without one word of enlightened interest in the problem of livelihood, which is assumed to be of such minor importance that it will solve itself. "History," he says openly, "teaches us that the equalization of landholdings by compulsory means is certain to fail," and instantly dismisses Dr. Sun Yat-sen's major contribution to the Chinese political scene as impracticable.

The old revolutionary flame, which burned so brightly in the time of Sun Yat-sen, had vanished by the autumn of 1942. It had been tended by many heroes and many martyrs, but the time of bureaucracy and unrestricted exploitation had come, the inflation was in full flow, the prisons were full, commerce with the enemy was beginning under the directions of the Bank of China, and the Kuomintang had produced an organization so rigid that it failed to allow a pattern of growth. Trade unions were suspended or placed entirely under government control, and already a beginning was being made toward an increasing violation of the rights of students and professors to think their own thoughts. Petrified, in danger of exploding as a result of the rigidity of its own structure, the Kuomintang was to lead the nation back to the stage it had left more than two thousand years before. All that the people are asked to have is "an absolutely sincere faith in their state and nation," and all problems will be automatically solved, "even though the future difficulties are as great as removing a mountain or emptying the sea." Nationalism alone, such as the ancients had never known, will replenish the granaries and give succor to the poor—to such simplicities had a corrupt regime descended in its efforts to convince the people that it possessed a program.

But there was no program, and there could be no program as long as the state remained in the hands of a single man, whose education had been limited by poverty and the circumstance that the greater part of his training took place in the Japanese field artillery. If the Kuomintang was to survive, other and more resilient policies would have to be introduced. Time was running out. The inflation was growing—a phenomenon that could not be exorcised by nationalism. Two other courses were open to China—the moderate liberals of the center, and the Marxists Communists advancing down from their valleys in the north. Between them there was still a possibility that China could be saved from the desperate destiny that the Generalissimo had foreseen.

Chapter 12

The Middle of the Road

FIVE large political parties had joined to form the Teng Men Hui, the predecessor of the Kuomintang; there was something in the feudal imperial history of China that compelled larger groups to swallow the rest, then consolidate. There were left and right wings of the Kuomintang, so different in outlook that they seemed to have nothing in common, yet the Kuomintang remained, dedicated to carrying out principles that had little application to the modern world. The idea of "a period of tutelage" had come to Sun Yat-sen at the moment when he felt most dispirited with the existence of the revolution, in 1924. The foreigner, coming to China for the first time, heard the words with bated breath. Were the Chinese too primitive to rule without dictatorship? It was not— the Kuomintang intellectuals were at pains to explain—anything more than a benevolent institution; the Chinese peasant was indeed primitive, the literacy rate was no better than India's, the period of civil wars was hardly over. Dr. Sun Fo had said that his father's intention was never to applaud dictatorship, but at least it was certain that he approved, without defining it, a period of tutelage. The Chinese were justifiably proud of their long and continuous traditions. A period of tutelage broke the tradition, for it disallowed the ancient right to overthrow the Emperor if he failed to follow the mandate of the people. There was no mandate of the people because the constitutional assembly was never called. The vicious circle was there, and there was no constitutional remedy except the inevitable dissolution of the "period of tutelage" in its own time.

In effect the "period of tutelage" marked the colonization of the Chinese people by the Kuomintang. Backed by weapons, secret prisons, a dependent judiciary, the Kuomintang could theoretically have maintained its power for any length of time it liked. The old war lords had either been thrown into the sea (like General Wu Pei-fei), or assassinated (like General Chang Tso-lin), or they had unaccountably surrendered their armies (like General Feng Yu-hsiang). By the end of 1928 no effective opposition to Kuomintang power remained; the Communists were an underground tattered army of intellectuals, peasants, and shopkeepers who had survived the Nanchang attacks. For the first time since 1911 one undisputed ruler reigned over China, with an army that could be truthfully called a national army. The growth of opposition was slow, though the National Army did not rule with the completeness that Generalissimo Chiang Kai-shek desired. Some areas still retained their independence; General Yen Hsi-shan, the last of the war lords, was to maintain a small enclosed area in Shansi. The independent "middle of the road" parties were too small, or too terrorized, to make effective contributions to the social evolution of the nation. Seeing the huge power of the Kuomintang, they could exert pressure at times by entering the left wing or center groups of the government, but their effectiveness depended on their contacts with the people through propaganda; but no propaganda other than Kuomintang propaganda was tolerated by the government.

The scholar-politician tradition had ended with the revolution of 1911, when the Reform Party, with its roots in the universities and among Han-lin scholars, came to an end, submerged in the rising flood of the Kuomintang or banished by the Peking factions into insignificance. Something of the influence of the Reformers, who were the first to break down the walls of imperial power, persisted as late as 1914, when Hsiung Hsi-ling was prime Minister under Yuan Shih-kai; but in effect the tradition of the scholar-politician within the Kuomintang had broken beyond remedy. Power was to come increasingly into the hands of soldiers and overseas or foreign-educated Chinese.

The tragedy of China's modern development is the tragedy of the misuse of her scholars. The great scholars of the past were prepared to take political action; there was Confucian testimony that scholarship should go hand in hand with ordering policy. In the Kuomintang government few outstanding scholars were given place. Chiang Mon-lin, once president of a university, became secretary of the Executive Council toward the end of the war; but he had neither the intellect nor the energy to face the task of reforming the whole government. Dr. Hu Shih was made ambassador to Washington, where, though he could transmit unpalatable facts to the highest governing bodies, he was deliberately isolated from policy making. He was followed, perhaps inevitably, by Wei Ta-ming, who had assisted the Generalissimo in the march to the north in 1927 and possessed close family affiliations to the Generalissimo. Scholarship, if it was used at all by the Kuomintang, was used as a screen. Occasionally the university students could use their natural power of protest, as when they protested against the Generalissimo's submissions to the Japanese, and when, still more bravely, they resisted in Kunming the undeclared civil war in December 1945. There they were alone; with the exception of nine professors, including the poet Wen Yi-tuo, who was assassinated by a Kuomintang officer six months later, the whole faculty opposed the demands of the students. There was no intellectual leadership of China; the professors were not the descendants of the great Han-lin scholars but of the pathetic family tutors.

The emergence of a third party, long expected as a result of the war, did not take place immediately. Small political affiliations had grown up, the Kuomintang itself was split among seven or eight powerful groups, but a third party that refused to accept the extremist theories of the Communists or the Kuomintang did not arise until late in the war. It owed its origin largely to pressure from the students in the national universities.

The universities presented an extraordinarily vivid cross section of the Chinese scene. By 1940 nearly all the universities had been nationalized—hardly any university could exist under wartime pressure as a private institution. At least half the students in Chungking, Chengtu, and Kunming, the three remaining university centers, were refugees from Japanese-occupied areas. They possessed a surprising maturity, and they were prepared to accept the Kuomintang if it remained faithful to the early promises of Sun Yat-sen. Until 1940 there were still hopes that the Kuomintang would clean its own house, and that the nepotism, by which every senior office of state became the appurtenance of the Generalissimo's own family, would come to an end. It did not come to an end. Discontent began to spread. Severe measures were employed. Students began to disappear mysteriously; occasionally professors vanished, and it was said that they were in prison camps, or they were being educated in Kuomintang doctrine. A distinguished professor of economics, Ma Ying-chu, author of textbooks used in all universities, disappeared after making a speech calling upon the Generalissimo to offer high posts in the government to men who were not his relatives. Professor Keh Fung, of national Chekiang University, disappeared on a visit to Chungking; he was last seen crossing the Yangtze river on a ferry steamer, and it was generally believed that he was killed by agents of the secret police and his body thrown overboard. Students suffered more than professors. If they were known to have political opinions not in direct conformity with those of the government, they were imprisoned, tortured, and sometimes killed; many of them went to "redistribution centers" for reindoctrination, of which the largest was in Sian. It was part of the duty of foreign professors attached to Chinese universities in wartime to try to release students whose political crime was usually to have been possessed of a faith no more radical than nineteenth-century British liberalism. These students provided the potential seedbed if any third party could ever be called into being. Most of them foresaw that the Communists and the Kuomintang would fight a civil war at the end of the war. Bitterness increased gradually. The people were too weary, too badly fed, too insecure to protest violently; only the hardiest, hearing of the agrarian reforms introduced by the Communists, dared to make the long overland journey to Yenan.

The students in the south were shielded from Cummunist influence by a paternal government. The Sin Min Chu I Youth League was founded by the Generalissimo to provide political indoctrination for the students. Expensive clubhouses were built on university campuses, and students who joined the San Min Chu I Youth League were provided with promises of future employment. At Fuhtan University, near Chungking, the University itself was built hurriedly of mud, plaster, and bamboos; the clubhouse was built of brick, the only comfortable and inviting place on the whole campus. About a quarter of the students joined the Youth Club. In spite of almost overwhelming pressure the rest refused to join and regarded the members of the League with detachment.

In the Southwest Associated University, the most famous of all, comprising the three exiled universities of Tsinghua, Peking, and Nankai, the influence of the Kuomintang was less dominant. The reasons were complex. Partly it was because Kunming was eight days by motor from the capital, partly it was because these northern universities had hammered out over many years a traditional defiance of arbitrary authority, partly it was because the University was protected against some extreme measures of Kuomintang influence by the governor of Yunnan, General Lung Yun, a descendant of tribesmen, who attempted until the last moment to maintain his decentralized power over the province. The presence of large numbers of Americans in Kunming helped the University students to be self-supporting. Until October 1945, when the Generalissimo declared war on the province, no students were arrested for reading banned books, and thought control hardly existed. During the five-day civil war, at the beginning of October 1945, the University was caught in the cross fires; seven students were wounded, and classes ceased. The civil war against the Communists in the north had not yet begun in earnest, though sporadic shooting had taken place.

The Generalissimo had ordered the Japanese to surrender only to his own forces. The Communists disobeyed and compelled the Japanese to surrender, captured their equipment and stores, and maintained defensive positions along railroads. The battle for Kalgan, fought southwest of the city on August 26-27, was the first large-scale assault on Japanese positions; it was followed by others in central Manchuria and in the western hills overlooking Peking. Once again the Generalissimo found himself compelled to safeguard his rear. There had been talk in high Kuomintang circles throughout the war of possible invasions against Lung Yun in Yunnan. The soldiers of the Fifth Army, secretly mobilized, were sent against the capital of Yunnan while the Yunnanese armies under General Lu Han, a brother of the Governor, were in Hanoi with full powers to receive the surrender of the Japanese in Indo-China above the sixteenth parallel. With the invasion of Yunnan by the Hunanese and Honanese soldiers of the Fifth Army, the curtain of the civil war lifted. The consequences could be mapped out almost mathematically; the students spoke openly of their despair— they could see no end to the civil war that had already dawned. American equipment had increased the fire power of the Kuomintang army; Russian soldiers were entrenched in Manchuria; already there were rumors from Shanghai that Kuomintang control over the treaty port was more disastrous than Japanese control. Old war lords were being sent back, like satraps, to rule over provinces. There was no sign that the government intended to introduce con- stitutional reforms.

On May 3, 1946, the association of three universities in the Southwest Association University came to an end; the three univer- sities split up and returned to Peking and Tientsin. With them went the firmest, most powerful, and least intimidated of the believers in social democracy in the south. But before the University finally broke up, four students had been killed by hand grenades, the whole province had come under the influence of Kuomintang appointees, and the last vestiges of democratic freedom had disap- peared from the province.

What was surprising was that the attacks on the University took place while the American troops were still in Kunming, and that the attack was so widespread and so carefully managed. The mili- tary governor, a graduate of Whampoa Academy, ordered the sol- diers of the Fifth Army to fire above the heads of the students when they were holding a mass meeting against the civil war on the campus of the Associated University. The students demanded that telegrams should be sent both to Chairman Mao Tse-tung and Generalissimo Chiang Kai-shek, warning them against the disastrous consequences of civil war. The meeting was held in the half-darkness of the evening of November 25. Shots were fired from behind the campus walls. The speakers, who had been selected from the faculty to represent all parties except the Communist party, continued speaking. The distinguished so- ciologist, Dr. Fei Hsiao-tung, said quietly: "I am coming to speak to you tonight because I view with the utmost seriousness the posi- tion of our country. If there is civil war—" The voice was drowned by the sound of machine-gun bullets rapping against the tiles of the large barnlike library. When the sound of bullets ceased, he continued: "My voice must be heard above the sound of bullets," and quietly went on to denounce both sides for preparing for civil war. "What is necessary above all is that neither side should regard themselves as the possessors of separate states; there is one Chinese people, and there must be no war among them."

The deliberate provocation was inexcusable, but the consequences were not easy to foretell. It seemed in Kunming unthinkable that the military extremists of the Kuomintang, who were later to be so bitterly criticized in General Marshall's farewell report, would allow themselves to be drawn into direct conflict with a powerful university, whose graduates held high posts in the government and whose scholars had been invited to the most famous universities in the world. The official *Central News Daily* appeared the next day with a brief announcement that there had been firing outside the city walls "against some tens of bandits." The implications were obvious; the students and most of the professors were incensed; in the afternoon of the twenty-sixth the students came out on strike.

The importance of this move became clearer in the following days. The government spokesmen were inclined to believe that the students were favorable to the Communists—a statement that was neither true nor possible, since the Communists had no roots in Kunming and no students were known to have connections with Yenan. The military governor, General Kuang Lin-seng, stated that Yenan had broadcast at 6:20 P.M. on the evening of November 23 an account of the coming strike against the Central authorities. No transcripts of the broadcasts were available in government headquarters in Kunming, and on enquiry in Yenan later I could find no evidence that such a broadcast had been made. The implication that the broadcast was fabricated became only too clear. The attack against the students was not essentially an attack against those who sympathized with the Communists, but against the Democratic League. To the government in Chungking the third party was as dangerous as the second.

On December 1, 1945, four students were murdered in the stone courtyard of the teaching college attached to the associated university. Two men accused of throwing the hand grenades were later arrested; both were former officers in the Kuomintang Army. At a summary court-martial on December 4 they were sentenced to death; the sentence was held over till the papers could be formally recognized by the Generalissimo, and some days later the officers' death was announced in the newspapers. The students remained on strike and refused to return to classes until January. They ignored the new orders against free speech and free assembly published by the provincial government, they bitterly attacked the acting governor, Li Chung-huang, and the military governor, Kuang Lin-seng, and demanded their punishment and removal. In all this they had the backing and sympathy of the Democratic party, which was represented in the University by the sociologist, Dr. Pan Kuen-t'an, who was then acting president in the absence of Dr. Mei Yi-chi. The fight for the democratic League had begun—there were four bodies in the library of the University to prove that the students were not unlike their predecessors who fought off the Peking police, and when the dangers of Japanese invasion were greatest, commandeered trains and made their way to the Chinese Foreign Office to lay their complaints before the Minister. Tuberculosis, malaria, dysentery, and vitamin deficiency had weakened them physically; but they had been nourished on the belief that they were the bulwark of democracy in China, and they took their responsibilities seriously. Small pamphlets printed on hand presses were distributed throughout the countryside; the pamphlets bore the American Declaration of Independence, quotations from Thomas Paine's *Rights of Man,* and the funeral speech of Gettysburg. From the surrounding villages peasants came to pay tribute to the dead students; throughout the famous campus there was an air of festive mourning. The Democratic League protested, but for the first few days after the murders almost no news of the attacks was allowed to leave Kunming. The government newspapers published wildly inaccurate reports of the events. The students were able to send more accurate accounts with the help of Chinese copilots on Chinese National Aviation Company airplanes; other accounts reached Shanghai and Chungking by diplomatic bag. It was a week before anyone of ministerial rank came to enquire into the situation; the prisons were beginning to fill with students, who were tortured and beaten; for merely writing the word democracy on a wall, a girl student was clubbed. Two students were shot at and knifed outside the American Office of War Information in Kunming, their lives saved by the presence of mind of the American director who allowed them to enter the building, releasing them two hours later and taking them to a hospital. The atmosphere was electric with danger. Unaccountably the streets were suddenly filled with armed thugs.

The Democratic League was fighting for its life. Without the students, no "middle of the road" policy would be possible in China. The League protested vigorously. The students were able to send messages to foreign universities. Though there was considerable evidence that the Generalissimo had ordered some kind of attack on the University, other issues were at stake. The Yunnanese armies

in Hanoi were getting out of hand; the presence of a purely nationalist organization, the Viet Nam, in Indo-China had put an
end to whatever hopes remained of forming in Indo-China a powerful political party under the control of the Kuomintang. General
Lu Han, in command of the Yunnanese armies in Hanoi, was
neither politically dependable nor averse to strong measures to
avenge the defeat of his brother during the civil war. The military
government of Yunnan was ordered to placate the students, the
president of the University, Dr. Mei Yi-chi, a Kuomintang member,
was ordered to do everything within his power to make the students return to classes. The struggle between the faculty and the
students began, with the faculty possessing at least one weapon
denied to the students—they could decree the discontinuance of the
University.

The struggle was short-lived; under the threats of the faculty the
students returned to classes. But the disparity, which had been
growing slowly throughout the war between the students and the
professorial body, only increased. Outside the University gates a
pathetic poster was hung: "To the professors. You taught us to
believe in democracy and constitutional government. Now when
we fight for it, why do you desert us?"

Among the professors who refused to use pressure upon the students was the poet Wen Yi-tuo, who had led the long overland
march of the students into exile from the universities in Peking. He
was a scholar whose interpretations of the classics were famous, and
whose popularity among the students had made him a marked man.
Though he was not the official representative of the Democratic
League, he was regarded by the students as their representative in
Democratic League affairs. He was a powerful speaker, one of the
founders of the modern Chinese literary movement, a painter who
learned painting in Chicago and New York, a calligraphist and a
seal carver. He lived in extreme poverty in spite of his position as
head of the faculty of Chinese studies in Tsinghua University. With
Chen Tuan-sen, Feng Chih, Chiang Hsi-jo, Fei Hsiao-tung, and
Wen Chia-tzu he represented the full force of the Democratic
League among the professors. When told that the military governor
had said, "Nothing would please me so much as to have Wen Yi-
tuo's head cut by an ax," he answered, "There is nothing to prevent
the military governor from having my head—the power of the

country lies in the hands of the wildest militarists." He survived six months longer.

Because the University was a national university, financed by the government, it could be closed down whenever the government thought fit. Some of the older professors began to believe that the refusal of the students to return to classes showed that they were "unfilial," and therefore deserved punishment—Confucianism, a doctrine against which Wen Yi-tuo objected vehemently—was firmly entrenched. Chiang Mon-lin, formerly president of Peking University, then secretary of the Executive Council, was writing articles for *Asia* protesting China's historic sense of democracy at the same time that he was countersigning orders for the imprisonment of students. Asked whether anything could be done to save Wen Yi-tuo's life, which was clearly in danger, he replied: "The man is a member of the Democratic League—he is a tail of the Communist Party." Asked why it was necessary to maintain in a country theoretically at peace a vast system of secret police, he replied: "A secret police is obviously necessary. If there was no secret police, my life and the lives of all government officials would be in danger." The two answers complemented each other, but the danger to Wen Yi-tuo continued.

Chiang Hsi-jo, an outstanding economist and dean of the faculty of political science, had taken little part in the formation of the Democratic League. He was ill during a large part of his stay in Kunming. Like all the other professors, he suffered atrociously under the inflation. He had once occupied a ministerial position in the government. He was the descendant of scholars, a man not easily aroused to anger. He published little and considered that his major task was to infuse in students a theoretical knowledge of politics and the social sciences. He would say of his own generation that "it lacked intellectual leadership and was more damnably lost than all others that have ever existed in China, because in our childhood we were educated under the Manchus and in our maturity we had no way to find our education except abroad." He had studied in America, France, and England. On January 13, a little more than a month after the murder of the students, he made what was in effect a valedictory speech to the students on the campus of the associated universities. He said:

"We have come to the stage when certain intellectual decisions are demanded of the intellectuals of China. The time is running short, and it is necessary that we make up our minds sooner or later. It is difficult to see clearly what the situation is, but our consciences demand of us that we speak the truth. I shall state the truth as I see it without regard to persons, even if those persons occupy high places." The impact of the opening words was prodigious. Under the burning sun, bareheaded, standing alone on the campus, surrounded by nearly four thousand students, he seemed for a while to be the conscience of China speaking. In a profound sense his speech was a charter for the third party. He continued:

"It is necessary that we should admit that the most important of the measures to be taken in this country are purely social measures concerning the livelihood of our people. Society grows sick; at such times doctors must be called, prescriptions must be written, medicine—even very distasteful medicine—must be taken. Today China is suffering because political power has been concentrated in the hands of an extremely reactionary, extremely unintelligent and extremely despotic political party, which is dominated by men who have never compelled themselves to make an intellectual study of the problem before them. I will name this party—it is called, for some reason, the Party of the People, and it is necessary that you should observe that the Chinese characters in this name include also the radical for 'darkness.' Yet there was a time when the Kuomintang did dispense light. That time has passed; at the present day the Kuomintang is a purely mercenary body of people who think only of their own interests. It issues statements 'for the nation' and the Generalissimo makes profession of encouraging 'the livelihood of the people,' but in fact neither of these things are done. The nation is allowed to sink slowly into misery.

"The Kuomintang still professes to be a revolutionary party—more's the pity. Its members still talk about revolution, but where is the revolution? There is no revolution—only the parrot-like repetition of the word 'revolution.' It claims to be the legal government. On what basis? Is legality sufficient for a government, without the support of the people? Legally the Kuomintang may be the government; in practice it is banditry, holding power simply by force of arms. It is even charitable to refer to them as bandits, for if you were to meet a bandit face to face, at least you are allowed to summon the policeman. There is nothing we can do against them, because they have the law on their side. They may be called legally recognized bandits, and this is the only term applicable to people who could take part as they did in the affairs of November twenty-fifth and December first.* The future of Chinese power therefore, has been monopolized by an ignorant, stupid, corrupt and despotic group. This is unfortunate for Dr. Sun Yat-sen, who is responsible for the principles which have now been exploited only for selfish gain.

"You may be disturbed by these conclusions, but they are supported by facts, and could not be changed even if we desired it. There are some people who see these facts and turn away, pretending they are not there. We should let the facts speak for themselves.

"One: The Three People's Principles. Every day the Kuomintang leaders will make at least one reference to the Three Principles. In the May sixth Draft Constitution of 1936 it is provided that China shall be a republic of the Three People's Principles. The first of these principles is nationalism; this does not mean only our sovereign independence; it means also that each national group should have independence and freedom. Yet the only positive achievement of the Kuomintang has been to recognize the independence of Outer Mongolia. The second principle is the people's rights. But the people have no rights. The only right the people have is to attend the Monday morning meetings, bow to the Kuomintang flag and read the Kuomintang principles. They have nothing else. I shall not waste your time in talking about the third principle—the people's livelihood. The streets are full of the starving, and the soldiers are treated worse than the beggars.

"Two: Limitation of capital and equalization of landownership. You would think that the Kuomintang, after talking about these things for twenty years, would have done something about this, but you have only to look at the war profiteers to realize that they have done nothing. Are there limitations on capital? How do they propose to introduce equalization of landownership? There may be many reasons—perhaps they are waiting until the peasant no longer is able to afford to plant his seed because of heavy land taxes. They have done nothing, and when I asked the Generalissimo what they proposed to do, I was told they did not have any plans whatsoever.

"Three: The period of tutelage. It has always been said that this period is intended to train the people for the assumption of their political rights. What training has there been? The real purpose of tutelage is to postpone constitutional government indefinitely.

"Four: The People's Assembly. Up to the present we have heard only about the construction of buildings for this assembly. You remember that Dr. Sun's testament called for the convocation of the Assembly 'in the shortest possible time.' That was in 1925. More than twenty years

* Refers to the two attacks on the students of the Southwest Associated University.

have passed since then. No wonder that foreigners are complaining about the peculiar Chinese ideas about time.

"Five: Thought control. It is only here that the Kuomintang has been superbly successful.

"Six: The two-year plan. At the beginning of the war against Japan, every single government department was provided with, or furnished, a plan. There was no co-ordination, of course, between the government departments. The Ministry of Communication wanted to build railroads, the Ministry of War wanted to build an army, the Ministry of Finance wanted something—no one quite knew what, and no one was ever able to tell exactly what the Ministry of Finance did want to do. Anyway, the plans are lost. During the second year of the war I was a delegate of the People's Political Council. The government produced a new three-year plan. I asked the head of one of the government departments whether the three-year plan also included the two-year plan, or whether it would begin where the other one left off. I was told: 'How can we possibly tell?' I say seriously that these plans were nothing whatsoever, or at most they were attempts to make us believe that something was going on.

"Seven: War first; victory second. These were ideal slogans, but what happened? Our armies, even in 1945, were never in shape to fight.

"Eight: Those with money, give money; those with strength, give strength. All we can say of this is that those who had strength gave their strength, and those who had money became war profiteers. In the end, when victory came, the government purloined several tens of billions of dollars to subsidize those who were so weak after giving their money at interest. When people asked for better treatment for the soldiers, the government always replied: "The money is not available."

"Nine: Administration in the former enemy-occupied areas. Well, the government heard of the scandal of the taking over of Shanghai and answered that the Japanese victory was so sudden that proper precautions could not be taken in time. There was, however, plenty of time to take precautions when we moved into Peking and Tientsin. Our officials came like conquerors, they confiscated everything, automobiles, money, gold, women. Newspapers have told how the people were prevented from telling this to the Generalissimo when he entered Peking.

"Ten: Turn the government over to the people, the Army to the nation. This is what they say, but has anything ever come of it. Who are the people? Are the people the Chen brothers? And is the nation the Generalissimo and the Chen brothers? Of course, if this is the case, the thing can be done very easily indeed. It is easy to invent slogans; what is necessary is to do things.

"Eleven: Then finally there is the question of the massacre of the students two months ago. I shall not dwell on it except to say that it is only one more example of the activities of a government 'filled with good words, which has not done a good deed.'

"Then what must we do? We must abolish one-party government, and alter the whole conception of government in this country. Let me suggest a few concrete steps. For the sake of our country and for his own sake, may I suggest that the Generalissimo should resign. If I could speak to the Generalissimo now, I would say: 'You are responsible for our evils. You should be punished. The lightest possible punishment is that you should go and make way for good people.' For many years he has been extremely presumptuous. Should we not ask him not to be presumptuous for once? In this way he could 'act resolutely and with dignity.' Let him resign before his own downfall. And with him there should go, too, all his lieutenants, who bear their share of responsibility and should be punished. A coalition government should be formed to include the enlightened liberal elements in the Kuomintang. Then, immediately it is formed, the coalition should call a convention to draft a national constitution.

"All this is perhaps too ideal, and if it cannot be brought about, I suggest another solution. We abolish tutelage and one-party rule, and we allow Chiang Kai-shek to remain. We do not want him, but we have a feeling that he will stay to the last possible moment, and so we are prepared to suffer him under certain conditions. These conditions must be made clear. First, he may be entitled to hold whatever rank he likes— Supreme Hero, President, anything as long as he conforms to the law, takes no part in legislation, and is not empowered even to change existing laws. Second, all policy making must be removed from his hands. If he participates, he should be allowed to have one vote, otherwise the whole purpose of the People's Consultative Council is brought to ruin. Third, the responsibility for putting laws and policies into practice must be vested in the group, not in one man. It is only under these conditions that ministers can become responsible officials. Fourth, the number of posts available to the Kuomintang must be reduced to a quarter of the total, or at most a third. This is necessary because of their disgraceful record in the past, and because the Kuomintang is badly in need of a purge.

"Then I suggest that if the tyrant refuses these demands, all non-Kuomintang members of the Council should resign *en bloc*. They would be better looking after their families than attending such a conference. Dr. Sun Fo has suggested that a few members from other parties be allowed to attend the Conference. There are at present about a dozen members on this committee; they have never held meetings. We must remember that if you attend such a committee, you are entitled to rice allowances and free automobiles.

"Then it has been suggested that a few minor ministries be given to other parties. Does this bring us any nearer to a coalition government? Dr. Sun Fo, the Kuomintang spokesman, is suggesting that we should agree to these tidbits of change. Something greater is required. The delegates must be elected by the people. Under present conditions, delegates are elected by the Generalissimo and by the two Chen brothers. When the coalition government is formed, the electoral law must be introduced, and the new delegates must be elected according to the law.

"I do not know how the Generalissimo will receive this statement, and I am afraid I do not care—I have spoken the truth. General Kuan Lin-seng, the military governor, has told me that he considers Dr. Chen Tuan-sen a Communist. I asked him why. The answer was: 'Dr. Chen Tuan-sen called him "senile" and gave him no courtesy titles whatsoever.' I am afraid, too, that I can only agree with Professor Chen Tuan-sen. For ourselves, our consciences, our love of the truth, our education demand that we speak out loud."

The speech of the Southwest Associated University campus was historic. Various versions were made by students, but the general tenor of the printed version was seen by Dr. Chiang Hsi-jo, who agreed to its general accuracy. In effect, he was saying as Amery said of Chamberlain and Oliver Cromwell said to the Long Parliament: "You have sat too long here for any good you have been doing. Depart, I say, and let us have done with you. In the name of God, go." The courage to have spoken in this way so shortly after the student massacre was convincing proof of the urgency of the theme; the long parliament of a single man had endured too long. There were undertones to the speech that did not pass unnoticed. He was speaking to the University students, and at the same time he was speaking on behalf of the intellectuals who were still exiled in the south, gravely and succinctly, and with the knowledge that nothing was more likely than his immediate arrest. He was not arrested. But in the history of the ill-equipped, often ill-informed Democratic League, a step forward had been made. Dr. Chiang was not a member of the party, but it was known that his sympathies were all in favor of such a party.

The history of the Democratic League is not easily defined. It possessed many platforms, some of them conflicting; at no time has it had a clear and coherent platform. It stood for "the middle of the way," and its leaders were sufficiently respected by the Communists and the Kuomintang to be able to act as mediators. Dr. Lo Lung-chi, who assumed the role of spokesman for the party, lived in Kunming throughout the later part of the war. He had been a professor of the Southwest Associated University until his dismissal was demanded, against the statutes of the University senate, by the Generalissimo. He had been educated in London and America; he had the toughness necessary in a man who willingly takes up a position between two gigantic parties.

The Democratic League had come about as the result of the fusion of a number of minor parties, all opposed in principle to the government, though some members were eventually inveigled into supporting the government. Dr. Chiang Mon-lin could report that "Wen Yi-tuo and the other members of the League are the tail of the Communists"; the Communists answered that they possessed considerable evidence that some members of the Democratic League were in the pay of the Kuomintang. At its best it represented the unnumbered millions who could not loyally support either the Communists or the Kuomintang. They were "the splendid body of men" mentioned in General Marshall's farewell speech.

Most of the leaders were sociologists or economists. The elected leader of the party was the seventy-six year old Dr. Chang Lan, a former civil governor of Szechwan and president of Chengtu University. The League included the Young China Party, the National Socialists, the Third Party, the Rural Reconstruction Association, the Vocational Education Association, and the National Salvation Association. It contained right- and left-wing elements, held fitfully together less by the personalities within the League than by the necessity of forming a counterweight that would help to dissolve the tensions introduced by the growing fear of civil war between the Communists and the Kuomintang. In a circular issued on the twelfth anniversary of the Mukden Incident, on September 18, 1943, the main points of the League were announced. The tone is similar to Dr. Chiang Hsi-jo's attack on the government. The period of tutelage must be concluded, and a democratic state, governed by elected officials, should take its place. Dr. Chang Lan demanded:

1. The immediate establishment of an open and legal consulta-

tive body to include all parties, working for constitutional government.

2. The immediate announcement that the people were to have freedom of speech and assembly, association and residence. Habeas corpus was to be entered on the statute books.*

3. The immediate recognition of the legal existence and activity of the different political parties.

4. The empowering of the various public bodies, the People's Political Council, the Provincial People's Council, the *hsien* (county) councils, to investigate budgets and check on unlawful use of public funds.

These demands possessed particular significance at the time; the barest essentials were mentioned—beyond those it was dangerous and unnecessary to go. The government paid no attention to them, nor was any attention paid to one of the ensuing paragraphs of the circular that stated simply, without prevarication, the nature of the conflict:

I must add here that for several years the officers of the government have been openly corrupt. The new officials imitate the old. The organs of monopoly and taxation have proliferated, and become burdensome and complicated. The result is that the government is hated on all sides, the people are harassed, the greater emoluments flow into the pockets of the middlemen. The people, who have no grain, are still made to pay grain. Where there are no men left, the conscription gangs still manage to take men. We must have democracy so that the people shall be empowered to supervise the government, check on officials and help the government to manage its own affairs.

The tone was deliberate. The League insisted that it was opposed to dictatorship in any form and believed implicitly in national unity as the prelude to victory. The government answered that every one of his claims had been made by the Communists, that there was no substance to them, and that a perfect form of democracy would be brought about after the conclusion of the war. More statements were issued by the Democratic League later, usually more cautious, because the government was making every effort to dissolve the League. Police spies followed its members everywhere. The Democratic League members ruefully stated: "We have increased the cost

* It was already there.

of government—a thousand more secret service agents have been absorbed into General Tai Li's organization to deal with us."

Perhaps it was an exaggeration; the attacks did not come always from General Tai Li's organization. The militarists were even more powerful. A secret service agent might think twice if he murdered a man; a regular army officer, guaranteed protection, would not even need to think at all. Though no one knew (and the Democratic League itself did not know) the total numbers of its members and sympathizers, it wielded considerable power during the meditations, which Dr. Lo Lung-chi attended. Attacks only strengthened it. The murder of Dr. Wen Yi-tuo and Professor Li Kung-po in July failed to weaken it; the students might be silent, waiting their time, but the government was conscious that the League represented a valid and very extensive proportion of public opinion. The weakness of the League was that it failed to make a simple platform completely dissociated from the Communist platform; it was a weakness that could not be avoided when the Communist platform in theory answered so many of the needs of the people. It suffered from being a party without traditions, founded in 1941, twenty years after the Communist party and fifty years after the Kuomintang. It was formed at one of the worst crises of the war, shortly after the New Fourth Army incident, during which the Communists claimed that their second most powerful army, placed voluntarily under the orders of the Generalissimo, had been decimated at the Generalissimo's orders while attempting to cross the Yangtze. The Communists refused to form part of the People's Political Council; permission was obtained for a Federation of Chinese Democratic Parties to take over the representation previously granted to the Communists. The Federation suffered inevitably from its origins. Unlike the Kuomintang, which possessed banks and arms, it lacked money and had no way of enforcing its claims. Its newspaper, published in Hongkong in September 1941, died in December, when the Japanese occupied the island. It was supported by purely voluntary subscriptions and by grants given by the brother of the founder of the National Socialist Party, who held high office in the government. With all its inevitable faults, the League had demonstrated its power in three directions: it had shown that there remained a body of intellectuals who were not terrified into silence, it had shown the possibility of mediation by members who were equidistant from the Communists and the Kuomintang, and it proved in March 1946, during the Political Consultative Council, which it organized, that agreement on outstanding questions could be reached. Unfortunately, the agreements were not accepted by the Kuomintang.

In one sense it was a party that had more to recommend it than either of the others; its physical weakness was its strength. When Dr. Lo Lung-chi received a telegram from a commander of the Shantung area saying he would like to surrender his army to the Democratic League, the offer was refused. The death by assassination outside the Yunnan University in Kunming of Professor Li Kung-po, who had been arrested by order of the Generalissimo in 1937 for declaiming against the government's appeasement policy toward Japan, proved that the government was determined to break the strength of potential leaders. The death of Dr. Wen Yi-tuo was a national catastrophe and could not be explained so easily. Brutal physical attacks were also made on Dr. Lo Yung-chi, Dr. Chang Lan, and others. The League could say with truth at the end of the year that "the Democratic League is an organization which believes in and works for the attainment of democracy by legal means. We have no armed forces. The fact that we are being persecuted shows that in present-day China a peace-loving democratic organization cannot enjoy the protection of the law, and has little chance of survival." They added, as a codicil:

The Kuomintang, which is still in power, has repeatedly declared to the whole world their intention of putting democracy into practice, protecting the freedom and rights of the people, and ensuring the freedom and security of members of all political parties. We do not know how they can account for the facts as they are. Facts alone, not empty words, will show whether they have the determination and sincerity to bring about true democracy in China.

Chapter 13

The Communists

TWO years before the publication of Chiang Kai-shek's *China's Destiny* the Communist Mao Tse-tung had written a brief outline of the course of Chinese political development as he saw it. *China's Destiny* was originally conceived as an answer to the program outlined by Mao Tse-tung. The Communist book is easier to read, contains no appeals to the ancients, and refers repeatedly to the sources of the Chinese revolution; it is humorless and impersonal, and like Soetan Shjarir's *Indonesia Fight* is more concerned with the technique of the revolutionary struggle and the possibilities of an alliance with Western capital than with formulating historical charges against the depraved nations of the West. One fundamental thread runs through the book—the Chinese state must first be fully democratic before any effort can be made to introduce socialism. There must be rule by ballot box before there is rule by socialist bureaucrats.

In all essentials Mao Tse-tung insists that the program he outlines agrees with the program outlined by Sun Yat-sen; he carefully demonstrates the differences that exist, and says that these differences are not such that the Kuomintang could easily find reasons for opposing them. Like Chiang Kai-shek, he will sometimes include the adages of wiseacres, such as "those who have the power of judgment are wise people," a phrase that possesses no devastating effect even in the original Chinese. Occasionally he will descend to scoring mere debating points, as when he remembers accurately that Chiang Kai-shek spoke in Swatow in 1925 during his expedition against Chen Chiung-ming in the authentic accents of the world revolutionary. The value of the book does not lie in its appeal to communism but in his recognition that changing forces are at work to produce in Asia a necessary evolution from feudalism to democracy, and so to socialism. Elaborating his arguments, he repeats three times that the passage is irrevocable and necessary; that democratic government is itself the weapon to kill feudalism, and that socialism cannot arise except in the form of a popular democracy. Socialism is not the weapon that kills feudalism but is the end product of a democratic evolution. This analysis is not an article of faith but a stubborn acceptance of things as they are in eastern Asia; and though the argument is introduced only in so far as it affects China, he implies that it is true of all Asia.

Soetan Shjarir, Prime Minister of Indonesia, accepted the major argument and introduced it bodily into the platform of the Indonesian Socialist Party. Nehru has similarly confessed that there must be a democratic interval between the present complex tenures of India and the enjoyment of socialism. Though the thesis is simple, and I have heard it repeated with an almost childlike glee in Communist China, as though the fact that there were two sages in the revolution solved all problems, the implications are enormously complex, and it may be that they are unpredictable. The differences between the democratic state and the socialist state are not fully analyzed. According to General Chu Teh's speech on May 1, 1946, the new democratic state includes an economy balanced between the co-operatives, which already exist in north China, and the introduction of foreign capital. Capital will be required in order to increase the wealth of the people, and it will not be rescinded until the state is self-supporting, or possesses sufficient capital to maintain livelihood at the desirable level. In its simplest form Mao Tse-tung's *New Democracy* is a statement of the recognition that an Asiatic agricultural economy is in urgent need of capital, and cannot exist without it, but having acquired sufficient capital, will in the end dispense with it.

Contrary to the practice of the Kuomintang, Mao Tse-tung demands that "a minority shall not monopolize the sources of power" —the Chinese Communists had recently introduced a system by which only one in three of the members of their governing bodies were *allowed* to be Communists—and that the government of the Chinese nation should not be in the hands of one party "but should be formed in a national polity which includes several revolutionary classes within a centralized democracy." He appealed for a coalition government, an appeal which was to be repeated two years later in his book *Coalition Government*. In a curiously involved passage he appealed for a larger absorption of the cultures of foreign nations, saying that the learning of all countries should be treated as food, "submitting our food to the mouth for chewing and to the stomach and intestines for digestion, then adding saliva, pepsin and other secretions of the intestines to separate it into essence and residue, and then absorbing the essence of our nourishment and passing off the residue," and at the same time approving of the "long, long period of China's feudalism which created such brilliant cultures in ancient times." Humorless, staid, and precise, with the accents of a university professor demonstrating applied mathematics, Mao Tse-tung outlines his plan for the future. In its crystallized form the argument could not be simpler:

The Chinese Revolution must be divided into two stages. The first stage is New Democracy, the second stage is socialism. But the duration of the first stage will be rather long. It certainly cannot be completed in a morning and an evening. We are not visionaries. We cannot divorce ourselves from the reality of the situation.

Unlike Chiang Kai-shek, but like most of China's scholars in the past, he finds the strength of China in her unawakened but awaking peasantry; his greatest praise is for the peasants, "who are our all," and for the famous writer Lu Hsun, whom he describes as "the bravest, firmest, truest, most correct and most zealous of our national heroes." The word "correct" is used thirty-seven times. It is at these moments that his arguments assume a slightly fallacious air; there are no absolute judgments, and his claim to correctness is in the last instance no better than Chiang Kai-shek's.

Where he excels is in his elementary premises—the reliance on the native strength of the peasantry, which Chiang Kai-shek overlooks. Mao Tse-tung sees the war in China as a race between the oppressed Chinese peasants and the rebirth of a new form of feudalism. Certain that the peasants will win, he can describe their inevitable victory as "correct" without elaborating his argument, except to emphasize that they are "correct" and that "anyone who disagrees or acts against this current will find his head broken." The principles of Sun Yat-sen are taken over bodily. Chiang Kai-shek dismissed the compulsory equalization of land rights as impracticable, quoting the failures in the time of Wang Mang and the Taiping rebellion. Mao Tse-tung, more simply and perhaps more judicially, accepts them as they are without further quarrel as the only method available for increasing the productivity of the peasants. "The land must belong to the tiller." The liberal declaration of the First Kuomintang Congress of 1924, at which Dr. Sun Yat-sen presided, is accepted in its entirety: "Enterprises, foreign or Chinese, which possess a monopoly character or which, because of their immense scale, are beyond the power of the individual to establish, such as banks, railways, aviation companies, etc., shall be managed by the state, in order that private capital shall not be allowed to manipulate the life of the people." But the restriction of capital does not include its total elimination—capital is seen to be a force of immeasurable value as long as it does not act as the rival of government.

Where Mao Tse-tung differs from Dr. Sun Yat-sen, he is careful to suggest that Dr. Sun Yat-sen would inevitably have differed from the original position if he had seen the consequences of the war. He says: "In the democratic stage of the revolution, we shall include the 8-hour day and the thorough agrarian revolution. The doctrine of Dr. Sun Yat-sen does not go farther than the democratic revolution—we intend to progress toward the second stage." The program of the Kuomintang appears to him full of inconsistencies. They have not seen realities; they have forgotten that the major task in China, as in all Asia, is an agrarian reform. Every schoolboy knows that the Chinese peasantry forms 80 per cent of the population of China. "Our great culture of the past exists, but now our task is 'to go up to the hills,' meet, work, study, publish, write and play among these hills, not for ourselves, but for the peasantry; for everything we have in a war against the Japanese comes from the peasantry." There are moments in his evocation of the peasants when the dry Marxist swaddling bands burst, and the passion of his respect for the peasants is suddenly revealed. His most forthright attack on the Kuomintang is a sidelong one: "Those who do not truly protect the peasants and workers, and do not realize the awakening of the people, must be extinguished."

New Democracy is important and should be required reading matter for anyone studying the Orient, because for the first time a blueprint of agrarian reform and democratic government was placed before the Asiatic masses. Nothing similar to this had come out of

India or the Philippines, yet the book was to be read eagerly in both countries later; the main patterns have been adopted by Shjarir in Indonesia. But some explanations are necessary. Mao Tse-tung assumes that the new patterns of civilization in the East will not be based on an urgent sense of nationalism—there are horizontal divisions of greater importance, and in the absence of any large-scale proletariat there can be class-warfare only between the peasants and the landlords, and this will pass. He mentions nationalism only once, toward the end of the study, saying that "the new national culture will unite with socialist culture and the New Democratic culture of other nations, establishing with them relations of mutual absorption and mutual development, and serve with them mutually as part of the new culture of the world." The shrieking emphasis of nationalism in *China's Destiny* is absent; in its place there is a human understanding of the interpenetration of all cultures.

What exactly is new democracy? He says succinctly that it is not communism: "We must separate the propaganda of communist thought and the communist social system from the practice of the program of New Democracy." The communist method, he adds, must also be put aside. "It is improper to mix the two. New democracy in its essentials is an adaptation of the political circumstances to the demands of the people, who desire self-government and the breaking-up of the agricultural pattern and will not rest until these things are brought about. In 1944 he repeated the main inferences of his book *New Democracy* to an American journalist in these terms: 1. We must drive out the Japanese. 2. We must realize democracy on a national scale by giving the people fundamental liberties and a government elected by the people. 3. We must solve the agrarian problem so that capitalism of a progressive kind can develop in China. But the major importance of *New Democracy* lies in its clear enunciation of the third principle, and in the emphasis he places on solving the problem of balancing a rural and industrial economy by private capital. Communism is thrown overboard. What is necessary is that the elementary rights of the people should be granted, and those rights include greater comfort as well as the ownership of the land they till. In this sense the book forms a deliberate plea in favor of a restricted capitalist-socialist state.

There are simplicities in the book that have not passed unnoticed in Kuomintang China. Living in a remote valley of Shensi, where the only industries are salt wells in the north, a paper mill in the east, and an arsenal in Yenan, Mao Tse-tung shows no comprehension of the vast problems facing large-scale industry. It is unlikely that he has ever entered a large modern factory. Stock exchange markets are a secret to him. The infinite complexities of modern industry have no place in the world as he sees it. Years before, he had founded an army and defended a mountain range against forces twenty times the number of his troops; his outlook has been consistently that of the intellectual guerrilla, foraging into enemy territory. When the soldiers of the Eighth Group Army found an abandoned Japanese tank, they were compelled to burn it, for fear that the Japanese might regain it—they had neither the oil nor the spare parts to use it for attacking the enemy. Reading *New Democracy,* one is conscious that the author is continually attempting to reduce complex problems to their ultimate simplicities. The enemies are the Japanese, Wang Ching-wei, who was then ruling from a puppet presidency in Nanking, and the Kuomintang; there is no mention of the industrial workers of China. The arguments are not always sound, and they are often delivered with a staggering simplicity, as when the man who is regarded abroad as an enemy of all forms of capital says that the aim of the Japanese invasion was "to prevent the Chinese from establishing a bourgeois dictatorship or develop her own national capital." The book suffers from the same kind of simplifications that haunt the pages of *China's Destiny,* but where Chiang Kai-shek has faith only in Confucius, Mao Tse-tung's faith in a socialist peasantry "awakened and made new" reveals the springs of his character. He makes no apologies for representing them as the greatest force in the land. The book was originally written in 1940, before Soviet Russia had entered the war; he can speak glibly of the second "imperialist war," but at the same time he emphasizes the dependence of the Chinese revolution on the success of British, American, and Allied arms.

Sun Yat-sen accused the Chinese of being "shifting sand," a claim that was to be repeated by Chiang Kai-shek in the passage of *China's Destiny* where he attacks the people for their wants and specifies that they should be protected from having too many desires. Mao Tse-tung, with greater reason, attacks the Chinese bourgeoisie for being double-faced, "for they have at once a revolutionary and a compromising character," and he points out that it was the bourgeoisie that fought for the first revolution, but it was also a part of the bourgeoisie that went over to the Japanese. His brief analysis of the forces at work commands respect—he claims that the bourgeoisie unites with the workers and the peasants to oppose the enemy when the enemy is endangering them, but unite with the enemy to oppose the workers and the peasants when they are awakening; but he does not explain why the Chinese bourgeoisie shows this more vividly than the bourgeoisie of other nations.

How communist, then, are the Chinese Communists? Mao Tsetung denies that they are communists at all, but the name is retained because their final analysis of modern political currents springs from Marxist sources. In the same paragraph in which he urges the abandonment of communist forms in government, he asks students to study Marxism more thoroughly. He says: "Our present culture is not socialism but New Democracy," and, "New Democracy is to be separated entirely from communism," implying that communism cannot be reached in China in its original form, because the conditions under which communism flourish are absent. There would seem to be no reason to disbelieve his statement that the "Republic of New Democracy is a republic of a genuine, revolutionary Three Principles of the People, which includes Dr. Sun Yat-sen's three revolutionary principles." He might have added that it goes farther only because it takes the original three principles so seriously that it is determined to enforce them.

China's Destiny suffers from a monumental dullness, relieved only by bouts of vigorous temper against the misguided scholars of China, to whom much of the failure of the Kuomintang is ascribed; something of the same monumental dullness appears in Mao Tsetung's book, which is repetitious and so full of words like "proletariat," "aggressive imperialism," "bourgeoisie," and the rest that the reader is perplexed and wearied beyond endurance. When in January 1946 two American airplanes secretly flew students from the universities of Chungking to the Communist-held city of Kalgan, the students were brought from an environment where discussion was still comparatively free. At Kalgan the discussion was, if possible, even more free, but "What we can't stand," one of the students told me, "is the look of pious horror on their faces if we criticize a single page of Mao Tse-tung's book. Oh, we are not sent to jail. What happens is that they come along and almost beg us with tears in their eyes to be converted, and then it begins—the same phrases, the same uncritical acceptance of it all. Mao Tse-tung's analysis is perfectly correct—one wishes there was less religious fervor, though."

The Kuomintang students, with their fervent adoration of the Generalissimo's conception of nationalism, may have had the same uncritical acceptance; what is certain is that Mao Tse-tung's new Democracy was infinitely less dangerous to the peace of the world than Chiang Kai-shek's imitation of fascism. It is not necessary to take Mao Tse-tung seriously when he repeats for the thousandth time that "revolutionary culture is a powerful revolutionary weapon of the people," but when he studies the implications of such a statement, saying that the scholars who are removed from the peasants and the workers are "simply officers commanding cloud castles," it is necessary to listen more carefully. At the very end of *New Democracy* he says: "It may be that even our language may have to be reformed, for the words we use must touch the masses." The revolution of the language is announced, and the success of the young writers who went to Yenan and learned from the peasants instead of teaching the peasants was only one more indication of the success of the new democracy, which demanded hardly more than Dr. James Yen has demanded in his mass-education movement—that the livelihood of the peasants should be the first consideration of all.

The sources of Mao Tse-tung's new democracy are already visible in the early work of Sun Yat-sen. From the beginning Sun Yat-sen seems to have had one eye turned to Russia, the other to America, admiring the Russians for their technique of revolution (an admiration which Chiang Kai-shek was to develop later) and for their agrarian reforms, and the Americans for their original revolutionary fire and their industrial technology. Caught in the cross fire of both, he could never make up his mind which course to pursue; there are elements of extreme capitalism and extreme communism in the version of the Three Principles of the People that he delivered in 1924. Toward the end of his life, his sympathy for the Russians increased, and in the year of his death he wrote an open letter to friends in Russia in which he made an appeal for co-operation between the Communists and the Kuomintang that reads strangely during the present civil war:

You are the leaders and vanguard of that grand union of free republics which looks to the future. That great federation of nations is truly the priceless heritage bequeathed to all the oppressed peoples by your immortal Lenin. Turning their eyes to you, the enslaved millions under the yoke of imperialism will nourish their faith and courage to win their own freedom, thereby working to liberate themselves from the shackles of the existing international order which is based on age-old wars of enslavement. What I shall leave behind me is the Kuomintang. It is my hope, while accomplishing its historical mission of ridding China of the bondage of imperialism and helping other fettered nations to free themselves, the Kuomintang will co-operate with you in the days to come as fully as possible. I have already directed the Kuomintang to establish lasting co-operation with you, earnestly believing that your government will gladly continue to lend its assistance unstintingly.

Dear comrades, while taking my final leave of you, I wish to express my ardent hope that before long the dawn will break. This will be the time when the Soviet Union as a good friend and an ally will greet a strong and independent China. Both countries will emerge victorious, I am sure, from their gigantic struggle for the freedom of the oppressed people of the world.

It is doubtful whether Mao Tse-tung would address the Communists with the same ardor. Though Li Li-san said that Russia had pursued the wisest course in removing the heavy industries of Manchuria to Siberia, there were some who wondered why the Russians were not able to allow the heavy industries to be managed by the Chinese Communists, who had fought guerrilla warfare throughout the war in Manchuria. Li Li-san's defense was not generally accepted at Yenan, where the Chinese claim for the heavy industries was openly acknowledged. The Chinese Communists had almost no contact with Russia, in spite of continual reports that Mao Tse-tung was making secret journeys to Moscow; one report was issued in Peiping, saying that Mao Tse-tung had left for Russia in July 1946, while I was in Yenan and seeing Mao Tse-tsung nearly every day. No evidence that the Russians supplied arms to the Communists was ever found. The relations of the Communists in China to the government of Soviet Russia was less close than their relations with the United States, which had at one time a large observation group stationed in Yenan. Both Chu Teh and Mao Tse-tung claimed that they were not a government in the real sense of the word; they were a provisional government elected by the suffrage of the people, content to have no relations with the outside world, because they were concerned only with problems of the interior. In the famous document signed by Dr. Sun Yat-sen and Dr. Adolf Joffe, the emissary of the Soviet Union, in January 1923, it was stated that: "Dr. Sun Yat-sen holds that the Communistic order, or even the Soviet system, cannot actually be introduced into China because there does not exist the conditions for the successful establishment of either communism or Sovietism." The Chinese Communists claimed that they were faithful to the agreement.

Then why should they call themselves Communists? There were at least four reasons. The practical and emotional reasons were stated by Mao Tse-tung in *New Democracy;* if they changed the name at this stage, they would lose the adherence of many of the peasants, who regarded the name Kan-chang-tang with the same veneration as they regarded the Pa-lu-chun, or Eighth Route Army. The aim of the party was still communism of an undefined kind, a breaking of all bonds with the existing framework of commercial exploitation, a discovery of a new and more exciting sociological method. By communism, he says, we mean "a proletarian system of thought and a new social order. This is different from any other ideological system or social system in that it is the most complete, the most progressive, the most revolutionary, and the most rational system in human history." Feudal ideologies and feudal social systems are only "the setting sun, breathing its final breath." It is strange to find the emphasis on the *proletarian* element, but what is clear is his belief that historical materialism is the most fruitful method in which social changes can be studied; but there is more faith than analysis in the claim. Yet *New Democracy,* with all its simplicities and inveterate brooding on the terms bourgeoisie and capitalism does provide an answer to China's most pressing problems. The argument may sometimes be wrongheaded; one has the impression that he presses points the more hardly when he is at least sure of his reasoning, but no conclusions could be more applicable to the times. The whole book is a defense of a new economic and social policy that will allow a bridge to be formed between the original plans of the Kuomintang as outlined by Sun Yat-sen and their more rigorous development. There were other reasons why the name should be retained. Thousands of students, farmers, and workers, whose crime was that they wanted a more equable distribution of the wealth of China, had been killed by the right wing of the Kuomintang on the grounds that they were Communists. Even in 1947 all liberals in Kuomintang China were in danger of being accused of communism—the greatest scholars and those who most loudly protested their indifference to both were accused of communism. Dr. Chen Tuan-sen was accused of communism because he addressed the Generalissimo as Mr. Chiang without the formality of titles. Both Dr. Sun Fo and Mme. Sun Yat-sen, the son and the wife of the Father of the Republic, were accused by War Minister Ho Ying-chin of being Communists. Historical materialism remained, rightly or wrongly, the method of the strange isolated leaders of Yenan, who were attached to principles with the same firmness as their rivals. The principles were dangerous—it is not certain that the Russian revolution has anything to offer the Chinese peasants—but at least they had been accepted as an article of faith, whittled down until they had assumed a purely Chinese form. The similarities between the program of Dr. Sun Yat-sen and the new democracy are amazing; Mao Tse-tung can find only four points of dissimilarity: the Communists demand an eight-hour day, they refuse to accept Sun Yat-sen's fundamental philosophy of *wei-sheng*-ism, an interpretation of history in terms of cycles of human life; and unlike Sun Yat-sen, who believed that the revolution could be achieved simply in a single throw, they insist that the revolution must pass through two stages, first democracy and then socialism. The fourth difference with which Mao Tse-tung makes great play is "the difference in the thoroughness of the execution." Applied to agrarian reform this means that the Communists demand that the law should be carried out which states that the rent of the landlord should not be more than 37 per cent of the peasant income. The law has been on the statute book of the Kuomintang Government since 1927. In all other respects their programs were the same.

Of one thing we can be reasonably certain: the Chinese Communists represent the Chinese peasants and have a passionate belief in the peasants' potentialities. Ignorant of industry and diplomacy, incapable of understanding the complexities of Western civilization, so secluded within their own valleys that they suffer from a kind of mental inbreeding, and so accustomed to fighting continual battles on all fronts that they are suspicious of strangers, they represent to a degree unknown elsewhere in the East the birth of a new social system in Asia. Chinese communism is not an end product; it is a seed that has still to flower, and no one knows what shape the flower will assume.

"If there is no rice, let us share it," said the old ex-President of the Chinese Republic, Li Yuan-hung, who absent-mindedly commanded the revolutionary uprising in Hankow that dethroned the Manchus. The word "communism" is too vague for the Chinese mind, which prefers the word *kan-chang-tang,* which means the "share-wealth party"; and it would be better for our understanding of the Chinese Communist, and their unending experiment, if we called them members of the share-wealth-party. Dialectical materialism can have no profound roots in China, but revolt against emperors who have relinquished "the mandate of Heaven" goes back to the earliest historical times. The significance of the Chinese communists lies in their realization of the peasants' desire for a greater share in the wealth of the country. In one of his rare passages of hard-bitten humor Mao Tse-tung describes the enemies of the peasants:

Oh, to whom shall we give credit for our fight against the Japanese? We cannot advance a step unless we have the workers, the peasants and the petite bourgeoisie on our side. Whoever dares to overthrow these people will surely stub his toes. Is this not common sense? But the stubborn elements (I say the stubborn elements) of the Chinese bourgeoisie seem to have learned nothing during these twenty years! Cannot you hear them still shouting there loudly for "the restriction of the Communists," "dissolution of the Communists," and "opposition of the Communists." Having issued "Regulations for Restricting the Activities of the Alien Party," they are at it again with "Regulations for Handling the Alien Party," and the "Practicing Plan for Handling the Alien Party Program"? Heavens! Where are they going to direct the destiny of our nation, if this "restriction" and "handling" are to go on incessantly? And how are they going to prepare for their future? We earnestly advise these gentlemen to open their eyes, have a look at China and the world, and see what the real situation is.

For them, and for many millions of Chinese, the real situation is the peasantry, and the destiny of China does not lie with the principles of the ancients, but in the immediate demands of the peasants, whose rueful humor is like Mao's. What was wanted above all was that the restrictions should vanish, and in their place there should be a constructive program for the future of China. Mao Tse-tung had written the blueprint; it would remain for others to fill in the details.

Chapter 14

Reading and Co-operation

THERE can be no society without co-operation, and no hope of stability in a land as vast as China when every province speaks its own dialect and savagely retains a quasi independence from every other province. Governments rise and fall, but the natives of Hunan, Kwangtung, and Hupei maintain their own dialects, their own habits of thought, their own physical characteristics, and their own undying loyalties.

A peasant from south China cannot understand the spoken words of a peasant from the north; he writes Chinese characters in the air or points them out on the palm of his hand—there is no common speech in China, though the characters remain the same throughout all China. The problem of illiteracy assumes urgent proportions in times of social change. In Indonesia it is a problem that can be solved comparatively easily; in China it will always be difficult, and in India it will be most difficult of all, though the introduction of Hindustani as a common language, easy to learn and simple in its fundamental form, may solve the problem of discovering a language common among people who now speak 222 vernaculars. But no short cut can be found for the arduous task of learning Chinese characters. Of the presumed 40,000 in existence, roughly 4,000 are necessary for reading a comparatively elementary textbook. The difficulty, however, does not end there, for the modern pei-hua language, as distinct from the ancient wen-li, is largely a dissyllabic language, the two characters together forming a single idea. It is necessary to know not only the two characters, but all their permutations and combinations; and since Chinese is a language infinitely more subtle than any Western language, learning Chinese with any understanding of its complexities is even now a task for a lifetime of undeviating scholarship. Short cuts exist, but none are wholly satisfactory. The Communists in the north attempted a form of romanization and still print their bank notes in romanized Chinese, but they are careful to add a purely Chinese translation. They have abandoned romanization in their night schools, where old farmers and the smallest children congregate in study. What is surprising is not that they have introduced new methods, but that in sheer desperation they have been forced to return to the old classical style of teaching—the students are taught by memorizing and humming aloud until the meaning and shape of the character penetrates their brains.

One short cut has been employed that may affect the whole current of Chinese literature in the future—a standardized and reduced vocabulary. The vocabulary of the peasants is never large. The peasants are taught the commonly used words; newspapers are printed that use only these words; political terms are expressed in their simplest conceivable form. The revolution in language accompanies the social revolution. A simpler, more dramatic, more *social* language is evolving with incalculable consequence to the future of Chinese education and even to the future of the Chinese people, for once the ancient parodies of refinement have been finally removed— nearly all terms employed in government and the bureaucracy are ambiguous—a more solid structure of thought may appear.

A revolution away from the archaic habits of the past cannot be brought about successfully without a rise in the rate of literacy. Less than 7 per cent of the Chinese people can write their own language. "Two thirds of the people of the world are in the coolie class," said Dr. James Yen, the director of the Chinese mass-education movement. "No nation can rise higher than its masses, and until these masses, the world's richest undeveloped resource, are developed through education—until the people are taught to participate themselves in their own reconstruction—world leaders can cry peace! peace! but there will be no peace. Mass education will make every man a complete man, and when he has reached that stage he is the brother of every other man. I humbly believe that the world needs this education for world democracy, for peace. Then not only can we have the Four Freedoms, but the Fifth Freedom—the greatest of all, without which we cannot have the other four—Freedom from Ignorance." The distinguished art historian Dr. Ananda

Coomaraswamy has spoken of the decline in real culture that accompanies literacy; the legends are forgotten because they are too easily put into print, the skilled storytellers no longer rely on their ancestral memories, and love songs disappear to give place to jazz. The thesis cannot be defended; a peasant cannot plant well, or build well, or live well unless he is in direct contact with the sources of modern learning; he cannot vote or take part in modern social life unless he knows what is happening beyond the borders of his village, by reading newspapers. In the wider social organisms of the future the newspaper dropped by air may have more importance than railways; until every family is provided with a radio, the problem of illiteracy will remain as one of the most potent factors in disrupting the social progress of communities.

Many of the 222 vernaculars of India will disappear, but the Chinese characters are so closely woven into Chinese thought that the most useful of them will remain. It is significant that Dr. James Yen, who has accumulated more experience on the mass education of the Chinese characters than anyone else, has never suggested that the solution lay in romanization.

He began in France in 1918, when he was sent to help the Army Y.M.C.A. War Council supervise 200,000 Chinese coolies whose presence had been required by Lloyd George. Finding that the coolies could neither read nor write letters, he devised a list of 1,300 basic characters. Out of 5,000 coolies present at a mass meeting he called, 40 answered that they were prepared to learn the 1,300 characters. A beginning had been made. When he returned to China, he was convinced that the experiment opened up immense possibilities. He quoted the saying of Confucius: "People are the foundation of the nation. If the foundation is firm, the nation will enjoy tranquillity." How could the people be firm, when nearly all were peasants at the mercy of the war lords, incapable of making decisions for themselves, with no understanding of the outside world? Ignorance and illiteracy were synonymous; there could be no hope till an attempt had been made to banish them.

Long before he became governor of Jehol and prime minister of China, a young Han-lin scholar from Hunan had been building libraries throughout his native province. Schools and hospitals followed, but Hsiung Hsi-ling was known chiefly for the innumerable libraries scattered throughout Hunan. Mao Tse-tung studied in his free libraries, which were built in a deliberate effort to increase knowledge and scholarship among the peasants. The principal products of Hunan have been for generations (according to the Hunanese) handsome men, beautiful women, scholars, and soldiers —in that order. Nearly all the great scholar-soldiers of China's history have come from Hunan; Hsiung Hsi-ling was determined to follow them, but when Dr. James Yen returned from France with his plans of mass education the Prime Minister was already aging, Buddhism absorbed him continually, he was building an immense orphanage in the imperial hunting park on the western hills outside Peking, and he suggested that Dr. James Yen should obtain help from his wife.

Mme. Hsiung Hsi-ling was a woman capable of considerable tyranny, a quality of fearlessness and complete lack of respect for the powers of the war lords, whom she bullied into offering large sums of money for the mass-education movement. Though ugly, her face lit with a merciless and supremely effective smile at moments when the money was received. She poured thousands of dollars into Dr. Yen's hands; a plan of campaign was mapped out. She was determined that Hunan should be the center of the experiment, and she ordered three Cabinet Ministers to become members of the Board of Trustees and presided over the meetings of the National Congress, making long speeches to anyone who cared to listen to her. This remarkable woman presided over mass education until her death in 1934, with the power of a ruthless dictator.

The organization in Hunan was planned to resemble a military campaign. Dr. Yen believed that if sufficient teachers were available, illiteracy could be made to disappear within ten years. An almost messianic hope uplifted the first experimenters. Dr. Yen would quote St. Paul: "Except ye utter words that are easy to be understood, how shall it be known what is spoken?" It was decided that the experiment should begin in the forgotten village of Ting Hsien, the teachers living in a corner of a ruined temple. Scholars from Peking joined in the experiment. Dr. Yen claimed with some justification that it was the first time the educated classes had "gone to the people" since the time when Confucius traveled and collected poems. The hours were strange—teaching took place at dawn or at dusk, when the farmers were not working—but stranger than the experiment in teaching them to read were the implications. Reading was not enough. New methods of farming, sanitation, the whole cultural pattern of 400,000 villagers living in this corner of Hunan, were put under review. The peasants were taught vaccination, elementary architecture, social hygiene; new groups of teachers from among the villagers were formed; by 1934 even radio was beginning to penetrate village life. They claimed that after four years they had taught 80,000 to be literate.

The movement, if it had been followed through, would have led to a complete social revolution. The same techniques were to be employed by the Communists in north China, who had advantages that were denied to the mass-education movement. On the death of Mme. Hsiung Hsi-ling, money for the experiment came largely from America, but the spiritual forces behind the movement no longer possessed its original fire. The Kuomintang government attempted continually to take the scheme under its wing; Dr. Yen was too great a scholar to become a bureaucrat, and he fought a losing battle against Kuomintang influence. He asked that the movement should be independent of politics. The government answered that by raising the standard of cultivation of the villagers and reducing literacy, he was making the peasants politically conscious. Under the Communists the experiments carried out by Dr. Yen were geared to the whole social pattern; that the peasants should read, write, form their own dramas, make their own newspapers, became part of the official policy of the government, fully supported by government. Suspicious of both parties, Dr. Yen attempted to form a pattern in which politics had little place. He argued in simple terms—unless there was increased education among the peasants, there could not be increased productive power, and without productive power the industrialization of China could not come into being. But how to form these groups without state aid? The greatest success of his movement lay in the fact that the groups could often be made self-supporting. Of 472 People's Schools that came into being, he could claim that all or nearly all were self-supporting.

He was beginning to see the mechanics of education in China as something simpler, and at the same time more complicated, than he had dreamed. The peasants were hungry for knowledge, not only in China but all over Asia. Left to their primitive farming and illiteracy, on the eve of an industrial revolution, they were malleable material for dictatorship; without powers of reason or experience of politics, their enormous potentialities would fall into the hands of unscrupulous leaders. In such circumstances industrialization would be neither practical nor beneficial. Two tendencies were at work: either the immense potential resources of the peasantry could be canalized through education, or they could be left in ignorance, to be employed according to the rigid wishes of their masters. Both tendencies were dangerous. The Kuomintang government would seem to have refused the first—only 7 per cent of the officially published national budget was used for education, and of this only a small fraction was employed among the peasants: the greater part went to the military schools, middle schools, and universities. The official budget, however, was known to be inaccurate; the actual amount of money spent officially on the education of the peasants by the National Government cannot have been more than 1 per cent of the total budget, though the Draft Constitution insisted that "educational appropriations shall constitute no less than 15 per cent of the total budget, and no less than 30 per cent of the provincial, county and municipal budgets respectively."

The success of the mass-education movement, in spite of many failures and the lack of interest shown in high quarters, lay in its self-sufficiency. The simplest weapons brought the dearest victories. The Chinese villagers possessed long traditions of village drama; this could be harnessed, the drama itself could become a means of advertisement. In Shensi the Communists employ the old village songs, called *yang k'o,* to express their own agricultural policies; around the songs propaganda plays are written, the words of the song are changed and instead of the lover's lament there is the instruction of the old farmer on the growing corn and the necessity of studying books. Like the Communists after them, the mass-educators formed a people's library of books rewritten to appeal to popular village taste. In China, where there is one modern physician for every 70,000 inhabitants, the essentials of the health service could be broadcast only through reading and radio. In a sense it was a race between radio and literacy—with every villager possessing his own radio, it might not be necessary to learn to read. Most necessary of all was that the villagers should be aware of their responsibilities, not as units, but as part of the immense peasant complex that forms the larger proportion of the inhabitants of China. By constant propaganda, by lectures, by films, poster, and radio, they were told of their own increasing importance. Mass education was gradually becoming a factor in the social consciousness of the people. Students and professors from the major universities became increasingly interested, not only in the movement itself but in the far-reaching implications. By tradition and by necessity the peasants claimed no attachment to politics.

Confucius saw a woman weeping by the road, and asked her why she was weeping. She answered: "Because my father was killed a year ago by a tiger, and afterward my brother was killed. Last month my husband was eaten by a tiger, and this month a tiger has eaten my only son."

Confucius said: "Why don't you move to a place where there are no tigers?"

The woman said: "O Master, why must I move, for there is no oppressive government here?" But what if it should happen that there were tigers in the place where the government was oppressive?

At the time when the western world was talking of the imminent danger of the "Yellow Peril," Liang Chi-chao, the most courageous of the reformers who attempted to dethrone the Empress Dowager in 1898, was saying: "We have a peril in our midst. There will come a day when the peasants will speak their own words and not listen to us. This peril is a blessing in disguise, and I truly hope to live to the day when the voice of the peasants is heard." But it was not heard, even when the mass-education movement was at its height, because it represented too small a grouping of the intangible strength of the peasant forces at work. When the Communists found themselves in danger of being beleaguered by the Japanese, they abandoned their doctrinaire persuasions for a more tangible reality—a conscious peasantry, whose demands were listened to and whose thoughts were armed. The mass-education movement under Dr. Yen began with an attempt to improve literacy among the peasants. Inevitably, it would be compelled to adjust itself to the rising social consciousness it had brought about.

In the autumn of 1932, at a time when the Communist movement was growing, the Central Government in Nanking sent Dr. Kan Nai-kwang to visit the experimental station at Ting Hsien. It was then agreed that the experiment should be enlarged to include the administration of the hsien, as an integral function of the educational movement. "After the people have learned to run their own

People's Schools, their modern farms, their co-operatives, their health clinics," Dr. Yen said, "what could be more natural than that they should run their own government?" It had been Sun Yat-sen's belief that the fundamental basis of government should be the self-governing hsien, but the hsien traditionally under the rule of powerful local gentry who combined the functions of chief magistrate, landlord, taxgatherer, rent-collector, and chief conscriptor of soldiers, had never possessed self-government in China's history.

In spite of protests, three self-governing centers were founded—Ting Hsien and Hengshan in Hunan, and Hsin-tu in Szechwan. The experiment was exciting and widely publicized, for if it had succeeded it would have stolen the thunder of the Chinese Communists, who also insisted that the hsien should be self-governing and placed outside the maladministration of the gentry. Dr. Yen has recorded the history of Hsin-tu in Pearl Buck's book *Tell the People*. The gentry conspired continually against the elected officials of the village, who exposed inaccurate land surveys and formed among the villagers a people's militia to defend it against bandits or the hired agents of the gentry. From time to time thousands of "citizens" would miraculously appear outside the gates, shouting: "Down with the experimental hsien!" In spite of the Generalissimo's approval, the experiments were unable to extend their influence—the Kuomintang party still had its roots among the landed gentry. Dr. Yen could insist that education, economic health, sanitation, and self-government were all interrelated, and that the success of one depended upon the success of another; but self-government depended upon political factors over which he had no control. The three experimental stations were part of a façade; the government could not resist the strength of the landed gentry but was powerless to offer opposition to the three experimental stations already formed. They could be used, and used well—the villagers from the Hunanese hsiens became among the best guerrillas in the war against the Japanese—but no new experimental stations were created during the war in Kunming or Szechwan. Villages remained under the power of the landlords; the young farmers were roped together as conscripts and marched off to their deaths by starvation long before they reached the Japanese fronts. In one sense the whole experiment had failed; the government, by not backing it to the full, had lost its opportunity of making direct contact with the self-governing hsien and harnessing to its best advantage the inexhaustible vigor that would have arisen from the peasantry.

Dr. Yen repeatedly denied that the scheme depended upon political considerations, yet he has explained that he was obsessed by the vast human wealth that would be released once the hsien were self-governing. There were more than 300,000,000 youths in Asia who had received only the rudiments of education. What if all these possessed learning and the ability to form self-governing village communities? "We started out to make people literate," he said, "and in the end we found that other problems were involved. The life of the village community had to be changed—not by us, or by the fellow scholars, but by the rigorous application of modern ideas, and these would become the property of the peasants themselves, and they would use them in their own way." At another time he said: "What good is it if they remain poverty-stricken? So we had to teach them how to be better farmers, grow better crops, breed better animals. Then we found that what they gained by being better farmers, they lost by being poor businessmen. We had to teach them how to market. When the farmers learned to be better businessmen, the economic level of the whole hsien was raised dramatically. In cotton alone production increased from $120,000 in 1932 to $1,800,000 in 1937." But by then the Japanese were pouring over the northern frontier, and the experiment could no longer be continued.

The significance of the experiment does not lie in its comparative success within three hsien in China, or in its adoption by the Chinese Communist party; for under wartime conditions no far-reaching conclusions could be reached. The significance lay in the discovery of the profound interdependence of reading, marketing, sanitation, bookkeeping, breeding, village architecture, and fertilizers. The peasant economy could not be improved only by literacy, and literacy itself, with cheaper and more dependable radios, might not even be necessary; what was necessary was the introduction of a more scientific form of agriculture and of husbandry. A new government department should have taken over the functions of the mass-education movement with far-reaching powers to reform the basic structure of the peasant community. The Communists were to do this later, with improvised tools and in the middle of a costly war, so that Mao Tse-tung could say: "They talk about communism, but all we have done is to give the people self-government and a few books—what they have done with these two things is miraculous!"

The mistake made in Kuomintang China was to begin with the famous 1,300 characters when a more fruitful beginning might have come about with "self-government and a few books." But the experiment had proved its worth. There could be no turning back, though the landlords were to remain for a few more years; and gradually the peasants were becoming conscious of their power.

Neither the mass-education movement nor the Chinese Industrial Co-operatives affected more than a few thousands of the Chinese people, yet their importance in the development of China's resources cannot be underestimated, and both are playing an integral part in the revolt of Asia. They received official encouragement from the Chinese Government but passed through checkered histories. It was not that the landlords and the banks were afraid of the unlimited potential power that might be released from these movements, or that they feared the implicit condemnation of a dictatorial government, but the very nature of these movements demanded a degree of independence from government control that a government at war is not always prepared to allow.

The Chinese Communists have accepted mass-education and peasant co-operatives as cornerstones of their own agrarian revolution. The Kuomintang government, seeing the sympathy aroused abroad for both of these movements, viewed them with alarm. An aroused and intelligent peasantry, financially independent, fed and clothed by its own co-operatives, was not likely to tolerate the abuses of power that became increasingly frequent as the war continued. Co-operatives suggested socialism, the vaguely socialist leanings of Dr. Yen might have an incalculable effect if he pursued them further. The mass-education movement came almost to an end in wartime China. It was more difficult for the government to control the co-operatives, which maintained their greatest influence in Kansu and in places far from the capital. If the inner struggle for power in the mass-education movement was complex, the struggle for power over the co-operatives was far more complex and far more bitterly fought. In the end the amazing founder of the Chinese Industrial Co-operatives simply disappeared from the capital, the scene of conflict, and retired to the hinterlands near Tibet, where he could continue his leadership untrammeled.

Rewi Alley would deny that he had founded the co-operatives, saying they were no more than an extension of the ancient guild system that has existed in China since the Chou dynasty. He would say they were indigenous to the Chinese scene and sprang from the simple communal democracy that exists still in the villages where the pressure of the landlord is not excessive, and like flowers in the desert, they would spring up overnight in great multitudes if any rain fell. The Chinese Industrial Co-operatives grew up with the war. Though the number of peasants who fled before the Japanese advance has been magnified, hundreds of thousands fled into the interior without means of support. The Industrial Co-operatives were founded in order to support them and to harness them to the war effort. The small committee that brought them into being included Rewi Alley, who had been chief factory inspector in Shanghai, Edgar Snow, who had spent fifteen years in the Far East and had a special attachment for China, Mme Sun Yat-sen, and the British ambassador, Sir Archibald Clark Kerr.

From the beginning the Chinese government distrusted the movement, which included within itself all the forces that were included in the experimental village communities begun by Dr. Yen. The peasants were to be taught simple mechanical handicrafts and to form communities among themselves, teach producers to work together, elect their own leaders, and assume wide social responsibilities. The initiators of the movement thought of it openly as a method to bridge the gulf between the guerrillas, who were largely Communists, and the armies of the National Government. Small-scale industrial co-operatives, which could be removed or hidden in the event of Japanese attacks, provided the answer to the loss of all the major industrial centers after the fall of Hankow. Co-operatives were divided into groups: the heaviest industries were placed in west and southwest China, the lightest of all were placed near the front lines. All were expected to be self-sufficient after being provided with an insignificantly small capital investment. Production, distribution, marketing, and accountancy were along generally accepted co-operative lines, but all were reduced to their simplest essentials. Schools were opened for the training of apprentices. It was hoped that in spite of the initial defeats, the economy of the country could be revived by introducing modern technical training to thousands upon thousands of these small peasant co-operatives.

Inflation would have been curtailed, because the country would not have to import goods from abroad or to import from occupied areas—it is significant that the greatest attacks against the Industrial Co-operatives by the Prime Minister occurred at the moment when the wartime frontiers between the Chinese and the Japanese were being opened for barter and exchange. The co-operatives flourished in the Communist areas, and in the regions bordering them.

By 1943 Professor Michael Lindsay could report that there were 4,200 co-operatives of all types west of the Peiping-Hankow railway and over 5,000 between the railway and the Yellow Sea. Under the Communists, every village supported its co-operatives; under the Kuomintang the progress was less steady and was too often involved in political considerations. In Kansu, far from governmental interference, they flourished, but their success here was due largely to the fact that the co-operatives provided urgently needed blankets for the army.

All branches of minor industry could be and were placed under co-operative control. The most important were military clothing and dyeing and weaving of all kinds, then soapmaking and alcohol distilling, then paper manufacture, salt refining, and drugs. Foreign assistance to these co-operatives continued; it was a form of assistance in which there was no element of exploitation, for the accumulated wealth derived from the co-operatives could only benefit the Chinese communities. The plans, the simple machines (nearly always of wood), the training of the teachers, were uniform, and the movement branched out in a hundred unsuspected directions—like Dr. James Yen, the organizers were faced with unforeseeable implications. Designed largely to reduce the risk of inflation, they were the first to suffer from the steady decline in the value of money that began three years after they were founded. The government, regarding the movement as the spearhead of a potential social revolution, became increasingly dubious of its success and increasingly determined to build up industries in places where there could be direct government control. Industry in Chungking, Chengtu, and Kunming expanded prodigiously. It was necessary that they should expand, but there were self-evident dangers. In Japan and in India the machine has penetrated the cities, but no balance has been found between industry and rural economy. The war might have produced such a balance by the expansion of small-scale industries in the villages, but by the time the war was over little was left of the original impetus which brought the co-operatives into being.

Attached to some of the co-operatives, and sometimes independent of them, were schools that came to be known as Bailie schools (after Dr. Joseph Bailie, an American missionary). These were industrial co-operatives especially designed for young apprentices, who were taught reading, writing, and simple mechanical engineering as a foretaste to work with machine tools. Dr. Yen called the students he taught "fellow scholars," because they would return to their native villages and act as carriers of the new technological knowledge; the boys trained in the Bailie schools were "technical fellow scholars." Like the village co-operatives they subscribed to the belief that the motto *Kung-ho* (work together) provided a successful basis for fighting the war.

The scope of the Industrial Co-operatives extended far beyond the bounds that Dr. James Yen had foreseen. Dr. Yen had seen the village as a whole social unit, in process of change from a peasant agriculture to a peasant agriculture of a higher pattern; the co-operatives introduced a more radical change—an industrial community, self-sufficient in prime needs, supported by a modernized agriculture. The scope widened beyond all existing bounds when the co-operatives began to introduce together with the new techniques of weaving, mining, technical and mechanical training, nurseries, hospitals, and clinics, and even hostels, cafeterias, primary schools, and clubs. The initiative that should have been taken by the government was left to the villagers themselves, who were more responsible for the success of the experiment than anyone else. By 1923 the co-operatives had organized five fully-equiped hospitals, twenty-three medical clinics, and fourteen primary schools.

What was strange was that the co-operative movement could survive at all in the atmosphere provided by the Kuomintang government. Rewi Alley, who had assumed the most urgent responsibilities from the beginning, was dismissed on the orders of Dr. H. H. Kung in July 1943, and one of his chief assistants was imprisoned. Supported by funds raised abroad, chiefly in America, Rewi Alley retired to Kansu, where he could open new Bailie schools and new co-operatives without direct interference from Chungking. Though great influence was used within the government, the movement continued largely because its resources in blanketmaking and cotton weaving could not be reduplicated by the government, but also because considerable American pressure was applied. The government could not deny that in Mme Sun Yat-sen's words "this new movement is based upon the fundamental principle of Dr. Sen Yat-sen—that the government should assist the livelihood of the people," but in December 1943, when the total number of co-operative members was 25,000, the movement was already declining. Since China was then under total blockade except for whatever merchandise was flown over from India and Burma, the implication would seem to be that the government no longer had the need for the articles that the co-operatives could supply; they could be, and often were, bought more cheaply from Japanese sources. The rot was setting in, the great market towns of central China and southern Yunnan were being opened for commercial exchanges between China and Japan. Cloth poured over the frontier. For the industrial co-operatives, though they were to survive the war, the time had passed when they provided the healthiest sign of the promised balance between agriculture and industry. With the end of the war the Kuomintang decided that industry should be isolated within the large cities. The Communists, who possessed no large cities except Kalgan for long, were content to search for the balance between agriculture and small-scale industries.

In different ways Dr. James Yen and Rewi Alley, and their hosts of helpers, had come to the same conclusions. The villages were changing; they were more conscious of themselves and of their potential power. By employing small-scale industries small capital investments yielded a large production of goods, the interval between marketing and investment was shortened, the substantial health of the village community increased. The new China would come that way—the balance between agriculture and technology would have to be found, as it would have to be found in all the other countries of Asia.

Chapter 15

Viet-Nam

AN air of mystery surrounds Indo-China, the least known of the southeast Asiatic states. The ruins of Angkor Wat and Bayon, the quiet temples buried under creepers, the suggestion of untold mysterious wealth still unexplored have only increased the mystery; yet today we can see films showing villages burning, young students taken out of their homes, put up against walls, and shot, of full-scale military attacks over apparently deserted rice fields. Suddenly Indo-China hit the headlines. When Chu Ta-kuan, a Chinese traveler, visited Angkor in the thirteenth century, he spoke of a palace "where there is golden pyramid, and above the golden pyramid a king sleeps. The natives of the place believe that the serpent spirit lives there, master of the earth and the whole kingdom, a spirit which appears every night in the form of a woman, with whom the king must sleep, and the king's principal women dare not enter. At the second watch of the night the king leaves and sleeps with his wives and concubines, but if one night the serpent spirit should not appear, the moment of the king's death has arrived; and if the king failed to be there on a single night, grave misfortunes took place." Through all known historical times emperors and kings have ruled over Annam and Cochin China, but on August 21, 1945, the serpent disappeared, the Emperor of Annam abdicated, and the virtual ruler of the empire was a bearded scholarly descendant of minor Annamese princes, who spoke Chinese by preference and possessed no known name.

They called him Nguyen-ai-Quoc, which means "the fellow over there." He had been known at different times as Ho Chi-minh, Song Man-tchu, *le petit Monsieur Ferdinand*. In Russia he was called Golin, and when he served in the Soviet consulate at Boston, he possessed still another name. He was short and wiry, with large eyes, he had never married; he spoke French, English, Russian, Japanese, Chinese, and various dialects of Annam, and he spoke sufficient Portuguese to suggest that he had spent some months in the comparative security of Macao. When his father was arrested, he escaped imprisonment in the island of Poulo-Candore by shipping as a cabin boy in the *d'Artagnan* to France, where he studied, worked as a photographer's assistant, and plunged into politics. At a socialist meeting in the Faubourg St. Martin he began to speak quietly of the problems of Indo-China. His voice was weak, but the fury of the man kept the audience spellbound. He attended the Congress at Tours in 1920 where the extreme left wing of the socialist party became separated from the second international and formed the third international. He edited a newspaper called *The Pariah,* thus antedating Gandhi's use of the same word as the title of a newspaper. In 1921 he formed "the intercolonial union," a union that attempted to include within its scope members of all colonial countries. In 1923 he visited Moscow as a delegate of the French Communist Party to the Congress of the Peasant International (the *Krestintern*) and remained there till the end of 1924 as a permanent member of the council. He assisted Borodin in the Russian consulate at Canton when Borodin was employed by the Kuomintang as technical revolutionary adviser; in theory he was simply a clerk whose duty was to transcribe documents into Chinese, in practice he was attempting a revolt on Indo-Chinese territory. Sun Yat-sen had begun his revolt against the Manchu government with risings on the Indo-Chinese frontier, assisted by French military officers. Perhaps the process could be reversed, and the revolt of Indo-China could be engineered with the assistance of Chinese officers on the frontiers. He visited Hainan, attempted once again to form a league of oppressed races among Hindus, Annamites, and Koreans, but in 1927, when Chiang Kai-shek ordered the counterrevolution, he fled to Moscow. He was next seen in Siam and Singapore. He was credited with being the representative of the Third International with vast theoretical powers of formenting revolution throughout south China, Indo-China, British Malaya, and the Dutch East Indies. On June 6, 1931, he was arrested in Hong Kong, where he had hoped to reorganize the Indo-Chinese Communist party. Banished from Hong Kong, he returned secretly to Singapore. The French

authorities in Hanoi placed a price of 50,000 piasters on his head.
Then he disappeared. It was rumored that he had been seen in
America, in Java, in Moscow, in France, in Portuguese East Africa.
During World War II under the name of Nguyen Tan Thanh, he
returned to French Indo-China, where he organized resistance
against the Japanese with the secret help of Kuomintang officers,
who realized too late that the Generalissimo had put a price on his
head in 1927. Elusive always, he reappeared in 1941 in Luchow,
in Kuomintang China, where the Chinese were preparing a military
school for training young Annamite officers and revolutionaries. He
attended a conference in Kunming in 1945 and then slipped over the
frontier by way of Tonkin, living quietly in a small village a few
miles from Thai Nguyen. After the abdication of the Emperor Bao
Dai, he was proclaimed the first president of the Viet-Nam Republic.
Asked why he was chosen president he answered: "It was because
I had nothing—no family, no house, no fortune, and only one suit
of clothes, the one I am wearing."

It was probably true; he was the anonymous representative of the
people, distinguished from the rest of the people only by the fact
that he had wandered more and suffered nearly as much as most.
His quietness was as singular as his power of making sudden decisions; his greatest gifts were silence and invisibility. Unlike Nehru,
but like Shjarir, he could disappear in a crowd of coolies and be
unrecognized. When he came to Paris to sign the accord for the
declaration of the Viet-Nam Republic, he was genuinely surprised
by the automobiles and hotel suites placed at his service; he had
occupied prison cells, tenth-rate Chinese hotels, miserable steerage-
passage gangways. His hotel suite was full to overflowing with
flowers. Those who still thought he might be a Chinese in disguise
realized that he was more Annamite than the Annamites when he
collected the flowers one by one and presented them to all the lady
secretaries of the French delegation. He was a man without crafti-
ness, but with great experience of the craft of revolution, and of how
to avoid being thrown into prison cells. He was embarrassed by the
presidency, and still more embarrassed by the responisibility of
power; for the first time he was compelled to face conflicting parties
within the organizations he had helped to build. His signature on
the treaty with France was small and cramped, with one immense
downward streak which testified probably to nervousness.

It is necessary that we should study him, and the movement he brought into being, at some length. The Viet-Nam revolt followed the pattern of the Indonesian revolt, sprung from the same causes, generated the same passions. Outwardly a nationalist movement, it remains essentially a movement of social reform. The Viet Nam Doc Lap Dongh Minh (The League for the Independence of Viet-Nam) was first formed in 1939 as a coalition of various groups including democrats, socialists, communists, and other less well-defined organizations representing only the demand for independence. In the same year a similar reorganization and coalition of groups had taken place in the Dutch East Indies. A program of agrarian reform and a greater distribution of wealth were demanded of the French Government, and a considerable measure of representation in the French parliament. In 1939 independence did not mean exclusive independence. It was a time when nearly all the political parties in colonial territories were forming coalitions for the same reason that coalitions were formed in countries fighting Hitler; national and social interests demanded the common front, with all its inevitable dangers and triumphs.

Ho Chih-minh, the son of a minor princeling at the court of Duy-Than, was a communist in origin, but his election to the presidency of a coalition group signified a change from formal communism. Russia had failed in Canton and Hankow in 1927 to devise a policy acceptable to the Asiatic masses, who remained predominantly moderate. The strikes in the rubber and coal industries in 1936, when transportation broke down throughout French Indo-China, had arisen as a result of the same causes that led to the revolt of the Dutch cruiser *The Seven Provinces* and the Boston Tea Party: there should be no taxes without representation, no exploitation without constitutional rights for the native inhabitants of the place. The history of French Indo-China had not, like the history of the Dutch East Indies, progressed through gradualness. Though Indo-Chinese students were welcomed in Paris, they were given no power when they returned to their country. No labor unions were allowed. The poverty of the peasants in the overcrowded Red River delta was greater than that of any other colony in the East with the possible exception of India. Ninety per cent of the population lived in crude thatched huts and earned less than a thousand piasters a year. An Annamite coal miner could get fifteen cents a day, but the general level of income was considerably less than ten U.S. dollars a year. The Governor General was advised by a grand council representing economic and financial interests, in which the Banque de l'Indochine was strongly interested.

In theory considerable powers were wielded by the courts of the Emperor of Annam and the king of Cochin China, but in effect these powers were subservient to French economic interests. In 1936, during the widespread strikes, the Minister of Colonial Affairs, Marius Moutet, could say that legislation would be introduced "to place the people of French Indo-China on the same level of moral equality, social justice and brotherhood as the workers and peasants of France." It was already too late. The pattern of exploitation had been laid down by the strange alliance of missionaries, diplomats, and colonial soldiers that began on November 28, 1787, when Monseigneur Pigneau de Béhaine signed, on behalf of Louis XVI, King of France, a treaty with Gia-long, Emperor of Annam of the dynasty of Nguyen, by which Annam ceded to France the sovereignty of the island of Poulo-Candore and agreed to an offensive and defensive alliance. The island of Poulo-Candore later became a prison as famous in French Indo-China as Dachau or Pallentaria.

The devastation of the Khmer empire by Siam in the sixteenth century produced in Indo-China a situation comparable with the situation when the Portuguese and the Spanish first invaded the East Indies. The oriental empires were breaking up of their own weakness at the time when the first foreigners came in contact with them. As with the East Indies, so with Indo-China the first foreigners to settle in these countries were missionaries. By one of those extraordinary ironies that are likely to occur more often in the East than in the West, when Indo-China proclaimed itself a republic in 1945, the chief French envoy was Admiral Thierry d'Argenlieu, admiral of the French navy, High Commissioner for the French Indies, and major superior of the Carmelite order of France. The tradition was preserved, but the Indo-Chinese people were inventing their own traditions during the revolutionary epoch that followed the war.

The significance of the revolt lay in its complexity. Among the parties that had taken part in the coalition of 1939 was the Viet-Nam-Quoc-Dsen-Dan, which could be translated literally as the Indo-Chinese Kuomintang. Heavily supported and financed by the

Kuomintang government, it was pro-Chinese, anti-French, and anti-Communist. The coalition therefore included incompatibles, and was basically unstable. Chinese merchants in Indo-China were not popular with the Indo-Chinese people, who lacked a middle class and saw the rise of a foreign middle class as a threat against themselves. Kuomintang envoys were continually entering Indo-China; two military training schools for Viet-Nam revolutionaries existed on Chinese soil during the later years of the war; Ho Chih-minh had considerable affiliations with the Kuomintang party—even when it was realized that he was a communist; his continual presence on Chinese soil offered hopes to the Kuomintang government that Chinese influence would predominate. An Indo-Chinese Kuomintang revolutionary party existed in Chungking. In the extraordinary enumeration of former imperial vassal states that forms the prelude to Chiang Kai-shek's *China's Destiny* the Middle-South Peninsula, presumably including the Malay Peninsula, Burma, Siam, and Indo-China, is given special reference, and the Generalissimo concludes after enumerating the widest frontiers of former Chinese empires, "There is no area that can be separated from the rest, none that can take upon themselves the function of an independent unit." The Annamite royal court retained the ceremonies last seen in imperial Manchu times, though its power was less rigorous. To the Chinese soldiers of the Yunnan garrison army who marched into Indo-China on the conclusion of the war, nothing could have seemed less unlikely than that China's territorial ambitions lay in the south.

Other elements entered the revolutionary pattern. Pro-Japanese factions existed; they were encouraged by the liberal employment of funds and propaganda from Japanese residents and the Japanese consulate in Hanoi. There were pro-French students, who were prepared to believe that M. Marius Moutet was about to introduce legislation that would deprive the Governor General of absolute powers and the four *Résidents Supérieurs* of their powers to arrest without the formality of charges or warrants. Indo-China had not gone through the process of gradual orientation under a single influence that characterized the Dutch East Indies, where the Chinese delegates of the Kuomintang could exert no political pressure on the Indonesians, and the Russians and the Japanese were equally powerless. In a very real sense Indo-China was the melting pot where all eastern Asiatic tendencies conflicted and harried one another.

The poverty of the country was extreme. As early as 1931 M. Moutet had expressed his fear of revolutionary risings. The Indo-Chinese budget provided a sum of 15,000,000 piasters for 30,000 Annamite employees and functionaries of the government; the same budget provided 40,000,000 piasters for 5,000 French employees. Nothing comparable to this appeared in the budgets either of British Malaya or the Dutch East Indies. Forty years after the conquest less than 2 per cent of the population received elementary education; there were one university, thirty-one hospitals, and eighty-three prisons. History lessons in the secondary schools were devoted to the history of France with considerable attention paid to the conquests of Louis XIV and only a brief chapter acknowledged the outstanding conquests of the French revolutionaries. Hatred grew slowly. The Annamites were tolerant people whose traditions attached virtue to extreme forms of toleration. The risings in 1930 and 1931 in Vinh province were small, ill-organized, and inevitably defeated; the more protracted rising in Yenbay in 1936 was the first of major consequence in the whole history of French rule.

When the Republic was declared on September 2, 1945, the proclamation was accompanied by an attack on French rule more bitter than any similar declaration in the Far East. One by one the errors of the past were enumerated. "They deprived us of all liberties, they imposed upon us inhuman laws, they built more prisons than schools, they have despoiled our ricelands, our mines, our forests." The proclamation concluded with a final burst of bitterness:

Therefore, we, the members of the provisional government, representing the entire population of the Viet-Nam republic, do declare that we shall henceforth have no connection with imperialist France. We hereby declare that we shall cancel all treaties which France has signed relating to our country, and we abolish all privileges which France has arrogated to itself in our territory.

We proclaim to the entire world that Viet-Nam has the right to be free and independent, and in fact has become free and independent.

For the first time since Monseigneur Pigneau de Béhaine's treaty with the Emperor of Annam, the government no longer consisted of appointees of France.

But the pattern of the revolution had been complex from the beginning, and the complexity of forces remained. Yunnanese garrison troops under General Lu Han, the younger brother of Governor Lung Yun, were marching toward Hanoi a week after the end of the war. Chinese influence predominated north of the sixteenth parallel. In the south the British had landed, and there was no General Christison to say that the territory was not being reconquered to give it back to its former governors. British troops from the Southeast Asia Command, under Lord Louis Mountbatten's orders, entered Saigon toward the end of August. With little knowledge of the revolutionary forces involved, they were at first prepared to believe that the Viet-Nam republican government represented the survival of Japanese influence. Orders were given against fraternization. By September 25 the French forces, liberated from Japanese prisons, were already moving to the attack, declaring that the Viet-Nam government was illegal and that Viet-Nam irregulars were attacking French troops, but the arrival of French troops and battleships at Saigon suggested that the military occupation had been planned in all its details many months before and was not solely concerned with disarming the Japanese. The situation was delicate, for the Indo-Chinese were talking continually over the radio, in teahouses, and in the paddy fields of the new dispensation that comes with freedom. A truce was arranged for October 4, but sporadic fighting continued in the outskirts of Saigon and Hanoi, where the French moved into the Chinese quarter, claiming—as they were to claim many times in the future—that they had come to protect Chinese lives. On October 13 the French Minister of the Colonies complained of the "vast anticolonial current flowing through the world," as though this was something unusual, and indeed a surprise. He blamed France's troubles on foreign support to "the rebels," but did not identify the foreigners.

The foreigners consisted generally of Chinese, who from Singapore and Penang in the south and from Kunming in the north supplied weapons. Former anti-Japanese veterans from the rubber estates of Malaya formed an "assistance brigade" and with false passports from the Siamese government were allowed into Viet-Nam territory. Other arms were smuggled by sea to Indonesia and Viet-Nam; the small fishing proas were continually stopped by Dutch corvettes and by French search-parties. But the Malayan support was neither so large nor so idealistic as the Singapore Chinese believed. The Kuomintang deliberately backed Viet-Nam, but the Viet-Nam government itself remained amazingly indifferent to the reasons for which Chiang Kai-shek offered aid. Viet-Nam was independent. They were determined to be polite to the Chinese, but the memories of former suzerainty went deep; the very name Annam, which meant "southern peace" or "the pacified south," was a relic of Chinese vassalage. On August 24, when Chiang Kai-shek stated that China had no territorial ambitions in Indo-China, the danger had become clear—in *China's Destiny* he had stated the same principle in still more ambiguous terms.

The fighting between the French and Viet-Nam continued, made terrible by atrocities on both sides. Some, perhaps most, of the released prisoners were from the French Foreign Legion and possessed no real loyalty to France. Germans and Russians predominated, and though they spoke French, they formed cliques among themselves; the Germans and Russians had been known to fight each other in the past. It was not surprising that the Foreign Legion, noted for a kind of chivalry in the Sahara, should fail in the moist autumns of Indo-China, where the rice fields offered better protection to the Viet-Nam guerrillas than the scrub sands offered Abd-el-Krim.

The Viet-Nam forces, like the Chinese Communists, were already in possession of arms before the legal government took over. The uncontested surrender of Indo-China by the Vichy government, transmitting its orders through Admiral Decoux, had been more shameful even than the oriental surrenders of the Dutch, the British, and the Americans; there had been no real fighting, the French contenting themselves with the *fait accompli* over which they possessed no control. But the people of Indo-China had revolted. There were no large scale attacks (the Japanese were too firmly entrenched), but riots, strikes, and demonstrations were continuous under Japanese occupation. The Viet-Nam, too, possessed its martyrs. And in this country where the cult of the dead is the strongest in all Asia, martyrs tend to absorb the consciousness of the nation. Ho Chih-minh announced, as the Balinese announced in 1908: "We will have independence or perish." The Viet-Nam, and their neighbors the Burmese, had no mental reservations concerning violence.

It is necessary to understand where the people of Viet-Nam drew their strength. The League for the Independence of Viet-Nam, after its meeting in Luchow in 1942, had formulated already the pattern of revolutionary independence, demanding almost the same things that the Indonesians were to demand in 1945. They demanded the election of a popular assembly with the task of drafting a democratic constitution, enforcement of all democratic rights and principles, the organization of a national army, confiscation of Japanese, French, and fascist properties (though this demand was withdrawn later in as far as it affected the French); a general amnesty for prisoners, promulgation of equal rights to national minorities, the abolition of the poll tax, the nationalization of the banks belonging to the Japanese, French, and puppets, the creation of a national bank, and the establishment of a national economy. They demanded an end to illiteracy and drew up special clauses concerned with the necessity for higher education and the creation of funds for intellectual and scientific research; they also demanded the eight-hour day, social insurance, the minimum wage, allowance for large families and state building of hospitals, lying-in hospitals, municipal theaters, cinemas, and clubs. These reforms, which entered very closely into the lives of all Indo-Chinese, derived their strength from their similarity to the reforms that were at that time being attempted in France.

The League's program of action was socialist, though nothing was said of the right to strike and the details concerning welfare and insurance were still vague; yet it would have been impossible to form the League from so many different parties without a program of action similar to the one they outlined. Shjarir's speeches have already been quoted. The proclamation of the League has much in common with the spirit of the early Indonesian proclamations:

We believe in the sanctity of the principles for which the world is shedding and will continue to shed so much blood, those principles which are being promoted by the world democratic powers, the United States, Great Britain, China and Russia.

In this struggle the whole of the Indo-Chinese people beg that they shall be allowed to co-operate in the common fight against the Japanese. We beseech the great powers, and particularly the United States, to give aid and assistance in our fight for national liberation.

We beseech the United States for recognition of our organization, the

League for the Independence of Viet-Nam, as an authorized and legal organization which represents the Indo-Chinese people.

We beseech the United States to come and help us in the struggle against Japanese fascism on our soil, by giving us arms, advisers and instructors.

In accordance with the letter and spirit of the Atlantic Charter, we ask the great powers to put into effect the clauses concerning the interests of the subject peoples who suffer from invasion by the Axis, and who take part in the defeat of Japanese fascism.

For its part the League for the Independence of Viet-Nam, in the name of the Indo-Chinese people, will be prepared to place all they have at the disposal of the allies, and contribute their meagre contribution to the Allied forces.

We will at all times supply useful information about the Japanese armies, and the French and puppet quislings.

We will back the Allied cause, and in agreement with them perform sabotage operations and commando raids.

We feel it our duty to inform the Indo-Chinese people always to welcome Allied arms, to give all needed aid, bringing immediate help and food to the wounded, to protect Allied flyers who bail out over our territory and show them to headquarters. This we swear to do in our struggle against the Japanese, and for our own liberation. . . .

In Kunming, the Viet-Nam leaders co-operated with the Americans and Chinese, and to a lesser extent with the French military mission under General Sainteny. They had mapped out bombing objectives and were continually attempting to harass Japanese garrisons. It was true that the Americans were sometimes suspicious of their actions, but by the end of 1944 forty-seven bridges had been bombed, innumerable barges had been sunk, and more than seventy concerted raids on Indo-Chinese territory had been made—all with the assistance of Viet-Nam.

The program of Viet-Nam was announced even before the landing of the French by the Minister of the Interior, Vo Ngyuyen Giap, who said on September 2:

A "liberated territory" comprising six provinces of north Viet-Nam is being organized along new lines of administrative and social policy. Meanwhile a nation-wide uprising has transferred the governing rule of the State into the hands of our people, thus materializing the unity of the country from Nam-quan to Cape Camau. Under the red banner with the central yellow star, with hope and expectation, joy and enthusiasm, we pledge a solemn oath to the fatherland.

In the program he outlined, he followed carefully the proposals made by the League, demanding that market and head taxes should be abolished, promising that once the threat to the national security had passed there would be complete freedom from censorship, and that national education would be the first charge of the newborn state. "We shall introduce a merciless fight against illiteracy, and make the study of Viet-Nam reading and writing compulsory." There would be an end to the free sale of pornographic literature, the government would adopt measures for feeding the famine areas and would be reorganized on lines of universal suffrage. It is as though the dispensation had arrived, and the provisions of the new republic thrown pell-mell to the people, who had no time to digest them but were carried away by these promises that seemed so near to fulfillment. The conclusion of his long sermon, however, is disturbing: no words are too bitter to describe either the French or the Japanese. "We have appealed continually to the French to join us in our fight against the Japanese, but not only did they ignore our appeal, on the contrary they continued their oppressive policy to an even more terrorist extent." The statement was at least half true. Significantly the Minister of the Interior looks toward China for the larger hope and quotes Chiang Kai-shek: "If the Asiatic peoples do not enjoy freedom and equality of status, a third world war will step into the shoes of the second, as the second stepped into the shoes of the first." It ends on a note that could come perhaps only from Indo-China: "We demand our happiness and an invocation of the names of the martyrs of independence who died a thousand years before."

The Indo-Chinese were living in legendary times. In the course of a thousand years of Chinese occupations, rebellions had been continual. In the streets and villages of the new republic posters appeared, bearing the features of the Trung sisters, who fought against the Chinese proconsul To Dinh at the turn of the century, of another woman, Trieu Au, who fought against the Chinese in 248 A.D., Ly Bon who fought between the years 544 and 548, and finally of Ngo Quyen who succeeded in driving the Chinese armies beyond the border, though he still offered tribute and gifts to the emperor. Pagodas and temples were erected to the national heroes; now, while the revolution flamed, the pagodas were surrounded with offerings of flowers.

What was surprising was that the Annamites did not at first suspect that the Chinese would leave. With supreme fatalism, remembering how three Annamite emperors had attempted and finally succeeded in driving back the Chinese invasions of the Sung and Yuan dynasties, they greeted the Chinese who stepped on Annamite soil for the first time since 1789, when the soldiers of the Ch'ing empire finally withdrew. So rigorous had been the dominant influence of China that Annam had derived its culture and all its ways of ceremonial life from the Chinese, as the French derived their culture from Greece and Rome. Every third year tributes were offered to the court in Peking, but the Annamites delighted in pointing out that the gifts they received in exchange were far richer than those they had given; they had been independent in all but name.

The new government and the prime minister and president were appointed. The Emperor had abdicated; no one knew for certain whether he had abdicated by force or by inclination—the presumption seemed to be that he took no delight in governing and realized that he could not maintain the dynasty founded by Nguyen Anh with the assistance of the French. One emperor had abdicated before—this was the famous Ham Nghi, who took to the Maquis and was finally deported to Algeria in 1888. At that time, too, the Chinese power had been in evidence, when De Tham organized armed resistance supported by the Chinese. The French war against China had followed, not only because the French wanted control of Yunnan but because they feared constant Chinese interference in their colonial territory. With the Chinese under General Lu Han north of the sixteenth parallel, history seemed to be repeating itself.

Chinese influence in northern Indo-China had been long-standing. Kunming had become the headquarters of a provisional government. The Chinese forces under General Lu Han who were ordered to cross the Indo-Chinese border numbered more than 100,000, and they were provided with three times as many bank notes as they would need under normal circumstances. It was said that the Chinese forces in Indo-China were ordered to prepare for an occupation of "from four to five years." What is known is that the bank notes printed for the occupation bore Kuomintang designs, that there were 500,000 Chinese in Indo-China who lived as precariously as the Chinese in Siam, and that on September 30, on his arrival at Luang Trabang, capital of Laos, General Lu Han announced that he would assume complete military and civil control of the zone. He instituted a few days later a provisional government of Annamites who were flown down from Kunming. Three days later there occurred in Kunming a civil war in which his brother was compelled to surrender all power; by December 10, when General Lu Han returned to Kunming, the Viet-Nam forces were already revolting against the Chinese in the north, while they were revolting against the French in the south. Peace was as far away as ever; the unhappy Vietnamese, seeing Chinese, Dutch, American, and British troops on their soil for the first time, could say that never had they suffered from so much foreign interference. The Chinese had one advantage over the rest; there was a heavily financed and well-equipped body of them within the Viet-Nam Lap Dongh Minh itself.

While battles raged against the French, there was to be civil war between the supporters of the Kuomintang and the supporters of a purely independent government later. The French were to accuse Viet-Nam leaders of subscribing to communism. To a limited extent it was true, but no one had ever worked out exactly what communism meant in Indo-China, and Ho Chih-minh was careful to say at the beginning of the revolution: "It is perfectly true that I was a communist. This belongs to the past. Now I am a member of Viet-Nam—nothing more."

The revolution had started a little too well. There were mass delegations to celebrate the birth of the republic. The Japanese-sponsored government under Tran Trong Kim had been overthrown. Appointed on March 5, it had lasted hardly five months. The Emperor's abdication and his appointment first as a counselor to the new president and then as a member of the legislative assembly had stirred the people to intense excitement, but it is still doubtful whether he acted wisely; under different circumstances and with a stronger will he might have assumed the place that Soekarno assumed in Java, and made the independence of his country more certain. His final speech from the throne, which was reprinted in

all newspapers immediately, was dramatic and moving. Delivered
on August 24, it read:

The happiness of the Annamite people and the independence of the
Annamite nation—for these I declare I am ready to make any and every
sacrifice. I wish my sacrifice to be useful to the fatherland. Knowing that
the most useful thing for our fatherland is the unity of all our countrymen, I declare that unity is life, division is death. Although I have
reigned for nearly twenty years, I have been near my people only for a
few months, and during that short time I have not rendered my country
any appreciable service. Therefore I have decided to abdicate and hand
over the country to a democratic republican government.

I advise all groups and parties, all the different classes of people, as
well as the Royal Family, to remain united and support the Democratic
Republic in order to consolidate our national independence. As for myself, during the twenty years of my rule, I have tasted much bitterness.
Now I feel happy to become a free citizen of an independent republic. I
will never allow anyone to use my name or the name of the royal family
to deceive our countrymen. Long live the independence of Viet-Nam!
Long live our democratic republic!

On the same day, he issued a rescript addressed to the royal clan:

I have always adopted the motto "The People Above All" and I have
always said that I would rather be a common citizen in an independent
state than the King of a subjugated nation; therefore I have decided to
abdicate and hand over the government to leaders capable of leading
the strength of the whole country toward consolidation of national independence and the happiness of my countrymen.

Independence of our fatherland, happiness of our countrymen—because of these eight words, for over eighty years many of our brothers
and sisters have sacrificed their lives in the jungle and in the forests, in
prison and jail. Compared with the sacrifices of these thousands of heroes
and heroines, the act of handing over my throne is but a small thing.
Therefore, after this reading of my imperial rescript, all my relatives will
place their debt to our country above the love of our family and they will
unite closely with our countrymen in order to support the democratic
government's effort to consolidate the independence of our fatherland.

Many Viet-Namese regretted the passing of the throne, not because
it had ever served a useful purpose—the Emperor, who was educated
in France, had fought a continual battle with the representatives of
the French governor general—but because at this stage in the revo-

lution, a focal point became increasingly necessary. Bao Dai's sympathies had been with the people at all times; stories, some of them legendary, of his deliberate rudeness to French officials were current, and he was known to have supported the families of Indo-Chinese who were imprisoned by the French.

From the very beginning of the revolution it was evident that the government of Ho Chih-minh was unstable and included elements wildly opposed to one another. Ho Chih-minh said, "The policy of the government is to fight the domination of France, and not the French as a people. We promise to guarantee the safety of life and property of Frenchmen. What we want is independence. This does not mean an end of all relations between France and Viet-Nam." Almost the same words had been used of the Dutch by Soekarno, but the situation in Indo-China, consisting of one colony, two kingdoms, an empire, and a protectorate, was infinitely more complicated than that in Indonesia, where the Dutch rule was more competent than the rule of the French, and there had been a less rigorous use of "divide and reign."

The French had brought the seeds of revolt with their conquest: a great Annamite scholar, Phan-Chau-Trinh, who founded the Tonkinese Association of Free Education, commented learnedly on Rousseau and Montesquieu, and on the leaders of the French revolution. De Tham, perhaps the greatest of Indo-Chinese revolutionaries, an associate of Sun Yat-sen, had also inbibed the products of Western democracy. He was assassinated in 1908, and thereafter the movement of Indo-Chinese nationalism veered away from court circles, a change already signified by the flight of Cuong De, a prince of the royal blood, to Japan after the success of the Japanese over Russia. Revolts did not cease. During the First World War the boy emperor Duy Than headed the revolt of the nationalists but was captured and sent to join his father and brother in exile. By 1917, when a continual drain of Frenchmen returning to Europe had depleted the reserves of the French, the Governor General, Albert Sarraut, was ruling over Indo-China with a force of hardly more than two thousand civil servants. No circumstances could have made the country more ripe for revolution. The Indo-Chinese say that their failure to revolt was not due to their love for France but to their loyalty to a French victory in the war.

The loyalty might have remained if the French had not come to

Indo-China in 1945, as the Dutch came to Indonesia, as conquerors returning to their own. Battles were continual. General Gracey, head of the Allied Control Mission, imposed the curfew, banned the carrying of arms, and suppressed freedom of press, assembly, and mass demonstration. At this date there seems to be no doubt that French troops, largely from the Foreign Legion, deliberately broke the order, attacked the arsenal at Saigon, looted, massacred, and raped very much as the Japanese had looted, massacred, and raped in Nanking at the hour of their triumph. The Annamites took to the paddy fields. The Japanese soldiers who were still not imprisoned saw their opportunity and joined forces with the Annamites, unlike the Japanese in Indonesia who joined forces with the invaders. An expeditionary force equipped with LST's and Spitfires was directed toward Tonkin, but before the attack could begin better counsels had prevailed, and the French, who on February 28 had concluded an agreement with the Chinese in Chungking for the eventual withdrawal of Chinese troops, signed a week later an accord with the Viet-Nam Republic, recognizing the Republic as "a free state having its government, its parliament, its army, and its finances forming part of the Indo-Chinese Federation and the French Union." At the same time the French would appear to have recognized that the authority of the Republic extended through the three provinces of Tonkin, Annam, and Cochin China.

On June 1, 1946, the autonomous respublic of Cochin China was formally inaugurated with a cabinet of nine under the presidency of Dr. Nguyen Van Thinh, who remained responsible to Admiral d'Argenlieu, the French high commissioner and special envoy. He had assumed the position in desperation, not daring to refuse and at the same time incapable of foreseeing the consequences of armed struggle. "We cannot go into a war against the French who have outnumbered us," he told his colleagues. "Therefore we must make peace." But the peace of Cochin China was short-lived, the Viet-Nam government protested against the French-supported government in the south, and civil war continued. On November 10 Dr. Thinh committed suicide in his private house in Saigon. He is reported to have left his cabinet suddenly after saying: "I am heartbroken to have led you on this adventure. The role they have made me play is only a farce, and the farce will remain even after the change of the cabinet." In one of those double-edged panegyrics that are more common to the East than the West, Ho Chih-minh expressed his regret at the passing of his Cochin adversary: "He was a man of a quiet character, who lacked nothing in his knowledge of medicine. It is the greatest pity that in times like these, when national reconstruction demands the services of all intellectuals, that so good a doctor should have been lost to us." In spite of Dr. Thinh's suicide, the Cochin-Chinese government remained.

Meanwhile in Cambodia French power was strengthening, the King remained in his palace with its fabulous silver pagoda, and the court ceremonies continued, in spite of the presence of French guards. King Norodom had ascended the throne in 1942 at the age of twenty-four. The Free Cambodia movement was at least as urgent as the Free Viet-Nam movement, but the Cambodians had always formed a smaller appendage of French rule. Communications with Viet-Nam were difficult. The Issarak, who wore red turbans and maintained intermittent communication with Viet-Nam headquarters, smarted under French, Japanese, and also Siamese domination, but found that they had greater freedom under the Siamese. They made relentless war on French rubber planters and threatened to murder the King unless he abdicated, with the inevitable result that the King was thrown into French hands. Cambodia, which possesses only 3,000,000 inhabitants and lies in the south, did not offer great obstacles to the Viet-Nam government, which maintained that it ruled over at least 15,000,000 inhabitants and governed from Hanoi in the north. It could wait.

The French suffered from an inferiority complex. They had lost two wars, one in France and one in Indo-China, and they were determined to right the balance. They had no particular liking for fighting in Annam, a place as legendary as the Sahara; there were diseases and floods and forests. They saw themselves with a mission —*civilisatrice et pacificatrice*. Soldiers were sent from France till the total number in Cochin China alone approached 100,000. The fighting went on till March 6, when both sides were temporarily exhausted; by an agreement between the two parties steps were taken "to create an atmosphere necessary for the immediate opening of amicable and free negotiations." Viet-Nam power above the sixteenth parallel seems to have been tacitly admitted; below that imaginary line the French retain their dominance, and the war goes on, with incident following incident, both sides maintaining that they are the heralds of the new civilization.

What is remarkable is the extraordinary similarity between the methods of the Indo-Chinese and of the Indonesians. There was less complexity in the movement in Indonesia, but the steps taken by the local popular governments have been consistently similar. In both, the first charge on the government is education, and especially the problem of illiteracy. Like Indonesia, the Indo-Chinese are faced with a comparatively simple problem compared with the problem that faces the Indians and the Chinese. The romanized Indo-Chinese language, *quoc gnu* (national language), is almost as easy to learn as Malay; the Minister of Education was able to announce a three-month course sufficient to provide an illiterate with a working knowledge of the language—exactly the same period of time was decreed in Java. As in Indonesia, an effort was made to make the peasants plant food crops other than rice extensively; and by an order of May 26, 1946, all fallow land was compulsorily acquired by government till the next harvest. More striking still, the basis of representation and popular suffrage followed the pattern of a village economy, all votes were by secret ballot or by a show of hands in the population was illiterate, and in villages where the inhabitants were of different races, proportional representation was demanded. The village committee by law was compelled to meet once a week, and every two months the entire assembly of villagers would be entitled to call the committee to account. The first charge on the committee was the abolishing of illiteracy.

For fifty years the French said the Annamites were incapable of government by election; the simplicities of the ballot system were foreign to them; they were illiterate, confused by a mystical religion in which the worship of the dead preponderated over other worships —how could they be taught to be citizens? Today, the democratic method the Annamites have worked out is in advance of the methods employed elsewhere in Asia. At the January 1946 election for the presidency, it was estimated that more than 82 per cent of the men and women over eighteen who had held the franchise had voted. The High Commissioner Admiral Thierry d'Argenlieu stated the month previously: "France claims the privilege and honor of protecting the minorities. She will protect the minorities against all imperialism, whether it comes from the exterior or the interior."

The classic claim of all colonizers was being repeated, for the statement could only mean that the Annamites were being protected from themselves.

By the agreement of March 6, 1946, Viet-Nam was recognized as a free state, Cochin China would be the seat of a referendum in which the people would be allowed free choice of the kind of government they would prefer, the relief of Chinese troops would be effected by 10,000 Viet-Nam soldiers and 15,000 French soldiers, and negotiations would be opened for representation of Viet-Nam abroad. None of these codicils was observed. The conference at Fontainebleau in June and July did little to ease the situation. On the very day that Ho Chih-minh left for France by air, the French inaugurated the autonomous republic of Cochin China in violation of the convention. A *modus vivendi,* signed in September, providing for mixed commissions to settle outstanding and urgent questions, a cessation of hostilities in Cochin China, and a formal guarantee to the people of Cochin China of their liberties, seemed to be only one of what would inevitably become an endless succession of agreements, to be broken at will. And since the French had the greater concentrated military strength, with small garrisons throughout the country, the onus of responsibility when there were clashes would always be difficult to prove. The French attacked Haiphong on November 20, 1946. All through December they were demanding the destruction of defense works, the creation of special zones of security, and the surrender of arms. The Viet-Namese, who saw themselves defenseless if they accepted these onerous terms, refused; and the belief began to gain currency that General Leclerc, in command of the military organizations, had deliberately attempted, by a slow absorption of important centers, to weaken all opposition till the time came when a *coup d'état* could be performed. There occurred in Indo-China the tragic spectacle of the "cease-fire teams," powerless or so dependent upon conflicting power that they seemed more useful as causes of war than as legitimate organs for its prevention. Mopping-up operations were fought by the French, who used gasoline dropped from airplanes to burn out villages. The list of atrocities committed by both sides was endless; but the justification for the continuation of French power was as small as the justification of the Dutch in Indonesia. "We have done our best," said Ho Chih-minh. "We are prepared only for the moment—what happens in the future no one can foretell. What we want is freedom to govern ourselves within the French Union. It seems a small thing, but is it too much to ask?"

Admiral Thierry d'Argenlieu, the descendant of the same Admirals who possessed power over Indo-China in the past, seemed convinced that Viet-Nam was communist. To this Ho Chih-minh, who admitted that he had once been a communist, could point to his government, which included many different parties, ranging from the socialists, the Democrats, and the Marxists to the Confucians, Catholic, Buddhist, and Landlord parties. He could point to the seventy-year-old minister of the Interior in the new government, Huynh Thue Khang, who belonged to no party but had been imprisoned for fourteen years in Poulo-Candore. "Our program is neither communist nor socialist in color. It is simply a program for the advancement of the peoples. We must produce enough food so that no one shall starve—last year we were able to avoid starvation. Then we must teach our citizens to learn how to read and write— last year we taught 2,500,000 citizens. We must make every citizen enjoy democratic freedom under a universal suffrage which gives every man and woman over eighteen the vote."

One disturbing factor seems not to have been noticed by the French—so many of the Viet-Nam troops kill themselves rather than surrender.

Chapter 16

Korea

LIKE China, Korea suffered from having no roots in any democratic principles. Traditionally Confucian and Buddhist, the
Koreans have been ruled by emperors since the beginning of
time; the sharpest feudalism remained until recently.

The Cairo declaration brought the problem of Korea onto the
international scene for the first time in forty years. Forgotten in
the main struggle, helplessly defiant of Japanese rule, occasionally
bursting with wild, panic-stricken revolutionary activity, the Koreans
had waged a silent battle to maintain their customs unharmed.
They were docile people, conscious of their past glories; like the
Chinese peasants, their calm exteriors concealed a maddened determination to be free of their overlords. The Japanese treated them
almost as though they were animals. Japanese nerves were spun
thin. In 1919, during the funeral procession of the former emperor,
Korean representatives prepared a declaration of independence to
be read in every city and village in the land, basing their claim on the
doctrine of self-determination offered by President Wilson. Huge
demonstrations were held, Korean flags were waved openly, flowers in the colors of the Korean monarchy were thrown on the coffin,
throughout one whole day there was open defiance of Japanese rule;
at night, when the cost was counted, it was found that more than
7,000 Koreans had been killed and more than 50,000 were imprisoned by the Japanese. The Declaration of Independence, signed by
thirty-three scholars, contained the following clause: "Our struggle
is breaking the sleep of four hundred million Chinese. China will
join with Korea, and India will also arise. This is a world movement, and it will continue." For the first time the theme of this
book was announced openly.

The fatal desire for independence had long roots that went back to the time of the Taiping rebellion, when the peasants of south Korea rose against the landlords and hoped to join forces with the rebels in Nanking. They had failed; on their own territory and with the assistance of Chinese soldiers, they were subdued; but the legends survived in the villages, as the legends of the Taipings survived throughout China. Though Korea by 1905 was under the strict rule of the Japanese, the Koreans continued to turn to Peking, where two months after their own merciless defeat after declaring their independence, they saw the students of Peking University demanding the same liberties from their own government.

The lesson of defeat only strengthened the movement. The Declaration had been based on the American Declaration of Independence and began with the same opening phrases. Many Korean leaders fled; some found refuge in Shanghai, but as many as possible went overseas to France and the United States. In Shanghai, in the winter of 1919, Dr. Syngman Rhee formed the first Korean government in exile, financed by exiles in Siberia, Manchuria, Hawaii, France, and America. It was a government-in-being, possessing few powers, without large contacts in the interior of Korea, continually split by factions; but it represented, in a world that had entirely forgotten Korea's existence, the only visible signs of Korean nationalism. The organization of the government was pacifist and amazingly idealist, in keeping with the instructions issued on the day when the Declaration of Independence was announced:

"Whatever you do,
Do not insult the Japanese.
Do not throw stones,
Do not hit with your fists:
For these are the acts of barbarians."

Three articles added to the original declaration emphasized the necessity of nonviolence:

1. Our task, undertaken at the request of the people, is to enable truth, religion and life to endure, and in order to make known our love for liberty. Let no violence be done to anyone.
2. Let those who follow us, at every hour, show forth with gladness the same mind.
3. Let all things be done decently and in due order, so that our behavior shall to the very end be honorable and upright.

Perhaps it was inevitable that a code so uniformly virtuous should defeat its own ends. Though the government possessed the semblance of revolutionary power, it was even in those early days too far detached from the Korean scene; the real power lay in the hands of the Korean terrorists.

Something of the spirit of Korean independence was demonstrated when Kim Koo, who became chairman of the Provisional Korean Government in Chungking, avenged the murderer of the Empress Min, whose death on October 8, 1895, had been ordered by the Japanese Ministry of War and carried out under the connivance of the Japanese minister in Seoul. Four years later Kim Koo found himself staying in the same village as a certain Captain Tsuchida, who had taken part in the attack on the Empress. Kim Koo murdered the Japanese at night with his bare hands and refused to escape. Instead, he wrote his name and address on a large sheet of paper, with an explanation of why he felt compelled to commit the murder, writing neither in Japanese nor in the literary Korean language, but in the language of the people. He was arrested and sentenced to death but later pardoned through the intervention of the Emperor Yi. Meanwhile terrorism had come to stay; there was no reason to believe it would soon end.

Some of the dangers inherent in the Korean independence movement are demonstrated in the characters of the two old leaders, Kim Koo and Syngman Rhee. Kim Koo was burly, of more than average Korean height, a swashbuckler, filled with a sense of quite extraordinary patriotism. Syngman Rhee was short, almost cadaverous, the pure student, falling under the influence of President Wilson at Princeton, a scholar who gathered degrees from at least four American universities and treasured scholarship in its own right. From the beginning the two leaders, though outwardly aiming toward the same end, found themselves in perpetual disagreement on means; and since both became exiles, when the Japanese made their third effort of colonization at the outbreak of the China incident, they gradually lost touch with their countrymen. Scholarship and terrorism rarely go hand in hand; the essential pacifism of the Korean people had little in common with the methods of these two self-styled leaders. The tragedy of Korea is threefold: the czarist government's desire for some kind of colony down to the thirty-eighth parallel, American interest in the industrial development of

Korea, and the absence of natural leaders. Of the three tragedies, perhaps the last was the most fatal.

Until the Japanese came, Korea possessed no middle class. A Korean middle class arose only after the Japanese invasion. Nor had Korea a proletariat of any size until 1933. Before 1933 less than 300,000 Koreans were employed in mines, factories, and construction works. Between 1935 and 1937, the number had been doubled; by 1940 it had been doubled again. By the end of the war the Japanese had brought into existence a proletariat of 2,000,000. Yet even this increase affected only 8 per cent of the country; for the rest, the country consisted largely of feudal landlords, peasants, and Japanese merchants. The economy of modern Korea has never been in a state of balance.

The sudden rise of an effective working class had the effect of an internal explosion within the cities, though the peasants remained unaffected, living in unchanging poverty, paying normal interest of 20 per cent if they were tenant farmers, their only security their next crop, continually at the mercy of the great combines like the Chosen Food Company and the Oriental Development Company, which between them controlled more than 60 per cent of the Korean economy. These huge companies represented feudalism at its height, and could be compared only with the Indian and Dutch East India Companies. They fixed prices, controlled banks, owned land, were dominant partners in all the shipping lines that touched Korea, possessed the greatest farmers' banks, and controlled the distribution and the sale of food. This authoritarian control extended even to the ownership of vast poppy-bearing lands. The sale of opium, prohibited under the Yi monarchy, increased twenty-three times between 1931 and 1940.

Meanwhile the peasants, like peasants elsewhere in Asia, were sharecroppers or cash-rented parts of the large estates. Few hospital services were available. Special passports were required, by which a peasant was effectively deprived of the right of travel; and no one could change his occupation without official approval. Shintoism was encouraged under the Japanese; all other religions were frowned upon. Newspapers were heavily censored; highly organized prostitution and a still more highly organized traffic in heroin and opium were employed to weaken the physique of the people. The same pattern that Japan used in Manchuria was used in Korea. In the history of Asia nothing so approaches the authoritarian world of Huxley's *Brave New World*. There was neither freedom of speech nor freedom of assembly. If ten Korean students wanted to hold a dinner party in Seoul in honor of one of their members, a permit had to be secured, and a Japanese official arrived at the party to sit with the group and take notes of the conversation. No Korean was allowed to draw money from the bank without the authorization of government. Discrimination against Korean workers produced a situation in which a Korean would receive one yen a day for the same work that a Japanese did for two yen. It was inevitable that Korea should have been caught up fatally in an atmosphere of nationalist revolution, the hatred for the Japanese so intense that it could never be disguised. It was also fatally inevitable that the parties in Korea should suffer the fate of all secret parties and be continually at odds. No real democratic alliance occurred till February 1946, and by this time the revolutionary heroes, Kim Koo and Syngman Rhee, had outlived their usefulness.

A previous alliance had occurred in 1932, when the provisional government broadened its base, but already it was becoming evident that the founders of the revolutionary movement were losing contact with the people. It was decided to work for independence along two entirely dissimilar lines. Dr. Syngman Rhee was to approach the League of Nations and make a final appeal to the League members, in the hope that the solution of the problem of Manchuria would introduce a solution of the problem of Korea; but in spite of the strong representations of the American Secretary of State, Mr. Henry L. Stimson, the Manchurian issue was never faced, and Dr. Rhee returned to become president of the Korean Commission in the United States. Kim Koo took charge of the illegal terrorist organizations based in China and largely financed by the Kuomintang. Nothing could be more dangerous. Dr. Sun Yat-sen had said: "It is comparatively easy to revolt against a single invading power, but how can one revolt against a plurality of powers?" The case of China, which fought or attempted to fight during the last fifty years against the Japanese, the French, the Russians, the British, and the Americans, and even for a short space of time the Portuguese and the Germans, offered an example that has never been witnessed elsewhere; entirely different from China were the fates of India and Indonesia, both occupied by a single foreign power. But the revolutionaries of Korea were hoping, as the price of Korean independence, to accept the influence of two friendly powers, China and America, whose friendship could not be calculated. The almost inevitable consequence was the introduction of a third power —Russia. But in order to overthrow the influence of Japan, there can be no theoretical advantage in admitting the influence of Russians, Chinese, and Americans. It was true that Hessians and French brigades had taken part in the American War of Independence, but neither the Hessians nor Lafayette possessed political power equivalent to that of modern armies.

The situation could hardly be worse. The division of the country into parts was fatal for the development of any kind of national resurgence: for the old split continued, and one cannot divide and rule a modern industrialized nation without bringing chaos. Like Manchuria, Korea was a heavily industrialized state in 1945.

A new working class had arisen, with an inevitable sharpening of nationalist temper. Even if the Japanese had not sometimes allowed their arms to be captured by Korean nationalists, the *means of revolt* were already in the hands of the Koreans. In Manchuria the heavy industries were removed by the Russians; in southern Korea at least they remained. The Koreans were faced with a situation that has no comparison in the Far East: the means of revolt were available in the shape of weapons and an educated working class, but the split was so deeply ingrained in the political shape of the new state that the means could not be employed. There could be no nationalism under a foreign military government, whether it was Russian or American; nor could there be real representation. "Korean economy," said General Hodge, "cannot develop without free communication between the two zones." A more brutal, and perhaps more necessary, verdict was offered by Dr. Arthur Bunche, who was dispatched by the State Department to head a mission of inquiry. He said: "South Korea faces the live threat of reversion to primitive conditions of life based on crude farming, forestry, and fishing." It was more than a threat; it was a description of what had happened over large parts of northern China, eastern Russia, and the states of southeast Asia during the war. The irony lay precisely here: on the verge of becoming great industrial nations, the states of Asia were first transformed into primitive farming communities.

It was not wholly the fault of the Americans, but American inexperience was to pay a costly price in Korean administration. The people were starving; there were no detailed policies worked out beforehand; American Military Government ordinances were continually changing. General Arnold issued "requests with the force of orders." Suppression of popular opinion had hardly been greater under the Japanese. There was a serious lack of trained technicians, the rolling stock had deteriorated, and the highway surfaces had suffered from neglect. Coal, hitherto imported from north Korea, was no longer available; the Korean peasant began to cut down the forests. Korean lawyers and judges who had acted under the Japanese were retrained, because in General Arnold's words "they were pledged to refrain from politics for six months." In February 1946 the American Military Government promulgated the famous Ordinance Number 55 which effectively destroyed any hope of creating live political parties, though in the same month the forces of the Republic were strengthened by the creation of the Korean Democratic National Front, representing the Korean People's Party, headed by Dr. Lyuh, the Korean Federation of Trade Unions, the Korean Farmers' Union, the Korean Communist Party, the Korean Youth Alliance, and the Korean Women's Alliance, altogether representing nearly three quarters of the Korean population. The Korean Democratic National Front also represented the forces of the famous religious organization known as Chun Do-kyo, or "The Doctrine of the Heavenly Way." This huge religious organization had taken a major part in the great revolt of 1893 when the religious revolutionaries marched from Chempulpo Bay to Seoul. The Emperor of Korea was forced to demand help from China. The help was given, but the Japanese saw their opportunity and invaded the country; yet the religious movement survived, obedient to the twelve principles of the founder. These twelve principles are in many ways similar to the principles outlined by other Asiatic revolutions and included the belief that "heaven may be obtained in this world, and belongs to this world, and men must fight for heaven." The battle cry of Chun Do-kyo was "The destiny of the whole nation—the three thousand li of mountains and rivers—depends upon the doctrine."

Nearly all foreign interference in the internal politics of states is tragic, but interference by the Russians and the Americans in Korea was more tragic than most because it came just at the point when the Koreans believed their independence was at hand. The dividing line between Russian and American influence in Korea represented the frontiers of two entirely different conceptions of life; there were even signs that the Russians and Americans were forming spheres of influence radiating from Korea—the Russian sphere including northern Korea, Manchuria, Inner and Outer Mongolia, Chinese Turkestan, most of China north of the river, and some south of the river, and the Kurile Islands. Against these huge empires there was balanced a complex consisting of southern Korea, Japan, the Philippines, large areas of China south of the river, and a host of islands in the Pacific. It is significant that not China, but the "small dagger pointed at the heart of Japan" was the place where these two powers confronted each other most nakedly.

On October 16, 1945, General Hodge proclaimed that "the military government was a provisional government established by the United States Army under direction of the Commander in Chief, by which the Allied powers will govern, guide, and control Korea south of thirty-eight degrees north latitude during the transition period between a state of Japanese domination and the establishment of a democratic government of the people, for the people, and by the people." The last phrase could hardly be reconciled with the earlier announcement; no military government has ever been known to rule democratically, or even to understand democratic rule. The examples of the Allied governments in Germany were perhaps less propitious than the examples in Korea; but both celebrated the same final fallacy—by definition a government backed by armed foreign forces cannot be democratic.

If the situation in southern Korea was bad, the situation in northern Korea was worse. A Russian military government was seeking the same advantages that the American Military Government was seeking: political long-range control against the day of evacuation. From Heijo, the capital of northern Korea near Manchuria, now known as Pyongyang, Russian ships could be seen in the harbor exactly as in 1905 during the Russo-Japanese war. Then the Koreans had hoped for a Russian victory, but as the struggle continued, sympathies turned toward the Japanese. "The conduct of the Russian troops angered the villagers. They oppressed the people, mistreated their daughters, and took the oxen." So wrote Kim San in the biography he compiled for Nym Wales. The same disregard for the country followed the Russian's second invasion. The communists received at last the power that had been denied to them for so long by the Japanese; but it was given with armed backing. A secret police was introduced; the Russian commander acted toward the Koreans with the same lack of knowledge of Korean history that distinguished the Americans. Yet the communists possessed one advantage over the rightist political parties in the south: they possessed an instinctive and theoretical knowledge of the forces at work among the peasantry. In the November elections the communists failed to win all the elections, which were won by 1,753 nonpartisan members, 253 Chun Do-kyo members, 351 members of the Democratic Party, and 1,102 Communist. Representation under these conditions suggests far less collusion with the occupying power than might have been expected. The American-controlled elections were less convincing. Out of forty-five seats in the Korean Interim Legislative Assembly in the south, thirty-eight seats went to members of parties affiliated either to Kim Koo or to Syngman Rhee, and two of the three representatives for Seoul itself were well-known collaborators.

Everything that can be said in indictment of the south may be equally said of the north. An investigation by the Korean Democratic Front issued in Seoul on November 1, 1946, admitted that the strikes in the south were caused by communist agitators, but they were not the only cause:

Granting the present affair has been caused by agitators, it is beyond imagination that the people would dare rise in revolt at the risk of their lives unless they were driven to do so by the difficulty of livelihood and tyrannical oppression which they can no longer endure or tolerate. In all parts of southern Korea all the right-wing terroristic gangs have been mobilized, and in collusion with the police they are comitting violence, massacres, arrests and imprisonments as they please. This resembles a punitive war.

This was not entirely the fault of the occupying power, which behaved with a studied deliberation and a determination to introduce democracy as understood by military minds; there was, however, great negligence. The surrender of the Japanese commander Abe in Soeul was hardly more than a token surrender. General Abe and his entire staff were retained in their posts. There was a strict ban

on fraternization; a curfew was imposed on the occupied cities; the
Americans entered the country as conquerors rather than liberators.
To the Koreans, who had risen repeatedly during the previous forty
years, the occupation had the effect of an anticlimax. The Cairo declaration had stated: "Mindful of the late enslavement of the people
of Korea, we are determined that in due course Korea should become free and independent." The Koreans asked themselves the precise connotation of the words "in due course."

The Koreans had behaved against their oppressors with fanatic
courage. Rising after rising, against almost insuperable odds, had
not blunted their messianic hopes of final freedom. In 1942 the
Koreans on the island of Saichu-do, southwest of the Peninsula, had
risen in revolt, fired the airdomes, killed the guards, and destroyed
the ammunition; but all were executed later. At least eight risings
in Seoul itself were recorded during the Sino-Japanese war. They
fought relentlessly, buoyed up by the hopes of eventual liberation,
and when liberation came there was considerable evidence that they
were being betrayed both by the Russians and the Americans. Once
before they had been openly betrayed; the minute written by President Theodore Roosevelt describes a betrayal that has no equal in
modern history:

To be sure, we solemnly covenanted that Korea was to remain independent. But Korea was itself helpless to enforce the treaty, and it was
out of the question to suppose that any other nation without any interest
of its own at stake would attempt to do for the Koreans what they were
unable to do for themselves. Moreover the treaty rested on the false assumption that Korea could govern itself well. It had already been shown
that she could not in any real sense govern herself at all. Japan could not
afford to see Korea in the hands of a great foreign power. She regarded
her duty to her children and her children's children as overriding her
treaty obligations. Therefore when Japan thought the right time had
come, it calmly tore up the treaty and took Korea with the polite and
business-like efficiency it had already shown in dealing with Russia, and
was to show afterwards in dealing with Germany.

No one before had provided so bitter a commentary on the purposes of modern diplomacy; in the history of diplomatic treason
the Koreans saw themselves as the perpetual scapegoats. They had
reason for their beliefs. Even under the most favorable circumstances, the task of raising Korea from a state of colonial backward-

ness to that of a self-governing and prosperous nation would tax the powers of the most skilled administrators, but was it necessary that there should be administrators at all? The decision to divide Korea into two zones remains inexplicable; the fact that the Koreans themselves had no voice in the Potsdam conference, where the decision was made, should have made the occupation illegal by international law. Yet the marked contrast between the two administrations, one working through the middle-classes and the rich, while the other worked through the overwhelming majority of the poor peasants was too significant to pass unnoticed. The Americans, insisting on "law and order," refused to accept the vast creative potentialities of the common people within the orbit of command —power was taken from the people and placed arbitrarily in the hands of those who possessed weapons of command. The Americans appeared dubious of the capacities of the Koreans to assume administrative positions, forgetting that the British during the American War of Independence had been equally dubious of American capacities to assume administrative positions. It was not only that the struggle between America and Russia was fought at its most naked level, but that the mere fact of struggle between opposing countries on Korean soil prevented any real or decisive evolution of Korean independence.

Mercifully the struggle for Asiatic freedom was not necessarily being fought on Korean soil only. Korea was not in any way the pattern for other Far Eastern states. Indonesia's independence had been proved; India was about to assume full independence; Burma and the Philippines in different ways were promised independence on surer grounds and with more complete guarantees. It was not true, as many commentators said, that if the Allied powers failed in Korea, there would be little reason to hope for a constructive solution of the problems involved in southeast Asia, and her liberation. But there was good reason to believe that the festering nerve spot, the place where two nerves met, might lead to incalculable harm on the whole evolution of democracy in the Far East.

Negligence and ignorance of Korea derived from ineluctable causes. The country had little trade with other nations outside Japan; a sealed province of Japan, visited by occasional missionaries who were only too likely to take sides with the Japanese for fear of being arrested, gave her the unenviable privilege of being as remote from men's thoughts as Tibet. These sturdy farmers, who dress in religious white, and live in thatch-roofed clay houses under the shadow of eroded mountains covered with pine scrub, seemed to be outside history altogether. Yet the same forces that were at work in the southern states of Asia were working here.

The revolt of Asia is largely an agrarian revolt. The Americans held that seizure of Japanese property was "contrary to international law," and no agrarian revolt has been allowed in southern Korea. In the north, however, agrarian revolt on a large scale was in full swing. It was not essentially communist in its origins. Land belonging to Koreans landlords in excess of fifteen acres per family was confiscated. All lands that were not cultivated by the landowners but rented for tenancy were similarly confiscated; and all land owned by shrines, temples, and religious foundations in excess of fifteen acres was confiscated. By Article IX of the Land Reform Decree all debts due to landlords whose lands were to be divided among the farmers were canceled, and by the following article no lands distributed to farmers could be bought, sold, rented, or mortgaged. All lands owned by the Japanese were confiscated outright; and except for the small forests adjoining farmlands, all forests became the property of the North Korea Provisional People's Committee. The unit of government became the village committee elected at mass meetings of farm laborers, landless tenant farmers, and tenants short of land. The move had become inevitable: in no other way could the farmers, who formed nearly 80 per cent of the population, achieve economic security. More important still, the way was open for the formation of co-operatives, with all its endless advantages and its inevitable stresses on Korean life.

A beginning had been made; there would follow necessary adjustments, but there was good reason to believe that with an increase in the crop yield, new adventures in irrigation, and an increase in the cultivated areas, the productivity of Korean soil would begin to show the amazing resources of this country, which until recently was known as an obscure nation on the borders of Asia.

Korea had advantages not possessed by China. Except where the Russians had removed her industries, her industry was unharmed. Enormous investments had been made by the Japanese in heavy industry. The production of coal reached 2,300,000 tons in 1936 and is now reported to be 5,000,000 tons, and new reserves are continually being discovered. Cheap hydroelectric power is available. The Japanese invested in large chemical industries, especially for the production of sulphate of ammonia, used for fertilizers and munitions. In 1938 chemical industries occupied the first place in terms of gross value of production, nearly a third of the total. Meanwhile communications were well developed; the military roads of the colonizers can be used as roads of merchandise under a new dispensation. There is no petroleum, but hydroelectric power can take its place. The difference between high and low tide at some places on the west coast is as great as forty feet; by constructing dams, a new source of electricity becomes available. Korea is rich in mineral ores, and though its yield of iron, lithium, aluminum, magnesium, lead, zinc, gold, graphite, and mica is not of the highest quality, she possesses the fundamental basis for an industrial state. There are close-knit advantages in Korea that might under different auspices have allowed her to become the model industrial state of the Far East, taking the place of Japan.

In time these advantages will return. No other country in the East has so glorious a history of resistance against invasion and tyranny; no other country has advantages possessed by Korea, which has combined the virtues of two distinct civilizations—the Chinese and the Japanese—and has acquired little of their vices. Though new leaders are rising, no one has yet risen among the Koreans of equal stature to Shjarir or Nehru. They will come; but before they come we must expect more revolts like the revolt that broke out recently in Taikyu. Korea is a test case, affecting the future of China and Japan and the Soviet East; but so far there has been only a dismal competition to see which of the two military governments is more inadequate and more disliked.

Chapter 17

Burma and Malaya

THE story of revolutionary Burma followed even in its details the story of revolutionary Indonesia. The same common front arose at almost the same time, and as in Indonesia the leaders were split among those who worked openly for the Japanese and those who fought continual guerrilla wars. Once again there was an armed national army, led by Burmese under the tutelage of the Japanese high command; and once again the Japanese played their hand too openly and found themselves caught in a net of insurrection. Like Indonesia, Burma was a country of many languages but one dominant language; of many religions but one dominant religion. Burma was the only invaded country that greeted the invaders with the spectacle of priests running to the assistance of the "liberators."

Burma's 17,000,000 people speak 126 native languages and dialects and are racially Mongolians, descended from the tribes that once occupied southern China. They are not Indians and were annoyed when the British included them within the Indian Empire in 1824. Political antagonism to India, however, is of recent growth; the revolt of Burma was directed at least as much against the Indians as against the British and the Japanese. The hostility of the Burmese toward the Indians, who formed the middle class, was so great that in 1941 agreement between the two governments curtailed the right of Indians to enter Burma. The Indians were moneylenders from southern India, photographers, skilled mechanics, skilled laborers; seven out of every ten skilled workers in Rangoon were Indian. Capital was largely Indian in origin, coming from the Chettyar moneylenders who demanded returns of up to 36 per cent per annum. For the poor peasants of the delta, there was no recourse until recently except the residual mortgage of his land. The British, who had invaded his country for teak, gave him the ricelands, but these in turn were taken away by the Indians. In three generations the Irrawaddy delta was transformed into one of the largest rice-producing areas in the world, producing before the war a surplus of 3,500,000 tons for export, more than her neighbors Siam and French Indo-China combined. Rich in timber, she exported more timber than all the rest of non-Soviet Asia, and her output of petroleum was exceeded only by Iran and Iraq. There were tin, iron, tungsten, bauxite in the Shan states and quantities of nonferrous metals; she was a richer prize than any country outside China except Indonesia, more compact than other countries in the Far East, dominated largely by wandering Buddhist priests in yellow robes. The Japanese could look forward to an uninterrupted occupation.

If they had played their hands better, the Japanese might have won out. Buddhism was a connecting link. The Japanese government could say openly that Burma was the one country in the Far East most like itself. Burma possessed imperial origins, and its practice of the Buddhist religion, though different from the Japanese, had enough in common to make a superficial understanding possible. Unfortunately for themselves, the Japanese did not exploit the similarities sufficiently; also, their uncouthness was only too evident to the quiet, dignified Burmans.

When the Japanese felled coconuts to get at the fruits, raped women, commandeered all transport, starved the peasants by commandeering all foodstuffs and haulage animals, it was already the beginning of the end. Even though on August 1, 1943, Ba Maw announced to the Burmese Assembly that General Tojo had graciously declared Burma to be an independent country, and though General Iida, the military governor, announced the liquidation of the military administration, there were good reasons for believing that independence and the liquidation of the administration were as far away as ever. A year before, on June 3, 1942, General Iida had invited the Burmese leaders to his house and offered them a vision of independence with threats:

"I am here to tell you that the Imperial Japanese Government will not go back upon the promises made by our Premier, General Tojo, regarding Burmese independence. But to grant it during the war is impractical and unthinkable. Your fate lies with a Japanese victory. After a victorious conclusion to the war, Burma shall achieve her freedom. Burma must be prepared for a long war and mobilize all the resources of the country for war, and those who jeopardize the war effort or refuse to respond to the war needs shall be dealt with ruthlessly by the military."

The speech was amazing for many reasons; the threats were so openly expressed that even those who believed in a Japanese victory were thunder-stricken. Moreover, the threats were so phrased that the peasants were immediately warned against the Japanese; once again, as with the Indian National Army, the Japanese were over-playing their hand. General Iida went on to discuss eventual libera-tion. Freedom would come gradually; railways, customs, and cur-rency would be reserved for the Japanese government for a period of fifteen years. Later the Americans in the Philippines and the Dutch in Indonesia were to practice the technique of slow with-drawal, attempting to retain the governing power in their hands as long as possible.

Among those present at the meeting with General Iida was a young student known as Thakin Aung San, with the rank of second in command of the Burmese National Army. The actual commander of the national army was a Japanese Colonel Minami, known as Bo Mogyo. The army consisted largely of half-trained troops of Burmans, Shans, Arakanese, and Karens: in each regiment there was a Japanese adviser with large and undefined powers. In this army Thakin Aung San occupied a decisive position.

He had come to fame during the student riots in Rangoon in 1936. Short, wiry, sallow, with fine eyes and an oddly commanding presence, in himself he assumed the responsibilities of the nationalist revolution. He had little knowledge, and not very much liking for social reform. His greatest contribution to Burmese nationalism was the decisive cast he gave to it, repeating continually that freedom on paper was less valuable than real freedom, the undisputed fran-chise of the Burmese people. He was a man of sudden impulses and a terrible temper. In 1940 he escaped to Japan with thirty other members of the Dobamma or Thakin Party (Dobamma means master) and helped to form the nucleus of the Burmese Independ-ence Army, later to be known as the Burma Defense Army, and still later as the Burma National Army. Like Bose, he entered into dealings with the Japanese with open eyes, prepared if possible to play one imperialist power against the other, and like Soekarno, he played a policy of pure opportunism, working in close contact with the Japanese until the spring of 1944 when he saw that their reverses in Burma were becoming more numerous. Throughout 1945 he succeeded in swinging the Burmese National Army over to guerrilla warfare against the Japanese.

The Burmese Dobamma has an old history, dating back to 1930, when the Indian Congress decided upon a plan of action against British occupation of India. Burmese envoys attended the Congress —until 1935 Burma had been governed from New Delhi as a part of of the Indian Empire—and there were already groups of university students inspired by the Declaration of Independence adopted by Congress in December 1929. There were other parties already in existence. The Sinyetha, or Poor People's Party, was founded by Dr. Ba Maw, who had the unique distinction of being the first premier under the 1935 constitution, and also the first premier under the Japanese. There was the Myochit, or Patriotic Party, founded by Dr. U Saw, a slow-moving and immensely wealthy Burman from the Irrawaddy delta, who had been educated partly in Calcutta in 1919-20 during the years when Gandhi's non-co-operation movement was beginning. U Saw, who owned a private airplane and represented the interests of the rich rice owners, had taken a small part in the short-lived rebellion of 1930, when Saya Saw had led a vast movement of protest against the dominant power. Saya Saw, known as Galon, after the bird of the Indian fable that could kill snakes, was later executed in Tharrawaddy jail; U Saw thereupon began to call himself Galon U Saw, and to regard himself as the leader of the movement of resistance. He was not a very successful leader. In 1932 he was arrested for sedition; in 1933 he became a member of the Corporation of Rangoon, and the editor of *The Sun,* a leading daily newspaper. During the following year he began his interest in Japan. He flew to Tokyo, traveled through Korea and Manchuria, and was given to understand that in the event of war breaking out he would be given important positions. He wrote a guide to Japan, and returned to Burma, where he was again sentenced to imprisonment in 1937. Twenty days after his release he received the important portfolio of minister of Forest Lands. In 1940 he became premier.

The Burmese were living through difficult times. Riots between

Indians and Burmans were frequent. U Saw openly expressed his fear of encroachments by the Chinese, and when the Generalissimo offered to arm Chinese troops and send them to Burma against an impending Japanese attack, U Saw took good care that the proposed Chinese army on Burmese soil should never materialize. The Burma Road, which brought constant small streams of Chinese immigrants, was also regarded in Burmese government quarters with suspicion. They pointed out quite reasonably that the existence of the road was a threat to the Japanese, with whom they were attempting to maintain friendly relations; U Saw had signed a secret treaty with them during his visit to Japan. In 1941 he visited Canada, New Zealand, Australia, and America, and during the course of his travels communicated at some length with Japanese envoys; on his return to England he was arrested by the British and held throughout the remainder of the war in Uganda as a political prisoner.

Meanwhile the power of the Myochit was declining; in its place there were the rising powers of the socialist federations and the Dobamma, still largely a party of university students. Riots in the oil fields at Yenangaung in 1938 were suppressed with bloodshed; the determination of the students increased, and a freedom bloc of dissident elements, comprising the Sinyetha, the Myochit, and the surprisingly named Party of the Bouquet of Five Flowers, an amalgamation of five parties, began to form a loose association. As usual there were internal stresses; the leadership was divided; Aung San was accused of fascist tendencies; the large-scale dominant united front came into existence only to be abandoned. As the war in the Far East came closer, the general opinion of the Burmese parties seems to have been one of hopeless fatality—the only solution lay in joining the Greater East Asia Coprosperity Sphere, on conditions.

What these conditions were became clearer when in the summer of 1940 thirty Burmans, largely selected from the Dobamma, reached Tokyo and made an agreement with the Japanese to found a national army of liberation. The war had not yet broken out in the Far East; the decision portended a supreme act of insurrection. The Burmese were prepared to accept a Japanese commander in chief and Japanese arms; the seizure of Tenasserin would be the signal for large revolts throughout the country; Japanese loans would be given to the insurgents, and in return Japan asked only for trade preferences and control of the Burma Road. The one-sided agreement, drafted and initialed in Tokyo, was an act of almost senseless despair, for without the eventual Allied victory Burmese freedom would have been as far away now as it was then. But the agreement was decisive. When the Japanese struck, there was already a large army of Burmese nationalists waiting to assist them, secretly trained and often secretly equipped, an army numbering more than 30,000 men who shared the same religion as the Japanese and were officered often by Japanese buddhist priests. Burma fell.

The circumstances of the growth of Burmese nationalism were therefore unlike the growth of nationalisms elsewhere. Nothing comparable to this invitation to an invading army had ever been made before; yet in its final effect it had the same results as in Indonesia—the puppets the Japanese had hoped to use were neither so foolhardy nor so useful as the Japanese had thought. General Iida could say that "the friendship between the Japanese and the Burmans will be perpetuated," but the Burmese peasants were as shocked as the soldiers of the Indian National Army at the rape of Burmese women and the intolerable destruction of property by wandering Japanese soldiers. Japanese economic exploitation was in the hands of the Southern Regions Development Bank. Japanese rule became more stringent the more they protested they were "assisting free Burma" through the premiership of Ba Maw. By 1944 the Burmese Antifascist League was becoming increasingly sympathetic to the Allies, and when the first Allied victories occurred, the Burma Independence Army was split for some months, some deciding to continue helping the Japanese, others deciding against the Japanese. Nothing could have been more heartening to the Japanese than the constant guerrilla wars between Burmans. Aung San sent emissaries to the British in India offering the assistance of his armies not only in securing the internal order of Burma but in the fight against Japan abroad, but Burma was still hopelessly divided; the guerrilla warfare continued for some months even after the Japanese surrender.

Partly it was due to the fact that there are four Burmas; the wild mountains and dense valleys of the north together with the thin tongue that descends to the strategic Kra peninsula, the eastern borders with their thirty-four Shan and three Karen states, and finally the southern plains. There are also unadministered areas in the northeast adjoining Yunnan where the tribesmen live out their almost paleolithic lives. Aung San claims there is a unity in Burma. Such a claim can be no more than a geographic claim, for the tribespeople belong to different ethnographical groups from the true Burmans. The Shans remained loyal to the British; the Burmese remained loyal to themselves after passing through a phase of loyalty to a common Buddhist religion. Burma was the one country that the Japanese might have colonized efficiently; once the colonization failed, the effects were disastrous. The country, held together for two years, exploded and once more assumed its original character, the minority groups seething with unrest.

The changing pattern of Burmese nationalism has not yet come to a stage where it can be analyzed clearly; in spite of Aung San, there is no generally accepted leader who represents the country as Soekarno and Shjarir represent Indonesia. Unlike Indonesia, Burma had the disadvantage of possessing few skilled native artisans—less than 90,000 people were engaged in factory work before the war. Even after the 1937 grant of a Burmese legislature, there was little evidence to show that the elected officials were representative of the people. In January 1947 the British Government announced that it was prepared to allow Burma to choose whether or not it would remain within the Empire; but no outstanding problems were solved by the surrender of power, for the new Burmese government contained the seeds of a disunity, and there were no signs of an agrarian reform. It could hardly be otherwise when the members of the government sprang from such different sources. U Saw had been a rebel premier; U Tin Tut, a brilliant economist, had no fixed political beliefs and represented simply the desire for independence; Thakin Ba Sein, who had been minister of Labour and Communications under the Japanese, represented the Dobamma Party; Aung San alone, in spite of his youth and his lack of any political philosophy, kept the strings together in a single hand. He was unlike any leader that the Far East had thrown up, and most resembled Peron of Argentina. "The Burmese," said Aung San, "will have no hesitation in using force if the demand for independence, desired by all of them, is not met." It was not quite true. There were unprotected minorities, and both the Indians and the Chinese could look forward to the same kind of hostilities that had been meted out to them in Siam, Malaya, and Indonesia. Yet independence had to come. What was disturbing was the absence of any finely wrought political and social philosophy, the failure to write a constitution, the growth of the purely nationalist concept unallied with a social philosophy. Shjarir had said: "Nationalism is worthless without socialism," meaning that nationalism by itself was a destructive force, and only a social program offered constructive forces. Burma might become, and indeed showed every evidence of becoming, a country ruled by a general who was a hero to his people but so lacking in understanding of the farmers that he would fail to introduce the necessary reforms.

Yet there were impressive successes. The demand for independence was met without chicanery. The original Conservative Blue Print, drawn up in 1942 by a group of parliamentarians under Mr. Somerset de Chair, had suggested a reconstruction period of six years under which a British governor would rule; less than three years later all thoughts of a reconstruction period were deliberately abandoned by the British Government. The pattern seemed clear: the British were prepared to leave Burma and India in complete independence, with no attempt to control their political destinies. If the Dutch, French, and Americans had decided upon a similar plan in Indonesia, Indo-China, and the Philippines, the fate of those countries might be more secure. History will almost certainly show that the British political loss was a moral gain; at this hour in the world's history procrastination is neither an asset nor a rewarding theme.

The Blue Print for Burma was followed six months later by a White Paper containing an official statement of policy regarding Burma's future development. By this all power was vested in the British governor until 1948, though the British Government aimed "to assist Burma's political development till she can sustain the responsibilities of complete self-government within the British Commonwealth." But the Burmese, in spite of their lack of unity, or even because of it, had decided otherwise, and Aung San's visit to London in 1947, following the visit of the Indian leaders, won control of Burma's finances and army, and an election for a constituent assembly in April 1947. It was a major victory, complicated only by the presence of two separate communist parties, and fifteen other parties, all of which would seek their own representatives in the assembly.

There were clear skies, in spite of coming storms. Elsewhere in

Asia, the Dutch forbade the export of goods produced within the borders of the Republic of Indonesia, the French continued for many weary months fighting against Viet-Nam, the Chinese were absorbed in civil war, and the Indians saw their country split by communal problems; none of these plagues were visited upon Burma. The future depended upon a young sallow-skinned general who had fought no pitched battles and who had received his rank from the Japanese, a man whom the Burmese trusted fervently and whose greatest merit was that almost without fighting he had assured Burmese independence.

Who was Aung San? Even in Burma little was known about him. He was born in Allanmyo in central Burma, but his schooling took place in upper Burma where nationalist feelings were strongest. He graduated from the University of Rangoon in 1935, pursuing studies in law. Here in the Rangoon University Students' Union, he first showed signs of his coming fame. Still a member of the University, he assisted Thakin Nu, the president of the Students' Union, during the famous 1936 strike; Aung San became editor of the *Oway,* a radical student magazine, and in the following year he became president of the Union. There he was known as a taciturn, strong-willed, and capable president, who seemed to think and act in sudden bouts of violence—a heavy violence continually under control. Some students were afraid of him, others worshiped him. The legend had begun.

In 1939 he joined the Dobamma and was immediately given the position of secretary-general. He took part in the strange mission to Japan and received military training in Formosa, training which was to become useful later against the Japanese. During the Japanese occupation he was puppet minister of Defense with the title of lieutenant general. He was known also as *Bogyoke,* an ominous word meaning leader. In January and February 1945, on the pretext of moving his army up to the front, he toured the places where the soldiers of the Burmese National Army were stationed, and gave secret orders for the soldiers to disperse into the countryside, where-upon guerrilla war broke out against the Japanese. Aung San had at last made contact with the British forces under Mountbatten in India. After the liberation the Burma National Army was incorporated in Mountbatten's army by virtue of an agreement signed with Aung San in Candy, Ceylon, but in fact only a small remnant of the army followed the British—the peasants returned to their native villages, taking their arms with them. Aung San became deputy chairman of the Executive Council of the Governor and finally headed the mission to London that received the promise of Burma's complete independence.

In devious ways, with a frankness and sometimes a rudeness that seemed strange in a political leader, he has carved out a position as Burma's national leader, resembling Chiang Kai-shek more than he resembles Mao Tse-tung, and entirely unlike Shjarir or Nehru. He lives frugally with his wife, who was a former nurse, and has no interest in his family outside the circle of his wife and children— there will be no danger of nepotism; the gravest danger would seem to lie, as in northern China, in his puritanism. He said once: "The man I admire most is Nehru." It was a curious confession, for no rise to power could have been more different from Nehru's than his own. The revolt in Indonesia had begun with the assumption of the presidency by Soekarno, the revolt in India had occurred as the result of a misleading statement by Gandhi and the Japanese ex- plorations of Bose; the revolt in China arose through the gradual accumulation of armed forces by the Communist leaders; the revolt in Burma was brought about by a man so young that he repre- sented the young forces of the country to a degree that existed no- where else except possibly in Indonesia. Aung San the opportunist was changing slowly into Aung San the responsible leader of his country. There were peasants three times his age who called him father. His views were socialist. Here, too, there were likely to be large co-operative farms supported by the state, state industries, an end to exploitation. The land that had been conquered for teak had become the center of the most youthful nationalism in the whole of the Far East, but the mystery of Aung San remained. Alone among the renascent nations of southeast Asia, Burma's leadership had fallen in the hands of a general.

Years ago, Sun Yat-sen said that nothing was so difficult for a colonized country as to obtain its freedom when the colonizers were many. Of Malaya the British could say with a fair show of truth that nothing was so difficult as to give freedom to a country where the races were so many. In Malaya, the sharp pointed knife that cuts across the China Sea and the Indian Ocean, all the races of the East are gathered in a vast melting pot. Here are Sikhs, Bugginese, Atchenese, Tamils, Malayalams, Chinese from four different provinces of China, each speaking different dialects; here are sultanates and ancient principalities surviving from the Madjapahit empire; here are free ports, a great naval base that was never allowed to demonstrate its greatness, and vast resources of rubber, tin, copra, and palm oil. Like Java, Malaya was rich while the war was being fought in Europe. Under those peaceful skies war seemed unimaginable; when it came, it came with unimaginable force.

Two of the greatest events of the revolt of Asia occurred in Malaya; the loss of the *Prince of Wales* and the *Renown* ushered in the new age of Asiatic resurgence, and the Indian National Army was the first Asiatic army after the Japanese to set out against the colonial powers. The importance of Singapore in the whole question of Asiatic unity cannot be minimized. "Singapore," said Jawaharlal Nehru, "may well become the center where Asian unity will be forged, for in future the peoples of Asia must hold together for their own good and for the freedom of the world." It was his first public declaration of the concert of Asia, and it was significant that it should have been made in Singapore. There is no other place in the world where the races of the East are so intimately fused together. Here, in an extraordinary balance, the three great Asiatic races, Indian, Chinese, and Malay, meet on an almost equal footing. And here, too, all the currents of the East meet in a fantastic assemblage of cultures on territories that belonged until recently to feudal princes.

The Chinese and the Indians have both acquired a permanent stake in the country, which is ruled by a small number of Malayan civil servants "of pure European descent on both sides." The large majority of the Indians are coolies on rubber estates, whose allegiance is to Congress; the Chinese are helplessly split between allegiance to the Kuomintang and the Chinese Communists; the Malays owe a double allegiance, first to their sultans and then to the British Crown. Already they are being outnumbered. In 1911 they constituted 53 per cent of the total population; by 1941, in spite of Malay immigration from the neighboring islands, they formed no more than 41 per cent and were already outnumbered by the Chinese, who formed 43 per cent. The number of British residents before the war was less than 1 per cent.

The Malays, like the Indonesians, were mostly tenant farmers, though a few were drawn into minor political and administrative posts. Poverty-stricken, they shared only incidentally in the boom of rubber and tin, which lasted till the early thirties and revived again at the outbreak of the war against Germany. They were the feudal peasantry, living in colorful squalor, too proud usually to accept service in the tin mines, the rubber estates, or the great shipyards of Singapore, though occasionally they could be found in these places. They were content to fish and plant rice and coconut trees, enviable in their beauty and laziness; but even before the Pacific war a rising nationalism was being fostered among them.

In no other country in the Far East had the adage of "divide and rule" been so sedulously fostered. In 1941 there were ten different governmental administrations, six postal systems, and seven sets of customs barriers. Nearly every federated and unfederated state was organized in a different manner, outward power residing in the sultan, political power residing in the British adviser. In a country so peaceful and fruitful, revolution was unthought of before the war. When the war broke out, the hidden springs of peoples' actions were revealed. The silent hostility of the Malays for the Chinese, due to the gradual increase of Chinese financial power and the more frightening increase in the Chinese population, became evident. There were massacres toward the later stages of the war. Chinese kampongs were attacked at night. The Malays openly sided with the Japanese, without any pretence of noncollaboration, and it was not until the inevitable ruthlessness of the Japanese showed itself that they realized they were being exploited. The Japanese fostered antagonism between the various racial groups and arranged a new caste system that placed the Japanese first, the sultans second, the Malays third, the Indians fourth, the Chinese fifth, the Eurasians sixth, and the Europeans seventh. The pyramid of rule was reversed.

By 1945 the pyramid was cracking. The exploitation of manpower in Malaya was reaching proportions that constituted an affront even to the Malays, who began to join the various groups of secret anti-Japanese organizations fostered chiefly by the Chinese. Unhappily, the Chinese were divided and fought among themselves. The MPAJA (the Malay Peoples Anti-Japanese Army), a federation of guerrilla groups supported by British liaison officers flown in and dropped by parachute or landed by submarine, and commanded nearly always by Chinese, began its last all-out campaign to cut Japanese railroad communications through Malaya. These minor guerrilla offensives were successful. Smuggling was becoming a fine art, so fine indeed that some of the most important contributions of arms for Viet-Nam were later dispatched from Singapore. With the end of the war there occurred the inevitable nationalist demands following the formation near Ipoh of a Malay nationalist party under Makhtarruddin, a native Malay and a Moslem. The party, which soon numbered 60,000 members, demanded the right of self-determination, a free and united Malaya, friendship between the three communities, civil liberties, lower taxes, better working conditions, and solidarity with the Indonesian republic. In the early days the Indonesian republic had laid claim to some kind of federation with all Moslem and Malay principalities in the Far East, including parts of the Philippines. But the Malay Nationalist Party was by no means the only party to come to prominence during the effervescent days following the British occupation. There was an Indian Democratic League, loyal to Congress; the Democratic Youth League; a women's federation; the Malayan trade unions. In the face of sultanates and colonial rule, all contended that there should be a legislative assembly elected by adult suffrage.

At the same time other forces were at work. The sultans began energetically to proclaim a program of "Malaya for the Malays." Dato Onn Bin, son of a former prime minister of Johore, advocated through his newspaper *Warta Malaya* an extreme form of Malay nationalism, which found favor at court, since the Sultan of Johore was the most powerful of the Malay princes. The Malayan Union, originally proposed by the British Government, was dissolved. On December 23 the British Government announced a federation of Malaya to be ruled by a British high commissioner in control of defense, external affairs, and with power of veto over the federal legislative assembly. In each of the nine states there were to be legislative councils, with the Sultan formally enjoying the powers he enjoyed before the war, advised by a British adviser, while Singapore was to remain a Crown colony, separate from the Federation. The process of "divide and rule" was to continue, with little excuse except the prevalent excuse of expediency; it was government on behalf of the sultans and the rubber and tin-making interests. The nationalists were too divided to proclaim with any great skill their desire for independence.

It was even questionable whether that independence would ever come about. No other Far Eastern country contained quite such a mixed balance of races. The political waters of Malaya had been stirred, but in the confusion of races no concrete nationalist program had been proposed. The visit of Jawaharlal Nehru in March 1946 gave the Indians a sense of solidarity with awakening India; the Chinese, smuggling arms backward and forward through Indo-China, were growing increasingly conscious of their ties with the Indo-Chinese, and still retained their weapons in hide-outs in the forests. Refused participation in the defense of Singapore until two days before the surrender, they fought well and learned to organize themselves in spite of the widening split between the followers of the Kuomintang and the followers of the Communists. The Indians had suffered grotesquely; after being given positions of honor by the Japanese, they were afterward discovered to be disloyal to the Japanese, and more than 80,000 of those who refused to participate in the Azad Hind were sent to work on the Burma-Siam railway, where they died in droves of hunger, exhaustion, cholera, dysentery, and beriberi.

The revolt in Malaya was sporadic, confused, and generally ill organized; there was no party that represented the interests of all the racial groups. The Chinese Communists by their strikes, the Indians by their assistance to the Azad Hind government, the Malays by their quiet upsurge of nationalism were each fighting the revolt on different political levels and with different aims. Racial riots, which had been fostered by the Japanese during the war, continued into the peace, to confuse the issues still further.

If Korea presents the extreme example of a nation being colonized by three other nations even at a time of native liberation, Malaya represents the contrary example of three nations in a single territory unable to form an agreement, each nation looking to another to protect it—the Indians looking to India, the Chinese to China, and the Malays to Indonesia. Moreover the Communists, working independently of the Chinese Communists, and including a considerable number of Indian and Malay members, appeared to be deliberately attempting to disrupt the economy of the peninsula; and as in Burma the Communist party itself split into two opposing groups, the Three Star group fighting a rearguard action against the One Star. There were evident signs that Malaya was in revolt, but the impetus of the revolt might splutter out.

Yet something remained. Gradually, against all difficulties, a Malayan political consciousness was being formed. The Indians and the Chinese were digging their roots deep into Malaya. Many had left their homes for generations; the most vocal Chinese supporters of the Chinese political parties were men who had never been to China. A local-born population was growing that regarded Malaya as its perpetual home; and there were signs that the power of the sultans was steadily decreasing. It was a time of effervescence, with few high hopes, the revolt almost impossible and fated to remain almost impossible until a greater number of the population considered itself Malayan. A Malayan consciousness was still to come.

Chapter 18

The Philippines

SHAPED like a sickle, the Philippines face Indo-China. The 7,083 islands run from Formosa to the tip of Dutch New Guinea. It is a country of large hills and rocky subsoil, great fertile plains and a population almost as mixed as the inhabitants of the highlands that lie between India, China, and Indo-China. The Spanish conquerors mingled with the native Negritos, Moros, and Malays. Three, or perhaps four, waves of colonizers had come centuries before from the Asiatic mainland, others came eastward from Malaya, and still others may have come from the south. The natives are people who have all the calmness and dignity of the Malays, but it is a calm that will sometimes change suddenly into Spanish ferocity. Handsome and agile, taller than the Javanese, the great majority of the peasants live in raised thatched nipa-palm huts and earn less than thirty dollars a year.

The tragedy of the Philippines is the tragedy of a feudal system that has long survived its usefulness. The mestizos who took the place of the original Spanish conquerors developed a caste system as rigid almost as the Manchus'; for over four hundred years the haciendas have remained as the symbol of feudal dominance, and during the whole of that time the Filipinos have been either in open or suppressed rebellion. There has been on an average one revolt every ten years, but only two revolts—one in 1892 under the brilliant physician and novelist Dr. José Rizal, and the other in 1942, which owed its origin to the saintly Pedro Abed Santos—have come close to success. Unlike the Malay and the Indo-Chinese, the Filipino has fought for agrarian revolution through all historical times. It could hardly be otherwise. The seasonal demands for rice-crop cultivation allow him only three months of actual work in the fields; the rest of the year the Filipino peasant must take on odd jobs, carpentry, river or swamp fishing, back-yard vegetable raising, the dregs of work. He is nearly always in debt. Cash crops like coconut, tobacco, and hemp (for manila rope) are almost wholly in the hand of large contractors or the owners of the large estates; if he sells, he sells at the lowest price. The national economy is geared almost entirely for the export trade, and of every hundred dollars of export trade, ninety-five dollars go to America. The Philippine governments have been proud of their literacy rate, which is the highest in Asia; but literacy alone has not succeeded in giving the peasant the social services he demands. No sound and balanced economy was achieved, no independent middle class arose. For the Philippines, American rule was no more advantageous than Dutch rule over the Indies or the British rule over India. They could repeat Nehru's cry: "They have conquered us, made us servile, taken our weapons away, frustrated us at every turn." Yet though the social services were meagre in the Philippines, they were far more numerous and more efficient than in the Indies or in India.

Mr. Paul V. McNutt has said: "Our businessmen and statesmen in past years allowed the Philippines to become a complete economic dependency to a greater degree than any single state of the Union is economically dependent on the rest of the United States." It was almost true; the prewar economy of the Philippines was based on the production of a few money crops for export to a free American market, and did not benefit the people as a whole. The capital remained in the hands of the mestizos and the foreign holding companies; no attempt was made to give the people a greater stake in the country. A single party, the *Nacionalista,* has ruled over the Philippines since 1907. It began like the Kuomintang with a purely nationalist program and found itself incapable of seeing the future of the Philippine economy in social terms. Ruled first by the quiet and dignified Sergio Osmeña, later by the vitriolic Manuel Quezon, and still later by Manuel Roxas, throughout the whole course of its development it failed to represent the social interests of the community. Being nationalist in origin, it became over the years subject to the distressing illnesses that obviate nationalism elsewhere. Like freedom and like sovereignty, nationalism lives in a vacuum and is sterile unless subordinated to a conception of community. This conception was lacking. When the Japanese landed, Quezon and Osmeña left the islands, but the greater part of the members of the Nacionalista remained, taking positions under the Japanese.

Throughout the history of the revolt of Asia, the revolutionaries have followed a strict pattern. Incapable of defending themselves against the Japanese, they were compelled to form united groups. In Burma, Indo-China, China, and to some extent in India, the threat of Japanese invasion led to a closing of the ranks. The peasants in the Philippines also began to close their ranks. By the end of December 1941 they were holding secret meetings in Manila and central Luzon to plan their operations against the Japanese. Representatives from the Socialist, Communist, Civil Liberties, Labor, youth, and religious parties met and agreed to a common plan of action—armed resistance if arms were available, and unarmed resistance if there were none. The parties had fought between themselves; by the end of February 1942 they formed one party. Like the Indonesians, whom they resembled most, they drew up almost messianic programs, believing that eventual victory was comparatively near and that the testing time for democratic forms of government had come. They demanded as the price of their resistance the complete abolishing of the feudal civilization of the islands; and in one of his speeches at the time Pedro Abed Santos, who advised the United Front throughout the occupation and died in the swamps near Candaba in January 1945, said: "We must have democracy in the villages as the price of tyranny over the islands." The principles of the United Front, stated in the posters that began to cover Manila and Central Luzon, said:

1. We must drive the Japanese into the sea.
2. We must co-operate with the United Nations.
3. Our aim is complete independence, unhampered by American rule.
4. The democratic government we shall establish must guarantee a minimum living standard for all.
5. All puppets, traitors, and collaborators must be exterminated.

These demands represented the will of the people; they did not necessarily represent the will of the Nacionalista, which could occasionally find good reasons for objecting to the last four demands and even to the first. Socialism was becoming a rising force. Several municipalities were electing socialist mayors in 1940. One other party, known as Sakdal-Ganap, was also not represented in the

United Front. It had been founded on a program for agrarian reform by Benigno Ramos, who openly expressed pro-Japanese sentiments and after the fall of Bataan helped the Japanese to recruit a Filipino army. The Nacionalistas who were in office when the Japanese arrived were confirmed in their offices by the Japanese; the party that had ruled since 1907 continued to rule under the advice of the Japanese general staff. The Nacionalistas became puppets. Unlike the government that surrounded Soakarno in Java, they seem to have acted consistently in favor of the Japanese.

In the history of the modern Philippines four names are outstanding. José Rizal, who led the revolution against the Spanish and was executed as a traitor; Manuel Quezon, the first President; Pedro Abed Santos, the founder of the modern agrarian movement; Luis Taruc, the leader of the Hukbalahaps. Of all these the most significant in his power of understanding the peasant movements was Pedro Abed Santos.

He was a man who wrote little and whose influence was manifested within the movement he attempted to create. He possessed nothing of Soetan Shjarir's intellectual force, or of Nehru's extraordinary capacity to see a problem through to the finish. Like many other agrarian reformers in the Philippines he came from the wealthy middle class; one of his brothers was secretary of Justice in the presidential cabinet, another was a judge in the Court of First Instance, and a third was an attorney for the Philippine National Bank. During the last years of his life he was lean and frail, with dark piercing eyes and a short trimmed beard and a high nose, so that he resembled a Spanish cavalier. Like a Spaniard he gestured and spoke in a low earthy voice, and like a Spaniard he was possessed of an almost unbelievable sense of dignity; and in this he showed only too clearly the traits of the Philippine peasant. He said once: "In our present age, what is heroism but to fight for those who have no rights?" He fought the power of the caciques, and whenever opportunity arose he raised his slow, deep, and passionate voice in protest. For him poverty, the exploitation by the landlords, and the terrible apathy of the peasants were the greatest evils. He said: "I am not an advocate of socialism or communism—I am an advocate of human justice." He could see no solution for the plight of the peasants except the peasant co-operatives, run for the peasants by the peasants. He said:

The average peasant family in the Philippines numbers five to six persons. If the head of the house can average twenty cents a day, he is considered lucky. But only 20 per cent of these farmers are readily employed and others are at work only three months out of the year. When they are paid, it is in the form of *palay* [rice in the husk], not cash. When a farmer needs money, say for a doctor or a funeral, he has to borrow from the landlord or the capitalist, at absurd rates, often 20 per cent. If a peasant borrows during the planting season, which is June and July, say two *cavans* of *palay,* at the next harvest time he repays this loan with four *cavans* or *palay.* If he borrows one *cavan* of rice, he pays back by means of five or six *cavans* of *palay.*

There is therefore only one solution of our agrarian problem in the Philippines, and that is better prices for the crops raised by our farmers, tenants or otherwise. Farmers need credit. We must have collective farms, supply them with proper farm tools, permit them to take advantage of modern farm methods, maintain their own stores, supply stations and marketing facilities for the disposal of the crop.

There was nothing in the least extremist about Pedro Abed Santos's desire to assist the peasants. Over all Asia the movement for agrarian reform is the most pressing; but with the exception of certain districts in China the movement in the Philippines was the least successful. The friar lands, the feudal estates, and the estates belonging to the private corporations possessed overruling rights that were denied to the peasant lands; and less than 52 per cent of the peasants possessed their own lands. The Dominicans, Augustinians, and Recollects had come into possession of large tracts of land covered by titles dating from the seventeenth and eighteenth centuries; by the treaty of Paris the United States Government was bound to protect the property of the friars. Similarly it was bound to protect the property of the private corporations and the landlords. By no treaty was it bound to protect the lands of the peasants. At the National Commission of Peasants held at Cabanatuan in Nueva Ecija on July 16, 1939, President Quezon declared:

"The rights of the *kasama* are no less sacred than the rights of the landowners. The landlords must realize by this time that the *kasama* is not a slave. The word *kasama* means partner or associate, and it is as such that the law contemplates him to be. Under the law the *kasama* is almost the owner of the land and cannot be ejected except for causes enumerated in the statute."

The peasant could take little pride in his title as "almost the owner of the land" when there were eighty-three clauses in the statute books relating to the reasons for which he could be dispossessed. When Dr. Karl Pelser of Johns Hopkins visited the Philippines and wrote his monumental *Pioneer Settlements in the Asiatic Tropics,* his indictment was all the more disturbing because it was expressed in purely academic colors:

Tenant indebtedness is desired by the landlords, who use various methods to involve their tenants in debt. One way is to force more advance money on the peasant than he actually needs, or the landlord may compel his tenant to buy clothing from him at exorbitantly high prices. Under the *cantina* system, common in Negros, tenants and laborers are obliged to make their purchases at the landlord's store, which charges more than other local stores. It is no wonder that the *kasamas* rarely, if ever, have a chance to rid themselves of debt, since the landlords are so anxious to keep them in financial dependence in order to prevent their leaving the land.

Pedro Abed Santos was not the first, but he was the most popular of the agrarian reformers, and it was due to the quiet intensity of his own determination that he was able to canalize the peasant movement. He lived simply in a one-story wooden building, where there was little beside a bed, a wooden table, rickety rattan chairs, and huge shelves full of books, the Spanish and English classics, and many in Greek and Latin. His early home life had been pleasant and comfortable. He passed quietly through law school at Manila, where he was a classmate of President Quezon and Vice-President Osmeña. On his way to classes at Santo Tomas he would pass barefoot workers, in torn shirts and trousers, sodden with rain. Like Gandhi he began to read Henry George and Tolstoy, and when the revolution broke out, he was suspected of rebellious tendencies and fled to the hills, where he helped to organize the insurgents. Later he fought the Americans, was captured, tried by court-martial, and sentenced to death. Pardoned by General MacArthur's father, he resumed his law studies, practiced law, served two terms in the legislature, and accompanied the second independence mission to the United States in 1922. He said of himself that he was the servant of the people.

His successor, Luis Taruc, was of an entirely different character.

Short, agile, speaking easily and rapidly, the dark face tanned by the sun, he had been for a while Pedro Abed Santos' secretary. He was born in San Luis, Pampanga, of lower middle-class parents. He completed his high school class with difficulty, because his family had little money; when he went to the university he was never able to complete his course. In 1937, when he first joined Pedro Abed Santos, he began to rise rapidly, becoming general secretary of the General Union of Workers. He was known in those days for his speechmaking and his organizing ability, the swiftness of his mind and the determination to succeed by practical reforms where Pedro Abed Santos had failed by theoretical reforms. He had a brute strength and a brute cunning; it was the first time since the revolution that a leader of this kind had arisen in the Philippines. He was no theoretician. He had none of Mao Tse-tung's brilliance, and nothing whatsoever of Nehru's determination to view the battle as a whole in its moral aspects. Pedro Abed Santos raised his vast audiences to a pitch of intense excitement; but he had never led them to revolt. On December 25, 1941, Taruc came secretly to Manila on instructions from Pedro Abed Santos to mobilize all the resources of labor in Pampanga against the Japanese.

There were difficulties everywhere. The Philippine Government refused to give arms, the Sakdal-Ganap officials were determined to prevent a rising by the peasants. As the Japanese gradually swept over the islands they set about organizing a single pro-Japanese peasant group called the Kalibapi; peasants were compelled to join the group or were deprived of their share of rations. Yet comparatively few joined. As in Java and in some parts of Malaya the peasants continued their village lives without accepting defeat.

The United States High Commissioner reported in 1942 that "as the enemy attacked and invaded Luzon, the mass of the population exhibited a calmness and stouthearted serenity that were quite striking. The people realized that our armies were being defeated, but they faced the situation without recriminations and with the typical self-confidence of an agricultural community reliant on the family and the village system. They adopted their own simple and effective decisions, and maintained an admirable solidarity." Meanwhile the caciques had for the most part abandoned their estates and fled to safety in the towns, afraid that they would be dispossessed by marauding bands of Japanese. Their absence gave the peasants the chance they had been waiting for. For the first time the peasants were masters of their affairs.

Inflamed by the war and the atrocities of the Japanese, the peasants became militant. As in China and Java, deprived of arms, they began to create arsenals of crude weapons—razor spears, clubs, sharpened pitchforks, knives. They raided Japanese garrisons. They murdered Japanese soldiers. By the spring of 1942 they were in a position to take the offensive. A barefoot, ragged army came into being when on the night of March 29 a group of United Front leaders held a secret meeting in a forest near Arayat in Pampanga. At this meeting the Hukbalahaps first received their name and their program, which in its simplest terms was declared to be "war against the Japanese and all oppressors." Luis Taruc was elected chairman, and Castro Alejandrino vice-chairman, of the new peasant military government. The advisers to the government were Pedro Abed Santos and Vicente Lava.

Secret dumps of arms were hidden in the hills and forests. A new peasant military government was vested with large powers, and the peasant soldiers swore pledges that they would fight to the death against the Japanese and for a free Philippines not dominated by American imperialism. Decrees were issued in the name of the new government, with stringent penalties for treachery; for the children and wives of the peasants special arrangements were made, allowing them to call on the government for funds if their fathers or husbands were killed. The armed militia was grouped into squadrons of about a hundred men each. Throughout the whole of the spring, armed groups were sent to the battlefield at Bataan, often by night, to collect the ammunition discarded by the Japanese and Americans. Arms were bought from Japanese soldiers wherever possible; other weapons were taken from Filipino civilians in Manila, from the Philippine Constabulary, from Japanese airplanes shot down over Pampangas. By the late summer the Hukbalahaps claimed they already possessed a fighting force of 20,000 with perhaps 50,000 reserves.

They had a multitude of aims, but their chief aims during the early course of the war were to act as guerrillas against the Japanese and to organize the nonpayment of taxes and agricultural produce to the puppet government under President Laurel. They confiscated outright the lands of collaborationist landlords and divided them among the peasants, destroying title deeds wherever they could be found, though special orders were issued to protect the church lands; collaborators were sometimes shot. By the spring of 1943 regular battles were being waged. The Hukbalahaps have claimed that during the course of the war they fought 1,200 engagements and inflicted 25,000 casualties. When autumn came they were so powerful that the Japanese were describing battles on the islands in daily communiqués. The Hukbalahaps began to build military training schools in the Candaba swamps; and with the military training school went the inevitable political training school, which included courses in Tolstoy, Henry George, Marx, the novels of José Rizal, and the discussions of Pedro Abed Santos. Filipino hatred—the tremendous force of juramentado—was stimulated by the victories of the guerrillas and the fantastic successes of the secret radio stations which broadcast against the Japanese in the name of a mythical Juan de la Cruz. The extraordinary youth of the guerrilla leaders— Luis Taruc was only twenty-six, a year younger than Aung San— gave added impetus to the movement, and the village councils with their autonomous local councils were often served by young guerrilla leaders elected by popular acclamation. The landlord's armies remained; so, too, did the puppet constabulary, strengthened by seasoned Japanese officers. The Philippines offer the same advantages for guerrilla warfare as north China—it is almost impossible to track down resourceful guerrillas among the hills. San Fernando in Luzon was for a while completely liberated from the Japanese. There were months when even Manila was almost completely invested. Raids were continuous. The murder of Japanese soldiers increased each month. The Japanese fought back by offering increasing power to the puppets, but the guerrillas, when captured, rarely gave away the secrets of their positions.

The Japanese failed, as the Spanish and Americans had failed before them, to produce a balanced economy or an independent middle class. Manila suffered more than most towns because it became the center of Japanese rule. Outwardly, prosperity ruled; but in a land that had rarely known starvation, though it had known poverty, starvation began to appear. The wealth of the Philippines was transported to Japan. In an atmosphere of terror, which increased when the bombing raids started, the Hukbalahaps were not always innocent of crimes. Occasionally men were arrested and executed because they were landlords, without trial. Puppets and collaborators were dealt with unmercifully. Some people were killed as the result of personal grudges. Opposition against the Hukbalahaps grew within the USAFFE (United States Army Forces of Far East) guerrillas in central Luzon, who were recognized by the United States Government. The Hukbalahaps, with a more popular following and a greater belief in a democratic party, found themselves fighting two wars—one against the Japanese and the other against the USAFFE, which included a number of Nacionalistas, and whose aims were to maintain the *status quo*. USAFFE was unpolitical and followed the deliberate policy of concentrating on political and military information. USAFFE guerrillas called the Hukbalahaps communists, which was less than a half-truth; Hukbalahaps returned the compliment by calling all USAFFE guerrillas Nacionalistas, which was equally untrue. The war was fought bitterly. A great deal of evidence had been brought forward to prove that there were massacres and assassinations on both sides, and that a reign of terror developed between the two forces. At times the USAFFE guerrillas combined with the Japanese-sponsored constabulary against the Hukbalahaps.

The Hukbalahaps were a popular force and suffered the vicissitudes that attend all popular forces. They were fanatic in their opposition to the landlords, the Japanese, and the Nacionalistas; they formed a united army. They controlled large areas of the islands, but they made no serious efforts to compromise with the middle classes, who would inevitably receive the support of the Americans. The middle classes were not powerful or numerous, but the main strength of the USAFFE lay in the fact that it represented them. The struggle between the Hukbalahaps and the USAFFE was class war.

Yet it could not be helped; this too was inevitable—as inevitable as that the peasants should be the most determined upon a new deal for the islands. President Quezon had spoken in harsh terms of the sorrows of Filipino life. "As he works from sunrise to sundown," said President Quezon of the farm laborer, "his employer gets richer while he gets poorer. He has to drink the same polluted water that his ancestors drank ages ago. Malaria, dysentery, and tuberculosis still threaten him and his family at every turn. His children cannot all go to school, or if they do they cannot finish their primary instruction." It was not only that the peasant was poor but also that his poverty made him politically conscious; he had chains to lose and a whole earth to discover. It was for this reason that the fighting among the guerrillas was so bitter, so endless, and so disturbing.

With the end of the war against Japan the situation was no easier. There would appear to be increasing evidence that Roxas was a collaborator, at least as great a collaborator as Soekarno; and that he was not placed on trial only because General MacArthur deliberately shielded him because of the long-standing friendship between them. Highly placed military officers rarely understand peasant movements. Both Taruc, the Hukbalahap leader, and Alejandrino were arrested shortly after the liberation of the Philippines.

In an article published on July 6, 1946, the date of Philippine independence, Mr. Paul McNutt explained the basis of the offer of independence:

We are already committed to maintenance of naval and air bases in the islands. They are not designed merely for the protection of the Philippines nor even for the defense of the United States. These bases are expected to be secondary supporting installations for supply, repair and staging activities for all our armed forces in the Far East. Committed as we are to a long-time occupation in Japan, to a strong policy in Asia, the Philippines are designed to play a major role in the diplomacy in the Orient.

It is not clear how the Philippines "are designed to play a role" if they have their independence, nor do Mr. McNutt's further statements on the importance of the triangle Manila-Tokyo-Shanghai appear to have much relevance to real power politics unless Shanghai is included within the American orbit; but far more important than the decision to retain military bases was the decision to make the Philippine economy accept parity with American economy. As far back as 1909 the Philippine Assembly petitioned Congress not to adopt free trade on the grounds that "free trade between the United States and the Islands would in the future become largely prejudicial to the economic interests of the Philippine people and would bring about a situation that might hinder the attainment of Philippine independence." The Bell Act, the presence of large American naval and air forces (shortly before the Republic was proclaimed

the United States Army presented Manuel Roxas, as commander in
chief of the Philippine Army, with a gift of $50,000,000 of military
equipment), and the presence of a feudalistic government intent on
terrorizing the revolutionary peasants into acquiescence were not
calculated to assist the revolutionary elements to follow a normal
course; they were calculated to embitter and to sabotage popular
and representative movements, as Taruc continually declared. Section 341 of the Bell Act read strangely:

The disposition, exploitation, and utilization of all agricultural timber
and mineral lands of the public domain, waters, minerals, coal, petroleum and other natural resources of the Philippines, and the operation
of public utilities shall, if open to any person, be open to citizens of the
United States and to all forms of business enterprise owned or controlled,
directly or indirectly, by U. S. citizens.

The act introduced an increasing tariff after eight years of free
trade, during which United States goods were free to enter without
restrictions, with the result that the Philippines could see the future
in terms of continual dumping on a hitherto unprecedented scale.
What terrified the Filipinos was that in effect they were given the
status of Burma in 1936, without real foreign representation, without control of their armed forces, and without complete economic
sovereignty—the "most favored nation" clause had been put to its
complete limit, and the Americans were not observing the two
principles expounded by Anthony Eden:

1. The receipt of economic and financial aid must not result in a
   loss of independence of the country.
2. Any form of assistance given to a country unpracticed in the
   art of self-government must be such as to help it achieve its
   own development.

The peasants, thinking in terms of large-scale co-operatives, saw
that social reforms under these terms were impossible, and co-operatives were almost impossible. Tied to the American dollar for eight
years, then suddenly placed at the mercy of incalculable tariffs, the
economy of the Philippines would be compelled to obey orders from
abroad. No basis for survival on its own merits remained; and
among the peasants at first, and then among the middle classes,

there arose a clamor of objections. On February 8, 1947, the *Manila Chronicle,* which had not previously been noted for any defense of peasant movements stated: "The agrarian system in central Luzon must be changed for the sake of objective justice. We must not serve justice only when there is danger of revolt." Arsenio Lacson announced: "The fires of agrarian revolt are spreading all over the Philippines. The present explosion in central Luzon, manifesting itself in terrifying outbursts of popular anger, is an ominous sign of gathering storm that heralds the approach of more uneasy tomorrows. Unless the government listens to the voice of reason and gives the peasant an even break, real civil war, more brutal and more savage than that which Spain only lately has passed through, will one day engulf us." Though parity was finally accepted by ballot, the revolt was still going on.

During the peasant campaigns that followed the liberation, Taruc repeatedly demanded the enforcement of popular liberties. His five-point plan became, like Mao Tse-tung's new democracy, a form of implicit protest against the government and the policies it adopted. He asked for:

1. Immediate enforcement of the Bill of Rights, especially the right to assemble, freedom from arbitrary arrest, ending of cruel and unjust punishments, trial by unprejudiced judges.
2. Dismissal of all charges against Huks, M.P.'s, and civilian guards alike, growing out of the events of the last five months.
3. Replacement of fascist-minded officials in municipal and provincial governments and military police command in the provinces affected by the agrarian unrest.
4. Restoration of all Democratic Alliance Congressmen to their seats.
5. Implementation of President Roxas's land reform program beginning with the 70-30 crop distribution allowed by law, and leading toward the social abolition of tenancy.

Taruc stated that if these five points were carried out, he agreed to place himself within the law. The principles were closely identical to those followed by other Far Eastern states in process of revolution. The danger was that the government might regard itself as the defender of tenancy to the last, failing to observe the revolution boiling beneath it, and in no way capable of preventing an explosion. It was certain that the explosion would come, and the Western historian, having seen too many revolutions, could only pray that it would come soon—delay would make it sharper, or give the peasants so deep a sense of frustration that the final revolt would be more terrible and more anarchic than anything anyone had imagined.

Long before the present wars an agrarian revolt had very nearly succeeded, during the last days of the Spanish Empire. In histories of the Philippines the Katipunan movement is rarely mentioned, yet for a while over 200,000 of them fought for agrarian reform. They drew up not a constitution but a list of the doctrines that moved them to action, a list that has validity for our own time, because the rigorous simplicity that underlies their code is still in evidence throughout Asia. Like Shjarir, they believed in a concept of freedom founded upon human dignity, but freedom itself was valueless to them unless it possessed social content. This moving document read:

1. We declare that a life not consecrated to a lofty and just purpose is like a tree that casts no shadow, and is no more than a poisonous weed.
2. To do good for some personal motive and not because of a true desire to do good is not virtue.
3. Real saintliness consists in being charitable, in loving one's fellow men, and in adjusting one's every word, action, and deed to right and reason.
4. All men are equal, be the color of their skins black or white.
5. He whose sentiments are noble prefers honor to personal aggrandizement.
6. To a man of honor his word is his oath.
7. Defend the oppressed and fight the oppressors.
8. Think not of a woman as a thing to pass the time with merely, but as a helper and a partner in the hardships of life.
9. Great and noble is he who although born in the woods and with no knowledge except that of his own native tongue is possessed of of good character, is true to his word and mindful of his dignity and honor; a man who does not oppress or help those who oppress; a man who loves and looks after the welfare of his country.

Preach and follow these doctrines, and when the Sun of Liberty rises in the midst of these unhappy Islands, and her splendor sheds everlasting light and happiness upon those united children and brothers of the same race, then the lives of those who have gone and the pains and tribulations we have suffered shall be well recompensed.

These words, first written in Tagalog fifty years ago, were still being recited by the Hukbalahaps in the Philippines. Once again in this revolt that affects all Asia we hear the authentic tones of the American Declaration of Independence.

Chapter 19

The Earth and the Men

GRADUALLY out of the confusing uncertainties of the Asiatic scene, one tendency is becoming clear. The checkered pattern of the administration and taxation of land is moving slowly to a stage where there must be uniformity. As communications become better, and more Asiatics travel through Asiatic countries, the disastrous land policies of the past will change, perhaps more quickly than even the Asiatics realize. In the long history of the East no problem has been so insoluble as land tenure.

In no country in the East is the pattern the same. They range from the vast feudal haciendas of the Philippines, which have remained undivided from generation to generation, to the small and compact systems of family ownership that exist wherever Hindu influence has reached. Unwittingly or deliberately, foreign rule has leaned toward a solidification of existing tenures. The foreigners came to the East at a time when feudal ownership was breaking up and the powers of the princes were declining, but the foreign invaders always assumed without change the powers formerly enjoyed by the defeated princes. When the Spanish arrived in the Philippines, land ownership reverted to Spain: 236 encomiendas were assigned to Spanish aristocrats, and the remainder were held in the King's name. California was luckier than the Philippines; for the vigor and magnitude of the gold rush of the Forty-niners obliterated the land-tenure system existing under Spanish rule. In the Philippines the large estates have continued unchanged to the present day, with disastrous effect on the taos, who found themselves in continual subjection to the hacienderos, reduced to peonage by bond slavery that had no equal in the Far East outside Korea and some of the landed estates in Szechwan. The feudal system of land tenure led inevitably to an economy that was not in the interest of the peasants. Of the six major crops in the Philippines four (coconut, tobacco, Manila hemp, and sugar cane) were grown for export, while only two were grown for domestic use—rice and corn. A similar phenomenon appeared in Malaya, where rubber plantations swallowed the land that might have been used more profitably by the peasants for rice. The history of the Philippines is the history of the uneven balance between the caciques and the obedient villeins.

It is difficult to appreciate the degree to which social distinction and the ownership of large tracts of land went together in imperial Spain. It is still more difficult to understand how such a system of land tenure has been allowed to exist to the present day. The spread of communism in China has been due to the same causes that gave rise to the Hukbalahaps, but in China the picture has been confused by the discriminatory pattern of government control, which exhausts the peasants not only by taxing the produce of their farms but by conscription and services demanded by the government without fee. In Malaya and the Netherlands the rights of the native have been protected only to the most limited extent. In India the complex, ever changing pattern of the zamindari system at least left the peasant considerable latitude; at most he could be deprived of half the produce of his farm, and the Zamindar was obliged to release him from paying the cost of his new working tools. The close-knit joint family system in India provides a palliative against excessive exploitation that is absent in the Philippines, but the principle of hereditary right—the Zamindar's functions could be bought or handed down from father to son—is open to enormous abuses. Under the zamindar system, if a tenant rents his own land for twelve years in succession in his own name, he may rent the same plot continually as long as he pays rent; but the process of acquiring title demands legal documentation that the peasant is not always able to provide. The first of the changes envisaged by Congress is an alteration of the system of land tenure in India.

In Burma, especially in the delta regions of the Bangkok plain, the system of land tenure is more arbitrary still; until recently the Burman peasant was continually at the mercy of Chettyar landlords from south India who had taken possession of the land by foreclosure of mortgages and hired the peasants as villeins. By 1936 the Chettyars, a subcaste of moneylenders, owned a quarter of the 10,-

000,000 acres of riceland in south Burma, their ownership deriving from the poverty of the peasants, who even before the arrival of the Chettyars were compelled to purchase their draft animals, plows, harness, and boats at usurious rates. The Japanese occupation which halted the export of rice and the import of consumer goods and led to an almost complete financial breakdown of the country, at least produced one good result: the Chettyars became absentee landlords who could not demand rent.

Absentee landlords have been the plague of the East from immemorial times. A shareholder of a rubber company in Java living in London owns rights and privileges over Javanese land. In the Philippines the picture is more confusing because the mestizos, who have survived through generations of intermarriage between the original Spanish settlers and the Fillipinos, tend to invest their capital increasingly in America.

In only one country in Asia do a large proportion of the farmers own the land they till. In north, south, and northeast Siam this rule is almost universal; only in the center, in the regions near Bangkok where the nobility have large established estates are tenant farmers common. The history of land tenure in Siam, unlike its history elsewhere, has not been one of increasing encroachment by the nobility or the rich, though the arrival toward the end of the nineteenth century of large numbers of Chinese immigrants has tended to develop an increasing number of large Chinese-owned estates. Yet the Siamese peasant is faced with the burden of continual indebtedness, which can only be avoided by co-operative marketing and by loans at low rates of interest from government banks. *Laissez faire* among the Asiatic farmlands has brought incalculable power, not only to the owners of large estates but to the wandering tribes of moneylenders who infest the whole of the East—Sikhs in Malaya, Chettyars in Burma, Chinese in Siam. In Indo-China moneylending has been a less remunerative profession, for the poverty of the people was so much greater.

The land economy of Indo-China has been ruined by the French, who sequestered title deeds or made claim to properties wherever they could prove the slightest doubt that the titles existed. By 1929 the Crédit Populaire Agricole, modeled on Dutch efforts to bring native cultivators out of their immense indebtedness, contained only seventeen rural banks. The well-to-do Annamite proprietor has benefited by the loans to the exclusion of the small peasant proprietor, who lost heavily with the decline in prices of merchandise and whose co-operative organizations were not assisted by private or public capital. Confusion of tax registers (which are kept with almost unfailing accuracy in large parts of British India and in Java) and the inadequacy of scientific surveying led to increasing poverty; the peasant, once reduced to poverty, had no method of reclaiming his mortgaged land or his supplies of seed and became a wandering villein. Communism has greater roots in French Indo-China than in any other country of the Far East. The reasons are clear. The roots of despair ran deeper and undermined the whole land.

Where there are co-operatives and "factories in the fields," the range of the economy increases; a farming co-operative demands an agricultural machinery co-operative, which in turn demands steel-worker and basketmaker and carpenter co-operatives. If the co-operative region is large enough, it can become self-supporting within wide limits. Co-operatives have given the Asiatics a sense of security and status. Still more important, they offer the individual farmer dignity within an enclosed community.

The pattern of Asiatic industry in the future may tend more to-ward large-scale barter rather than the manipulations of banking interests. The needs of Asia are well defined and can be calculated according to fixed and settled barter accounts. Recent events have shown that barter provides, in the absence of a controlled money economy, a method of solving most of the outstanding industrial problems of the Far East. The exchange of cloth and rice between India and Indonesia is more than a passing phase; large-scale barter between governments may include, as in the Cheribon oil-well agreement, the stipulation that part of the "price" may be paid in the training of students; for ever since the time when America re-voked the Boxer Indemnity Treaty, education has become a com-merciable asset. We are faced with the prospect that Indonesia will sell oil against university degrees and the training of vast numbers of students. Already the Indonesian Republic has declared that at least 20 per cent of the national income must be spent on education.

Agricultural economy in Asia has always been marginal; the small peasant proprietor, who might make more money from pig bristle than from a year's arduous toil in the fields, has been regarded in China as the strongest link in the economic chain; in fact, he is the weakest. The great Hunnanese famine could not have taken place if co-operatives extended throughout the province. To prevent the drain of the soil's wealth, the Chinese Government will be compelled to form large peasant co-operatives, for only the government has the financial and moral power to induce the peasants to form them.

The Asiatic primary producer must be protected and encouraged; there are no great Kansas plains in Asia where large-scale agricultural groups can be formed under private enterprise. The mere configurations of the land, the delicacy of the boundaries, and the lack of capital for widespread irrigation cry out for government control and scientific management. The future guardians of the Asiatic heart lands will not be the feudal owners but the trained agricultural chemists.

Through the whole of Asia commercial agriculture is still largely in the hands of the small producer. When Chu Teh called for an alliance of capital and democracy within the Chinese Communist areas, he was simply demanding an inevitable, and probably permanent, source of increase for the co-operatives, which could return profits to the shareholders against the guarantee supplied by the whole community. Those who say that capitalism is dead under a socialist state fail to grasp the urgent necessity of capital within the structure of industrial and rural co-operatives—there can be no beginning without capital, and no end without the productivity of capital. The Russian co-operatives, relying on state grants, are beginning to acquire the over-all efficiency that results from careful planning; but in the incalculable economy of the East, planning can never be so certain as in Russia, except perhaps in India, where the great plains can assure a certain harvest. China and the countries of southeast Asia are too mountainous, too dependent upon seasonal variations, to offer this certainty. In the future pattern of Asia, the great plain agriculture may be taken over by the government; for the rest private capital will always be needed.

Together with the violent sociological change there goes a violent change in national economy. For centuries China had been known for her exports of tea and silk. Nylon silk has probably announced the doom of all mulberry trees; the increasingly restless West has found coffee a better stimulant to the nerves than tea. The war, by encouraging the search for artificial chemical products, has thwarted two of the largest industries in Indonesia—the rubber tree and the cinchona tree may go the way of the mulberries that once crowned the walls of nearly every Chinese town. Crops traditionally associated with tropical zones can now by careful selection be grown in temperate zones. Meanwhile new crops are rising to sustain the ever increasing inhabitants of India, southern China, and the Indies, whose stunted growth is due largely to their choice of rice as a diet. A change to potatoes might well within twenty years make every Asiatic as tall as the northern Chinese, who live huskily on maize. A careful exploitation of grazing lands would give milk for babies and children—some of the best milk in China came from imported cows driven overland during the war years to Chengtu, which is in sight of the Tibetan border. When Mr. Henry Wallace made his famous cry for milk for all the inhabitants of the world, and was greeted with resounding cries of: "Even for the Hottentots?" the idiocy of unplanned economy became apparent, for the Chinese and the Indians realized that under the guise of Hottentots the Asiatic demand for a higher living standard was being assailed.

The rubber trees planted in Malaya and Indonesia did not grow originally in east Asia, but was found in South America. Sugar is not a native product of Indonesia but was introduced because cheap labor was available to an extent unknown elsewhere. Starvation wages were paid only because the fertility of the Indonesians was itself a cause for cheap labor; but the impact of cheap labor and foreign-controlled enterprises led to an increasing strain on the economy, and thence to nationalism. Nationalism grew in Java from three main sources—the Islamic religion, which could find nothing in common with Dutch Protestantism, the sugar plantations, and the University of Batavia, now renamed Jacarta. This strange alliance was profitable because, as one Indonesian said to me, the greatest forces for change are precisely a fervent religious faith, economic distress, and knowledge of Western technology—in that order.

Even in the self-governing nations of Asia, the unrest is continuous. The excesses of the Hukbalahaps, which even their best friends have been unable to deny, cannot be excused on the grounds that revolutionary intractability is a virtue; but the cause of the unrest is too clear to be dismissed easily as a result of communist propaganda. Communism has little real foothold in Asia, but it is essential to remember that the Asiatic sees nothing very startling in combining the communist manifesto with the Four Freedoms. Indeed, for him they complement one another, and though a dictatorship of the proletariat is meaningless to a Javanese farmer or an Indian peasant, the statement that the worker is entitled to the full value of his work is at least as important as that he is entitled to freedom in all its four manifestations. Moreover, the peasant must measure his toil in the future against industry, he will be coming increasingly in contact with industrial resources, and though he will not immediately derive advantages from them, hospitals, sanitation, and education will no longer be unknown to his children. The communal center of his life may be the nearest market town, in the center of which there will be not the ill-famed headquarters of the police militia but a hospital and recreation center. It may not even be necessary for him to go through the stage of the internal combustion engine industries; employing plastics on a large scale from soya beans, his house prefabricated, he may jump from the stage of physical labor straight into the electronic age. He will have advantages that have been denied to us; he may enjoy the fruits and end products of mechanical civilization without the travail of years of mechanical development. There are tribesmen near Kunming who joined the Chinese air force; they jumped from the paleolithic age into the age of jet airplanes.

The war, which harmed the Asiatic nations at least as ruthlessly as it harmed Europe—an estimated 20,000,000 were killed or died of wounds and disease in China, 4,000,000 in Java, and 4,000,000 in India—hastened the processes by which freedom is acquired. The rapid progress of technological development may not be easily spread over the countries that remain basically agricultural; there may be, and almost certainly will be, concentrations of technological power in the hands of governments. The Ichang barrage and the vast dreamlike industrial plans of the Kuomintang government suggest that the Kuomintang is deliberately attempting to regain control of China through industry. Recent attempts to shed the control, reducing large filatures and sugar plants from governmental to private control, may be indifferent efforts to mask the real character of ownership, which remains in the hands of Kuomintang appointees. If industry remains largely within the financial power of a political party—the Moslems' fear of the Hindus arises as much from religious causes as from their dread of Hindu financial power—it may be used as a weapon of authority, and with it political parties may entrench themselves in power, as in Japan. Hitler's capture of the Ruhr steel magnates was indispensable to his authority. In Asia the dangers are even greater. Unless the heavy industries are completely nationalized, or industrial power is exercised through nonpolitical organizations, the power of the people will inevitably diminish. A political party geared to heavy industry cannot be dissociated from the power that heavy industry employs; the police state follows.

When Shanghai fell to the Allies, American exporters began to plan their exports to China. The rising inflation of the Chinese dollar, the steadily increasing corruption within the government, and the hoarding by the government banks led to a financial collapse; the cost of transportation soared, not so much as a result of communist infiltrations as the inevitable spiraling of labor costs. American cigarettes, oranges, and tinned pork were cheaper in Shanghai than native cigarettes, oranges, and pork produced in villages nearby. The effect was exactly as though Japanese cheap labor, which could compete with the cheap labor of the rest of Asia because it was more highly organized, had returned to disrupt the internal economy of China.

The vacuum created by Japan has still to be filled. Some kind of protection against foreign merchandise would seem to be necessary, and greater governmental control on imports to Asiatic countries is almost certain. No free economy is possible during the transition from an agricultural to an industrial age; the balances are too delicate, the possibilities of unrestricted exploitation too dangerous for unrestricted free trade. The Open Door in China deprived China of her last hope of bridging the gap between two technical eras. The tragedy can be measured in its simplest terms: the peasants in the hinterland gained no advantages from foreign imports. No tractors appeared. The failure of the Open Door can be seen in every remote village of China that remains to this day untouched by the arts of technology. There was no electric light in Yenan till it was brought by the American Army. Yet if foreign capital had been available for the village co-operatives on a large scale, and if regional co-operatives had found some method of raising credit, the industrial exploitation of the Far East would have begun in the years before the war. One of the ironies of Asia is that though lamp bulbs are made in Shanghai, Calcutta, and Batavia, villages within five miles of these towns are without electric light.

Western capital, unless it enters the economy of these new states soon, may never succeed in gaining a foothold. The descendants of Chinese, Arab, and Indian immigrants have already achieved an industrial stake in the future of southeast Burma, and Indian moneylenders who once traveled barefoot in southern Burma have become the presidents of rice cartels. Chinese industrialists tend to have a monopoly of rice and lumber mills in southeast Asia; they possess large interests in Malaya, in rubber, pineapple, coconuts, and kapok, and whole cities belong to them—the richest shops of Malaya are nearly always Chinese. The power of the overseas Chinese may diminish in proportion to their political exuberance, since Kuomintang nationalism is not always acceptable to the renascent nations of Asia—hence the murders of Chinese in Indonesia, Malaya, and Indo-China. But wherever Chinese capital is available, they will have advantages over the West—they have a closer understanding of the new Asiatic states and a greater indifference to the dangers of hard work under tropical conditions. The race is no longer for the strong. It is for those who understand Asia best. We shall fail unless we accumulate a deeper understanding of the forces that have brought the new Asia into being.

Two dangers must be faced: our ignorance and our indifference. We shall not understand the forces that move Indian nationalism by a cultivated distaste for the evolution of Indian politics. These are things we must know, for among these emergent states politics is an expression of a national ethos. Gandhi's mysticism, the strident claims for Pakistan, the legends that have grown around the names of Nehru and Prakash Narain, concern us more than the results of the Polish elections or the appointment of a new premier to France. We tend to look westward, forgetting the tide of the East and the clamors of the Asiatic millions. We can no longer afford to regard a drought on the Yellow River that kills a million Chinese as of no importance to our lives; the Yellow River is a day's walk by airplane from San Francisco. Ignorance and indifference are cruel weapons that cut their users. They are more dangerous now because Asia is at our gates, hardly more than a stone's throw away; and if our indifference arises, as it sometimes does, from a kind of inferiority complex before the vast wealth of Oriental traditions, then it is less excusable—we have everything to offer Asia, and they have everything to offer us.

Three dangers must be faced by the Asiatics: the danger of an unrestricted rise in population; the danger of political or military command over industry; the danger of introducing social programs that do not represent the demands of the Asiatic masses. To the West, still awakening from its stupor, the vast potential increase of Asiatic populations is one that should make for quick action—nothing is more certain than that by the end of the century the population of Asia will be at least twice the population of the rest of the world put together. It is too early to calculate the effect that birth control may have on Asiatic nations, but there is little reason to believe that the peasants will accept it enthusiastically. Traditions and the farmer's livelihood tend to convince him in the belief that a large progeny is a blessing, and fertility never a curse. Technology may solve the problem for many generations to come by the adventurous opening out of all hinterlands; the Indonesians have already made plans for government-controlled emigration to Borneo and Sumatra from Java, and in Bengal the marshlands are being made safe for agriculture. Any picture of the future Asiatic world must take into account a natural rate of increase of births, without advantage of birth control, a rate that will increase at compound interest when the full effects of modern sanitation and medical progress are known. The shape of things to come includes an Asia so overwhelming in population that Europe in comparison will become a deserted island.

Though eight years of fighting, beginning with the Japanese attack on China in 1937, left Asia breathless, the prey to widespread diseases, starvation, and economic ruin, she is arising now with prodigious force. The leadership of Asia is passing from the hands of its legendary leaders into the hands of the students who were attending classes when the war began. Nothing is so necessary as that on American and British soil there should be built up universities for these Asiatic students, with engineering, agriculture, and the social sciences the major courses in the curriculum. One of the more curious mysteries of our contacts with the Far East is that we have not realized the immense good will which would flow to us if we built universities in the West for Asiatic students. Mr. Bevin's "Bevin boy" scheme is clearly insufficient. What is needed is something far more comprehensive and adaptable to the needs of Eastern students. There should, for example, be a University of the East—the name has been suggested by Mr. Henry Luce—in California, and another in the English Midlands; in these universities Eastern students should learn the technological and social sciences—precisely those sciences which have brought greatness to the West, and they should not leave England or America without a knowledge of our history, for as Shjarir has observed, the Eastern student finds the greatest difficulty in understanding our motives if he does not know our history. Meanwhile the economic and social problems of the Far East are of such a scale that there is needed immediately a concentration of all available forces to study and assist the development of these new nations. Palliatives will not help; what is needed is a long-range plan of support on a scale immeasurably greater than any hitherto undertaken, because the populations involved are greater than any hitherto envisaged. Greece, Turkey, and Hungary fade into insignificance in comparison with the rising tide of Asia.

The greater part of the Asiatic earth is still unplowed, the greater part of the Asiatic minerals is still undiscovered. If there is to be peace in Asia, it is to our interest that we should help them to plow their earth, discover their minerals, train their students, and see that the age-old feudal anachronism of land tenure should come to an end. Ultimately our interests lie in the earth and men of Asia—and the men are all peasants.

Chapter 20

The Revolt of Asia

WHAT are the chances that the revolt will be successful in the sense that it will bring the people of Asia into the community of great powers and along the road of the Four Freedoms?

Inevitably, much depends on the course of events at the present time. The seedtime is now. Small errors committed this year may become magnified next year; every decision made now is frought with danger. Liberty, democracy, the two undefined and miraculous words that stare down at you from the placards of half the streets of India, China, and Indonesia are no longer words with sharp, critical definitions; they have belonged since 1789 to a new historical mythology. Yet they are useful and necessary; they can inflame, but they can also point to a basic solution of the system of government. They have tragic overtones. Translated into Asiatic languages, they may have significances that are denied to us—they may mean more or less, but it is certain that they are deprived of their Western significances, and they are measured in terms of the existing concepts of the young nations now rising to power.

Yet some things at least would appear to be clear. It is no longer true that the success or failure of the governments of the world depend only upon the rivalries between the U.S.A. and the U.S.S.R. A new emergent concept of government, more closely related to the Fabian system in England, is rising in the East.

The Asiatic states are not yet rivals of the West; they are too young, and in their forms of government too experimental, to offer a challenge to the West. That challenge may come if the West fails to take account of their implicit desire for independence; and if this should happen, the West would have forfeited whatever leadership in the affairs of the East it has ever possessed. Darkly suspicious of all imperialisms, the people of Asia have as much to fear from Russia as they have from America, Holland, or Britain. They would prefer to be left alone to work out their governmental system, but increasingly they desire technical assistance—not to exploit their manpower but to exploit the natural products of their soil and earth. In every village of the East the revolution is making its demands on men; a new consciousness has arisen; the lowest coolies and the greatest princes are pledged to reform. The hungers must be assuaged, the people must be given a new dignity, the will of the people must be made representative, and the old monarchic and colonial systems must be destroyed; and what is surprising is not that it should have come at this time, but that there should be so much unanimity in the minds of the Asiatics upon the methods by which reform must come about.

From now on Asia is one and must be regarded as one. It is no longer possible or desirable to view the Asiatic countries as separated from one another by centuries of opposing traditions. The old village patriarchies of China, the caste systems in India, the logic of the Indonesian adat remain, but they are pared of their most harmful qualities; and there is more in common between a prince of Bali and a ricksha driver in Peking than between any Asiatics and Europeans. The movement was inevitable. The first signs of it came at the beginning of this century with the dawning collapse of China, the Boxer rebellion, and the determination of the Balinese to surrender by suicide against the Dutch invaders. Normally the movement might have taken a hundred years to flower. Later ages may view the Japanese occupations with their merciless techniques of supression as a merciful quickening; under the war machine of the Japanese, exploitation reached its height; yet if the war had lasted another year, the determinations of the Asiatic people under their control for independence might have been poisoned at the source; there might have been no intellectuals, no engineers left to guide the people when war came to an end at last. In this sense history has fought on the side of the Asiatics, and by the road of oppression they have come to their place in the sun.

The greatest danger for peace is that we should disregard their rights. Obsessed by fear of Russia, we tend to forget that the Asiatic half of the world has sent in its bill for settlement—we have done nothing to repay them for three centuries of imperialism. In man-power and resources they constitute potentially the greatest menace imaginable to the peace of Western civilization, but it is a menace we have brought on ourselves. The people of Asia refuse to be sub-ject any more. They demand their most elementary rights and will continue to demand them; and as long as the 75,000,000 of Indo-nesia and the 100,000,000 in Communist-held China are forbidden to exercise their rights in world councils, we can hardly expect them to show gratitude while we continue to assist those who are opposed to them. The Asiatic peoples have demonstrated their power, and if we fail them now, we shall be in danger of losing their minimal respect in the future.

A new leadership has emerged in the East. Their revolutionary record has been one of progressive success. In India, Communist-held China, and Indonesia the blueprints of the revolution were formed on the basis of the American War of Independence. Soetan Shjarir, Chu Teh, and Jawaharlal Nehru have all pointedly indicated that they owe their success precisely to their understanding that in Asiatic time they had come to the stage which, in American time, is represented by the Boston Tea Party. Their slogans, their speeches, the particular form of government they envisage, their relations with foreign powers, their desperate search for allies, and their impulse to create a new kind of nationhood—all these spring from motives that were more apparent in America during the Revolution than in France or Russia during their later revolutions. Like Jeffer-son, they realize the intractabilities of extremes, and that an extrem-ist government of any kind introduces by its very existence an entirely opposite extreme. Singlehanded in 1927 Chiang Kai-shek created the Chinese Communist party, which rose from 3,000 mem-bers in 1930 to more than 2,000,000 in 1940. China would have been a happier place to live in if the Whampoa reaction had never taken place; for it was the reaction that produced the Communists. Tan Malakka has failed in Indonesia for the same reason that Mao Tse-tung has succeeded in north China. Those who offer dignity, food, and stable government will always succeed; those who offer violence and instability and refuse to take into account the traditional graces of the Asiatic civilizations will fail. The splendors of the Madjapahit empire may be forgotten or buried in mangrove swamps, but no

Russian *diktat* on religion or customary rule can succeed in the face of the extravagant belief of the Asiatics in the value of their traditional customs. Adat remains, more powerful than nationalism or the urge toward independence. There are gods and laws that must not be defiled; the tragic graces of the East remain to temper all special pleading. To an extent unbelievable in the West the scholars, the priests, and the wise still rule. Character counts more than native cunning; the grapevines speak louder than published words.

The emergence of the new leadership in Asia presents an extraordinary problem to the West. In Europe as in America the highest officers of state have been offered power as a result of their party affiliations. This has happened also in Asia, but more often men have rocketed to power because they fulfilled a necessary historic mission at a time of revolutionary emergency. As in revolutionary Spain, a carpenter and a blacksmith may assume command of armies, but the leader of the Spanish Republican government was a scholar and an internationally famous surgeon. So in Asia, the scholars have been dominant on the revolutionary governments. Jawaharlal Nehru is known even in the West for his historical writings, but it is not generally known that he is an accomplished poet in his native Kashmiri, or that he has made a particular study of Buddhism in Ceylon. Mao Tse-tung possesses an omnivorous knowledge of history, a subject to which he has dedicated himself since his thirteenth birthday, and he is famous in China as a poet in the classical wen-li tradition. Soetan Shjarir at the age of thirty-seven had produced seven books on political economy. Abdul Azad, the Moslem President of Congress, is known from Morocco to the Philippines as a commentator of the Koran. Wang Chung-hui's treatises on law have established new principles. The list is endless. In the West few scholars have power; in the East scholarship is still revered as it was revered in the past, the tradition remains unchanged.

It would be the greatest tragedy to assume that the revolution of Asia is led by freebooters or storm troopers, or to believe that because the revolutionaries demand their independence, they are necessarily extremists. What is true of Washington cannot be untrue of Shjarir, Soekarno, Nehru, Ho Chi-minh, or even (in as far as his agrarian revolt represents the will of the Chinese peasants) Mao Tse-tung. Of all men from the West who are revered in Asia today the name of Washington is uppermost. There can be no government without independence, nor can there be any hope of a gain in friendship if the Western powers continue to bargain for a settlement, like divorced wives. There are no Renos in the international marriage market, and marriage must be bought at the dearest price —true friendship.

The East faces us with its challenge. Already in embryo we can foresee the shape of things to come—the overwhelming manpower and resources placed under the control of an Asiatic bloc. Asia for the Asiatics has come to stay. The Japanese militarists and the Atlantic Charterers have given the impulse for revolution, without being conscious of the effects of their words, which were taken, as usual in the East, in their most literal and finite sense. Since Asiatic nationalisms spring from different causes than our own, it is all the more probable that they will not regard independence as an end in itself. Having achieved it more easily, they will value it lightly; and the Asiatic bloc will be more powerful than the individual Asiatic states. In this bloc the India-Indonesia axis, rather than China, will play the dominant role.

The present leaders of Asia are conscious that it is a race against time. There can be no government without independence, but there can be no stable democracy without education; hence their intense efforts to raise the standard of literacy. Speaking of Congress plans for mass education the day before he became vice-president of the Indian Council, Jawaharlal Nehru told me: "If we can educate the Indian people sufficiently during the next five years, we can save India for peace." In Kalgan and Yenan in Communist-held China I had seen during the previous month the prodigious efforts of the government to teach the oldest and youngest inhabitants to read. Everywhere you went there were night schools where grandfathers and granddaughters sat side by side over the Chinese characters. Technical training has government priority. Even with inadequate facilities available to the Communists, fighting continual defensive wars against the Japanese and the Kuomintang, education held priority only second to the army. Again and again in his speeches Soetan Shjarir has spoken of the value of education, insisting that every village council strive to banish illiteracy *in a single year*. The main problem is still illiteracy, but technical competence and a greater knowledge of the principles of democracy and administrations are also desperately necessary. In capacity to give them these skills the Western powers have advantages that are not possessed by Russia—we know Asia more intimately, have sources of information denied to the Russians, and have longer (and more open) contacts. For all the effort we make in offering them these skills, we shall be repaid a thousandfold. Loans may help, but skilled technicians help more; and once the battle for literacy is over, we may expect to find the Asiatic more politically conscious than ourselves.

The major task of our generation is the understanding of Asia, for Asia represents potentially the mastery of the world in manpower and resources. We, who are accustomed to think of power precisely in those terms, forget that the riches of the East are as inexhaustible as they were in the times of Columbus. It is true that the mineral deposits of China are less than we had expected, but Indian steel and the unknown elements in the soils of Borneo and Sumatra may yet change the power configuration of the world. Burma's wealth of bauxite is still unexplored. Kuomintang China, financing its war on the export of tungsten and wolfram alone, showed the incalculable power of mineral deposits in the modern Asiatic world. No one has dared to dream up the number of oil wells that have yet to be tapped in Sumatra and Borneo. The East has it in its power to redress the mineral losses of the older world. Meanwhile, the Asiatics themselves are extremely conscious of their potential power, a theme that recurred continually during my talks in India and China last year. "We are self-sufficient," said Nehru, "on a scale of which we hardly dreamed, except in rice—and that was only because we have been suffering temporary drought and because the British mismanaged the crops of Assam and Bengal, and took it all to feed the troops." Chu Teh turned proudly to the Yenan arsenal and asked how much of the weapons of war against the Japanese were produced there; then answered his own question: "Nearly all, except those we have taken from the Japanese." The Burmese campaign should have taught us that the Chinese peasant has an enviable aptitude for mechanics, and nothing was more heartening for the future of Asia than the spectacle of the Singapore Naval Base before the war, where Malay, Chinese, and Indian mechanics worked in harmony. From a patriarchal agricultural civilization the East can jump fully armed into a democratic mechanized age, retaining much of what is valuable in the older and more graceful civilization that overlaps into our own times. Anachronisms may remain; the power of the Javanese princes and the Kashmiri pundits is retained in an age when the common man comes to his final triumph.

The prodigious momentum of the revolutionary movements in the Far East have blinded us to their true worth. It took the American colonies fourteen years (1775-89) to establish representative government; it was forty years later before political democracy for the white male population was finally realized. Even so, the patterns of American government have become confused, and the legislature is not yet entirely divorced from the executive. In Indonesia the government was formed and functioning within three months of Japan's defeat in all the territories of the Islands, and within less than eighteen months a communist uprising was quashed, Dutch and British armies were fought to a standstill, and peace was signed with Holland. The judiciary is independent of the executive, and a vast program of education is under way. No other Asiatic state has achieved so great a triumph. "We are the servants of the people," said Soetan Shjarir, "and what the people order us to do, we shall do. But let us first take to education and learn how each one of us must learn to govern himself, and through himself the community. In this country all men shall have equal rights; there will be no great riches and no poverty; we shall stand or fall together, as brothers."

Meanwhile, the boundaries of Asia are continually increasing. The revolt that began in Bali and Peking has spread to the Atlantic. Another scholar-leader, El Fassy, has raised the flag of independence in Morocco and is determined upon a program that differs hardly at all from the program outlined for the Republic of Indonesia. "There must be independence and democracy—the people must govern themselves by secret ballot and open treaties openly arrived at among themselves. And the French must go." The warning has been heard in Paris, where immediately after the end of the war with Germany orders were given for his release from the prison camp in Tetuan.

The triumph of Indonesia has given impetus to the movement for independence in India and for democracy in China. Early in 1944 Sun Fo, president of the Legislative Yuan and son of Sun Yatsen, said: "We have already spent sixteen years in political tutelage, yet there is not a single councilor of the hsien People's Political

Council or a hsien administrator elected by the people." Indonesia
proved, though no proof was necessary, that the political consciousness of the Asiatic peoples could be awakened without the need
of the monstrous machinery of tutelage. China did not deserve her
Kuomintang dictatorship, nor did India deserve to be administered
by a succession of viceroys in council. Yet both were unwilling
victims of their own philosophies. Gandhi's nonviolence, the traditional Chinese incapacity to think outside the walls of a single family
unit were proved to be weaknesses; the greater virtue, and the
greater historical necessity, lay in struggle. The Chinese Communists, who alone of the Chinese governments since the short-lived
presidency of Sun Yat-sen, had given effective leadership to the
peasants, did not proscribe the teaching of Confucius, but they were
relentless in exposing its feudal weakness; Chiang Kai-shek will
quote from Mencius: "It is necessary that the father be obeyed by
the children," and on such slim fabric find excuses for eternal tutelage. With better reason, and more profound philosophy, Mao Tse-
tung will quote the Confucian *Book of Songs* where the community
of the peasants is celebrated, or else the ageless adage of the Chinese
people that "all men are brothers." Nations are built, come to flower,
and die in the names of these simplicities. Can we hope that "freedom" and "democracy" will perform the same miracles?

What is certain is that freedom and democracy in their Asiatic
connotations will differ profoundly from our own. For the moment
they are ours, borrowed from the charter signed in mid-Atlantic but
well-worn since the days when the Greeks and British fathered
them. But once they are translated into Eastern terms they lose the
vagueness they have acquired in the West. In Malay, democracy is
pemerintah rayat, which can mean only "government by the people." The Chinese *min-tzu* means the same thing, and was so used
by Sun Yat-sen; but it has acquired already a theoretical connotation. Freedom is more difficult to define in Asiatic terms—*swaraj*
means "self-rule" to the Indians, and *merdeka* has the violence of a
battle cry to the Indonesians—the old warriors went into battle with
this cry on their lips. And this perhaps is what might be expected:
the Indonesians were more rebellious and conscious of their former
empire than the Indians, their symbol a rampant bull rather than
the unmoving spinning wheel of the Congress Party.

Today, when democracy is under fire, it is important that we should understand the impetus given to history by the majestic rhythms of words. Nations have been formed around words, men's aspirations congregate around the most pregnant utterances of leaders. Sun Yat-sen has explained how, one evening in a rooming house in Chicago, he overheard as in a vision a mysterious phrase of Lincoln's that changed the whole course of his political philosophy. Nehru, reading Blackstone, half poet and half visionary, saw the world as Law, and tempered his horror of British imperialism in action with the vision of the theoretical freedom announced by the continuity of British law. Gandhi, Jinnah, and Nehru were all lawyers. If Britain perishes, she will still have left an abundant mark on the East.

For the moment neither China nor India are the most politically advanced states in the East; that honor belongs to Indonesia. The least advanced is Korea, split mercilessly between rival camps, made hideous by rivalries. Meanwhile the tide flows on; no winds, no reefs, no crosscurrents can prevent it from gaining its necessary shore. There is an Indonesian story of a farmer who planted a strange seed that had been thrown up on the sand. Within three weeks the seed had sprouted, within six months it was already as tall as a house, in a year it was as large as a whole garden of trees. He was frightened and decided to cut down the tree, in spite of the sweet fruit and the glossy leaves; but he was powerless to do more than chip the great gnarled trunk. He tried to poison the roots, but the tree grew more splendidly, swallowing up the whole land. The tree became as large as a forest, and then as large as a kingdom, but the leaves were so thick that he was able to live on its topmost branches—and this was how Java came into being. Today another seed has been planted, as inexorable as the old and as deeply rooted. For this tree he will fight and die.

Everywhere in the East the dangerous seeds of liberty and democracy are bearing fruit. We can no longer proclaim that the Atlantic Charter is specifically directed toward the Atlantic states; the Four Freedoms hang in the schoolrooms of the Balinese villages, you will find them in Mongolia, in India, in China. If the revolt of Asia is the greatest and most portentous event in human history, the declaration of the Four Freedoms, whatever the intention of its framers, must be accepted as the greatest deliberate impulse toward the changing of history ever invented.

Today there exists a totally new equation between East and West. The vacuum left by Japan has been filled by the clamorous peasants of the Asiatic states, no longer content to live on a bowlful of rice a day. The Americans and British must realize now, before it is too late, that they have debts to pay; centuries of exploitation are not easily forgotten or forgiven. Political consciousness, which came to the Asiatics from the West, is a two-edged dagger, one edge directed toward their own past, the other toward the West. It is not sufficient to assume that they are pacific; what is certain is that they will not remain pacific if they are continually exploited according to the old patterns, or subjected as in China to foreign intervention, however well disposed. The Russian invasion of Manchurian heavy industries shocked the Chinese Communists, who were equally shocked when they heard that British, Dutch and Japanese troops were engaged in "mopping-up" campaigns in Java. In the eyes of the Asiatics all Western nations were equally guilty.

In conversation with Jawaharlal Nehru I have heard him speak bluntly and hopelessly of the British campaign in Indonesia as though it was only one more sign of British perfidy, forgetting perhaps that the responsibility did not lie with the British alone, and that America, by authorizing the despatch of troops from the Southeast Asia Command, was equally responsible. Even the violently reactionary General Ho Yin-hing, shortly after the beginning of the Pacific war, could say: "I drink to the day when every Englishman is out of Asia—and by Englishman I mean every foreigner." In saying this, he expressed a desire common to millions of Asiatics. Chiang Kai-shek's obsession against foreigners in *China's Destiny* represents the accumulated anger of generations, an anger still stirring and fanning into flame. It is to the advantage of peace that the anger should die down, but it can hardly die if the West behaves with the old arrogance, continually protesting its visionary authority and superiority. Nazi Germany and Russia have taught us that broken nations rise with lightning swiftness. Once Western pressure is removed from the East, we can expect them to take their place in the sun more quickly than anyone has dreamed.

Now for the first time since the age of Tamerlane undreamed-of possibilities lie before the East. Machines will take the place of the innumerable wretched coolie lines; huge capitals will arise in the deserts of Mongolia and the fertile vastnesses of Sumatra, their names still unknown, their sites unthought of; the scientists of the future will be the sons of the Balinese peasants, Indian ryots, Chinese farmers. The marriage of Eastern and Western philosophies cannot be long delayed. All renaissances of art and culture have been due to the mingling of intrinsic strains; we await now the final flowering that will occur when East and West meet on common ground. Today a thousand million people of Asia are still struggling for the barest livelihood. Once that has been assured, the unpredictable strength of these people will begin to sway the world in whichever direction they think best. In the most complete sense, the West will be at their mercy unless it co-operates with them hardily, now and in the future.

What is strange is that the danger has not been foreseen in its essential clarity. We have deliberately assisted the men who most hate the West as though some fatal instinct deprived us of choice. We have assisted Chiang Kai-shek, who fulminates against the West in *China's Destiny,* forgetting that Mao Tse-tung in *New Democracy* has expressed his undeviating respect for the forces that brought modern Western thought into being, and whose heroes, unlike Chiang Kai-shek's, are all Western. For a year and a half Dutch, British, and American guns were leveled at the Indonesian revolutionaries, who fought often with bows and arrows, and whose elected leader had written: "We have learned to handle instruments of power, but we do neither worship nor swear allegiance to power, we have faith in a future of humanity, in which a life on humane principles will no longer be suppressed by power, in which there will be no wars and no reasons for hostility between human beings." It is not strange that Soetan Shjarir should talk in the authentic accents of the Western tradition; what is strange is that such an announcement, made exactly a year after Hiroshima, should have passed unnoticed.

We have come to the turning of the ways, to the last and most exquisite flowering of human potentialities. It lies within our power within the next few generations to bring about the marriage of East and West; but this marriage can only come about as the result of certain predetermined conditions:

1. That the Asiatic revolution should resolve the main problems of land tenure.

2. That the revolutionary strength should not be diverted into civil war.

3. That the education of the young should have priority over all other reforms.

4. That they should be able to obtain from the West, under conditions that exclude human exploitation, the mechanics for exploiting the earth.

5. That government should be by representatives elected strictly by secret ballot.

6. That no extremist parties are allowed to gain power, for all extreme parties invoke the presence of contrary extreme parties.

7. That there should be no secret prisons, and the judiciary should be exclusive of the executive.

8. That minority groups should be allowed to exist unharmed, and that there should be continuing freedom to speak and report without interference of the police.

The policies of the West are now equally clear and equally decisive. We cannot continue the course we have continued to the present. We can no longer hope to receive huge dividends from investments, or to rely, as the Dutch have relied so long, on the cheap labor of colonial enterprise. There is not room enough in the present world for colonies. The more clear-sighted and most productive of modern statesmen must be content to wipe from all balance sheets the products of cheap labor—labor of all kinds will inevitably increase in money value as men continue to value their own efforts most highly; and in terms of the lives and deaths of nations, nothing could be more productive. The right to strike must remain, since it is the only weapon remaining in the hands of labor against the inevitable concentrations of bureaucratic power—a right that was guaranteed in the constitution of the United States of Indonesia, though it would appear to be denied in the Chinese constitution of 1946. All these are important, but more important is that we should accept the revolt of Asia as a fundamental issue of our times and assist it with all our power. To describe all "leftist" tendencies in the East as the product of Russian leadership would be the grossest folly. Even in Communist China, where there exists a deep ideological sympathy for Marxism, the tendency throughout the years of revolt has been toward a purely democratic and representative form of government, with the Communists *by law* disallowed from occupying more than one third of the seats in the chamber. We must recognize that what we regard as leftist in the Far East is more often a purely Asiatic expression of the kind of government they desire, with the least possible connections with the forms employed by Russia, and the greatest imaginable desire to be free of all ideological tendencies except those that are rooted in the primary conception of habeas corpus. From the fields of Runnymede and from battlefields in Massachussetts the Asiatic revolt has its origin and seed.

By assisting the revolt of Asia with all the power at our command, we are not committing ourselves to acts of charity. Within six months of the end of the war the pattern of the Asiatic revolt became clear; yet no efforts were made to assist the revolutionaries, and in many cases oppressive measures were taken against them. Great Britain has been the least unscrupulous in assisting the colonial powers; India and Burma have demonstrated that nationalism has come to stay in the East, but in its wider aspects the revolt is not one for national sovereignty—a social antithesis cuts across nationality and wealth, and in its final analysis the revolt is almost wholly a sociological revolution. The demand for nationalism was assisted by the Atlantic Charter—"Respect for the rights of all people to choose the form of government under which they live," but this stimulus, however intoxicating, was not the cause of the revolution, nor can we judge the forms of the society that will evolve in terms of nationalism. The social antithesis cuts across religion, foreign concessions, even foreign exploitation. To the Asiatics coming for the first time out of the somber shadows of their villages, none of these can have supreme importance in comparison with the labor of evolving new social organizations in the face of potential vast increases of population. The intricate and old-established patterns of culture are breaking down under the pressure of a new economy, new political forces, new social concepts, new education; no one can piece together the broken tapestries. Among the urban populations, then in the villages, then in the undiscovered hinterlands, the social revolt will spread its doctrine of the necessary dignity of man confronted with new tools with which he can seize the treasures of earth. It has come late; the pressures are formidable; no effort to constrain the revolt can persist without weakening the source of pressure. The revolt of Asia, the most terrifying and at the same

time the most necessary revolt of all, has begun; and though Jawaharlal Nehru claims that there is no difference between East and
West:

> There is no such thing as East and West except in the mind of those
> who wish to make an excuse for imperialistic domination over those who
> have inherited such myths and fictions from a confused metaphysical past
> —differences there are, but they are due chiefly to differences in economic
> growth. . . .

yet differences do exist—there are vaster populations, and richer untapped resources in the East than in the West. What is certain is
that the Asiatics will not be content like the red Indians to live out
their lives in solitary confinement within reservations. They are part
of the world and very voluble as they make their first inexperienced
experiments.

The revolt of Asia will change the pattern of America. With the
Pacific becoming the Middle Sea of the world, a new Mediterranean
around which the powers of the future will be gathered, the inevitable trend toward the West will gain in momentum. The West
Coast, and more particularly California, will assume immense and
ever increasing importance, if only because the mineral resources of
America are running out at fantastic speed and the mineral resources of Asia remain untapped. From California there are daily
flights to Honolulu; there will soon be daily flights to all the important centers of the East. Soon there will come a time when more
trade will flow from the West Coast than from the East, and nothing is more extraordinary than the refusal of Californians to believe
that their destiny lies in the Far East. Meanwhile there will be
changes in Britain. Though British economy will become increasingly rooted in Africa, Britain has the opportunity to assume the
political leadership of the East, since the political experiment she is
pursuing is the same in all essentials as the experiment that is being
pursued in Asia. Her destiny, too, lies among the unnumbered millions of the East.

All existing patterns will change. To the advantage of the West
for a short while is the presence in positions of power in the East of
men who have been educated abroad. Quezon and Osmeña were
American-trained lawyers, Soekarno, Hatta, and Shjarir owe their
education to Holland, Luang Pradit owes his training to France,

Nguyen-ai-Quoc studied in Paris, the two leaders of the Indian conflict were trained in London. Others will follow them who have had no training in the West, and possess no particular sympathies with Western doctrine or Western habits of thought. We cannot expect indefinitely to see the emergence of such Occidental patterns of thought. Out of the East new doctrines will appear, based as ours have been on the configurations and problems of government; neither communism, nor capitalism, nor socialism can be expected to survive for long in their present forms in the East. The Indian joint family villages and the Javanese *desa* will eventually disappear; in the new patterns, new forces will evolve. At the beginning of the century Raden Adjeng Kartini, the daughter of a district ruler in Java, wrote to her Dutch friend: "We are not giving battle to individuals but to old man-grown edicts and conventions that are not worthy of the Javanese of the future, of which we, and a few others, are the forerunners." The emphasis will not be on war, on "battle with individuals," but on the social struggle, on the emergence of a purely Asiatic society owing much to the West but still more to the native adaptability of the East. It is necessary that we should realize not only that nothing comparable to this in magnitude has ever occurred but that the experiment cannot be repeated. The decisions made now can affect the future of the East till the end of the world. A mythology unlike any previous mythology is being created; a social state unlike any existing social state is coming into being. In all the countries of the East the struggle is the same and will obey within limits the same laws. Asia is conscious of herself, and the Asiatic Century has begun.

Index